THE AMERICAN CENTURY SERIES

MIDDLETOWN

IN THE TWENTIETH CENTURY

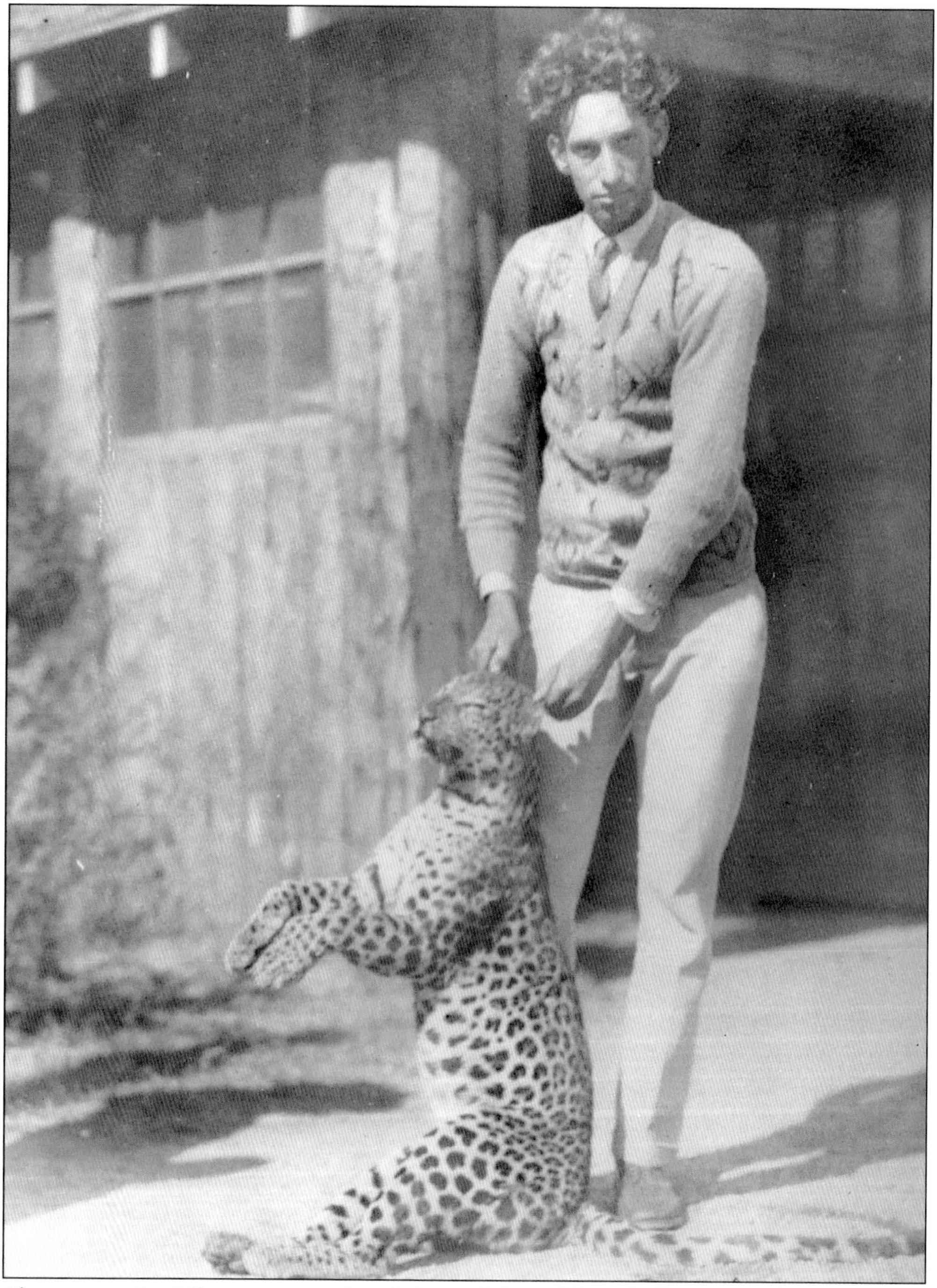

The escape of a full-grown spotted male leopard from Oliver Holton's Twin Brook Zoo on August 5, 1926, prompted anxious alarm and caused a zealous search that resulted in numerous false sightings. Stimulated by safety concerns and Holton's offer of a $100 reward, armed hunting parties eagerly sought the critter. The leopard took an incredible journey, winding up in Island Heights, Ocean County, where he was caught in a trap and killed on October 15. The man holding the leopard remains unidentified.

The American Century Series

Middletown

in the Twentieth Century

Randall Gabrielan

Arcadia Publishing

ISBN 978-0-7385-6401-2

Published by Arcadia Publishing
Charleston, South Carolina

Printed in the United States of America

Library of Congress Catalog Card Number: 2008940649

For all general information contact Arcadia Publishing at:
Telephone 843-853-2070
Fax 843-853-0044
E-mail sales@arcadiapublishing.com
For customer service and orders:
Toll-Free 1-888-313-2665

Visit us on the Internet at www.arcadiapublishing.com

Cover Image: A beauty pageant *c.* 1953 at McGuires Grove presents a bevy of local beauties and an opportunity to appreciate the great progress the bathing suit industry has made in the last half-century.

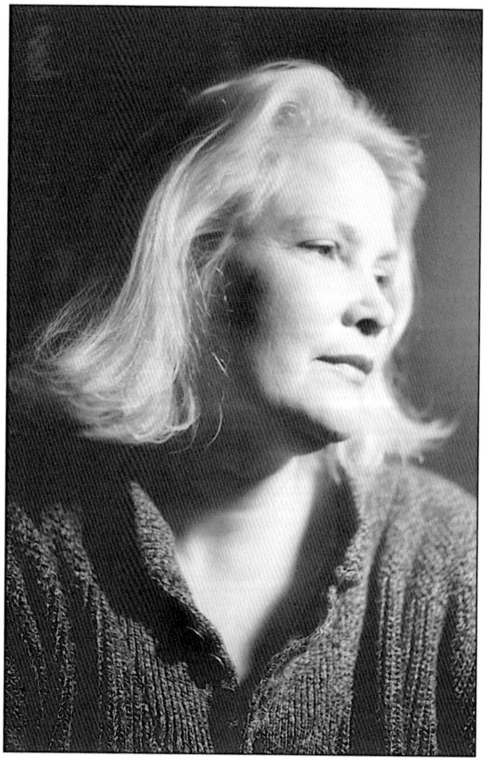

I dedicate this book to Margaret Lundrigan, a kind, genial, gracious person. She is a fellow writer and Arcadia author. Her pleasant manner makes her a welcome colleague and friend. Her dedication and concern for others makes her an effective writer and empathetic social worker, her professional calling.

Contents

ACKNOWLEDGMENTS

This collection of photographs is an extraordinary gathering for which I offer my sincerest thanks to a fine and generous group of people. I deeply appreciate their contributions, which have been special in so many ways; however, I merely list them in alphabetical order, taking brief exception to note that the names of Robert A. Schoeffling and John Rhody have appeared in nearly all of my books, making their long-term support deserving extra notice. Also, Photography Unlimited by Dorn's has in their Red Bank shop a collection of Middletown photographs that is particularly rich in the 1950 and 1960 decades. Many thanks to the following: AT&T and Joseph Norton; Elizabeth Albert; Edwin F. Banfield; Jane Bartlett; Katharine Bartlett; Richard Bingham, Ph.D., Command Historian, U.S. Army Communications-Electronics Command, Fort Monmouth; Olga Boeckel; Lois Bodtmann; Michael K. Brady, Public Affairs Officer, Earle Naval Weapons Station; Paul "Pete" Brady; Virginia Brady; Margaret Thomas Buchholz; Michael Cassone; Morgan Cline; Ronald I. Cohen; Moe Cuocci; Photography Unlimited by Dorn's; Gary Dubnik; Adam Finck; Lynn Jelliffe Friis; Gail Gannon; Barbara Guerrieri and her parents, William and Rose Marie Hansen Coyle; June Truex Hoffmire; Catherine Ann Jacoby; the late Thelma Jelliffe; Susan Kline of the VNA of Central Jersey; Robert Bade Leidner; John Lentz; Scott Longfield; Margaret Lundrigan; Robert Manson; Monroe Marx; the Middletown Landmarks Commission; the Monmouth County Historical Association; Thomas and Ruthanne Morford; Eugene F. O'Neill; Ole Palludin; John Rhody; the late Alice Robinson; George Rudolph; Special Collections and Archives, Rutgers University Libraries; Robert A. Schoeffling; the Seabright Lawn Tennis and Cricket Club; the Shrewsbury Historical Society; Harold Solomon; Patricia Stikeleather; Mary Thompson; the late Charles Toop; the United States Military Academy, Special Collections; Peter Van Nortwick; Sandi von Pier; and Richard C.Winters.

INTRODUCTION

One wonders how future generations will perceive Middletown at the end of the 20th century. Although many strive to assure a kind environment and well-planned town, the toll taken on our historic properties and the number that are slipping into a precarious future can make one fear that the destruction of our historic and architectural patrimony might be one of the legacies of this generation. One despairs over the lack of widespread public concern when a significant building is threatened. Frustration grows over many preservation proposals having to justify themselves on a business-like profit and loss basis to attract needed support. It seems that so many people like the idea of being in a historic area, but too few are willing to make slight sacrifices to help keep it historic.

Progress cannot and should not be halted. After all, most of us live in 20th-century houses and seek reasonable balance between change and stability. We cannot turn back time, but we can assist its moving in an orderly fashion. One assist would be greater preservation constraint in the planning process, specifically by forcing developers to preserve historic structures found on properties on which they seek to build. Moving an old building because a genuine Colonial structure would look "out of place" in the midst of ersatz new "Colonial"-style construction should not be an acceptable act. Since there is a limit on the number of museums or restored publicly owned houses that our society can absorb, making the old places appeal to new buyers should be a developer's imperative. Dedicated owners and prospective custodians of historic properties exist and must be cultivated; most give more than they receive from their historic properties.

Middletown is not the only municipality needing to grasp this problem; it runs across our society. However, Middletown was a leader with its local preservation ordinance (its later difficulties in the court room notwithstanding), and could also lead in putting teeth in regulations regarding preservation at the planning stage.

Middletown in the 20th Century focuses on the history of our time, more the latter half than the earlier decades. It is intended to be a stand-alone work, yet must be considered in the light of its three predecessors in the Images of America series. An effort was made to avoid subjects that were well covered in the prior books, regardless of their significance. There is some overlap, however, as additional information or imagery with a "must include" quality offset plans to avoid duplication.

Many captions reflect the progress of a subject over a lengthy period, an intention of the 20th-century focus. Thus, some subjects were chosen as representative of an aspect of history as much as for their own intrinsic qualities. Some of the commentaries reflect on-going change or processes. History can not be written in its own time, of course, so the historical merit or insight of these remarks is subject to the impact of changing times.

One

The Domestic Scene

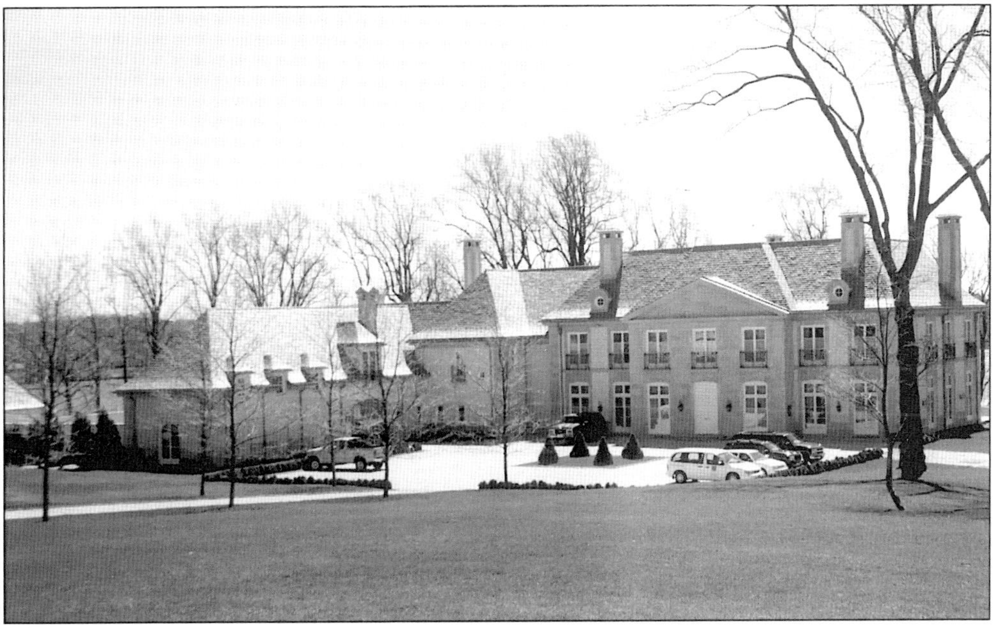

The 1870 opening of Navesink River Road facilitated the construction of large country houses, initially occupied seasonally, along the riverbank. Many were located on large former farm tracts, a number with houses along Cooper Road to the north. This recently completed house, designed by Robert A.M. Stern and located east of Sailors Way, dwarfs any others in the area and provides an opportunity to review trends. It is the largest since Warren Barbour's 1931 house at 901 Navesink River Road, now called "Seascape" (see Volume II, p. 124). Seascape and the road's 20th-century highlight, the 1918 "Brick House" that John Russell Pope designed for Andrew Varick Stout, employ classical motifs in their design. Today's lots are typically smaller than the early century plots, although this 7-acre plot was the largest remaining available tract on the river.

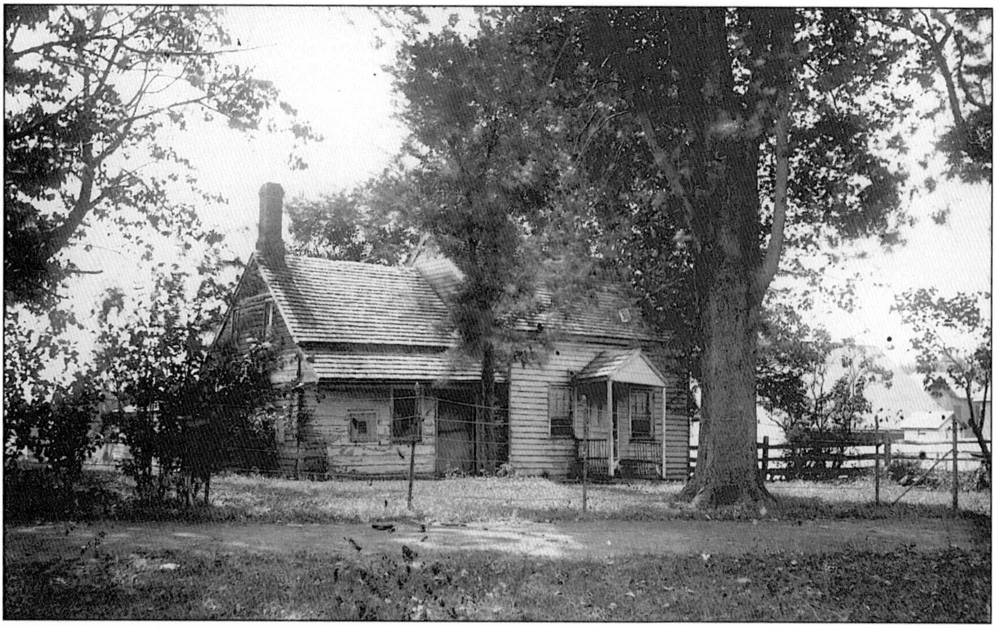

The age of the former Christ Church rectory would appear to offer it stature as one of Middletown village's oldest structures if it had been permitted to stand. It was located adjacent to the church on the west side. The house's history is obscure, but it was demolished *c.* 1899 for the building pictured below, with historic preservation probably not a factor in the decision.

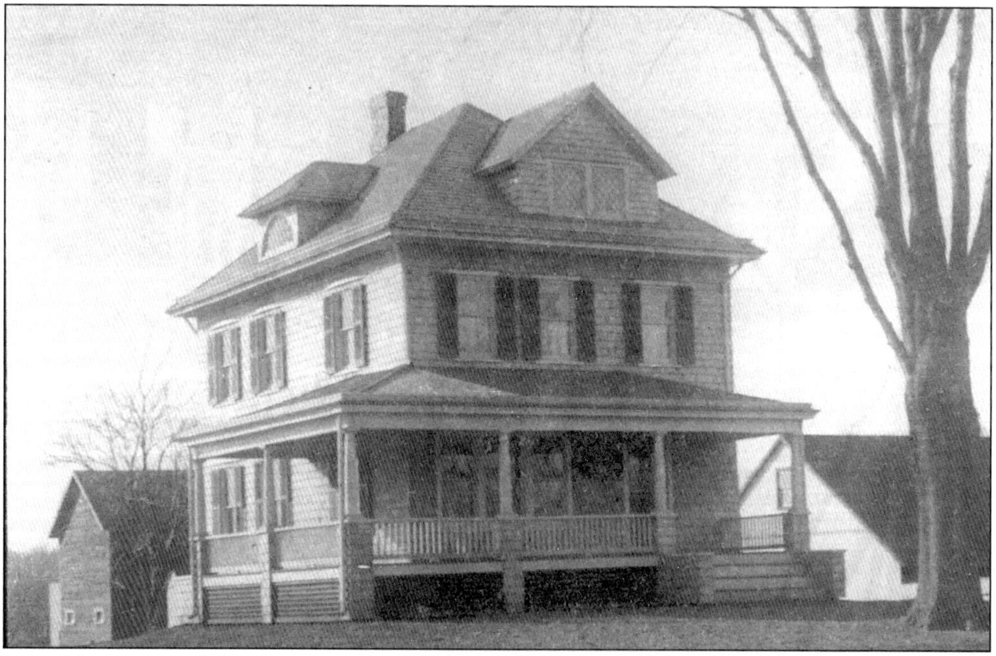

It may be presumed this Four Square-style house, built *c.* 1899, had conveniences that made it preferable to Christ Church as a rectory, its architectural lack of distinction notwithstanding. It was converted to a hall-education building and was taken down in the 1960s together with an adjoining hall for the construction of the brick church annex now adjacent to the old structure on Kings Highway.

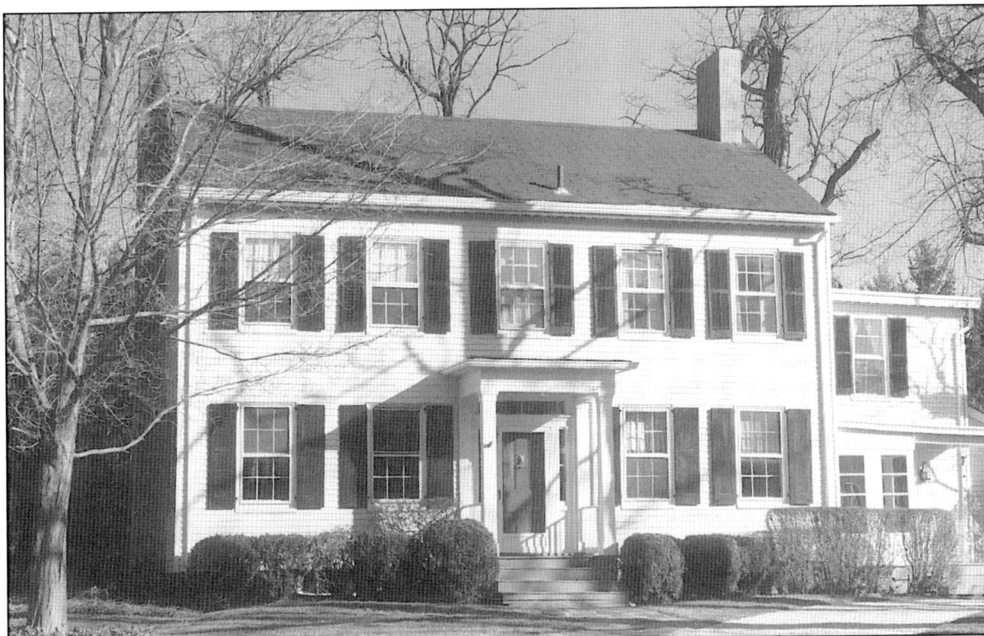

Later expansion disguised the probable 18th-century origins of Brookside Farm, located at 3 Van Schoick Road, a house once owned by the Luyster family. Construction c. 1860 made the main block appear to be one five-bay unit in the Greek Revival style, but the two bays on the west (left) are older. The ell at right is a later addition. Thomas Van Schoick named the farm when he bought it in 1922. Development shrank the farm to an acre lot, but preserved the old place on site.

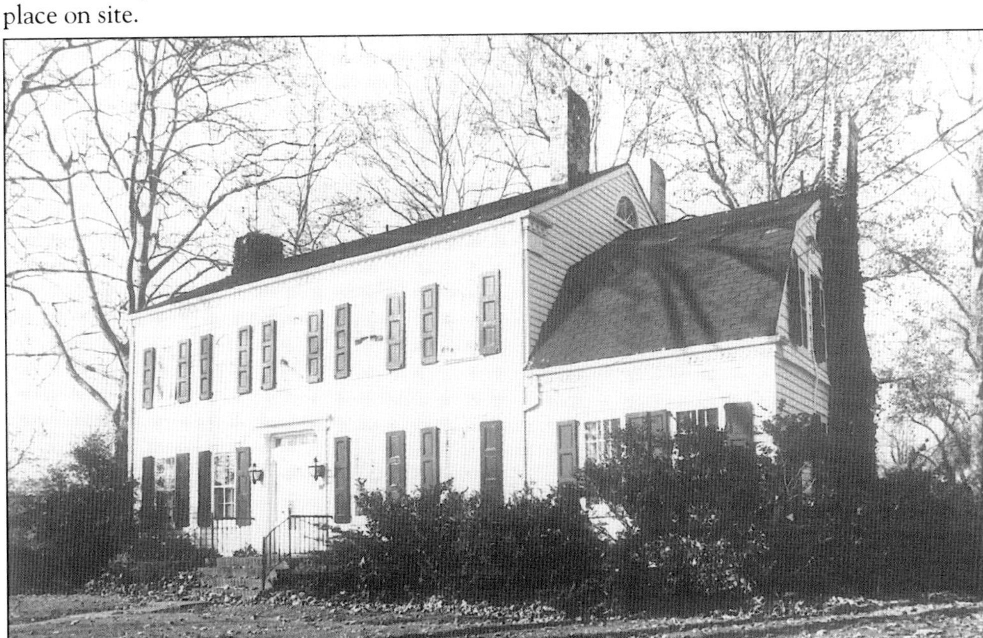

An old Cooper house, located at 7 Conover Lane and later owned by a Van Brunt, was apparently built in sections (the interior was not seen). It was later remodeled as offices. The house stands over the Navesink River's bank.

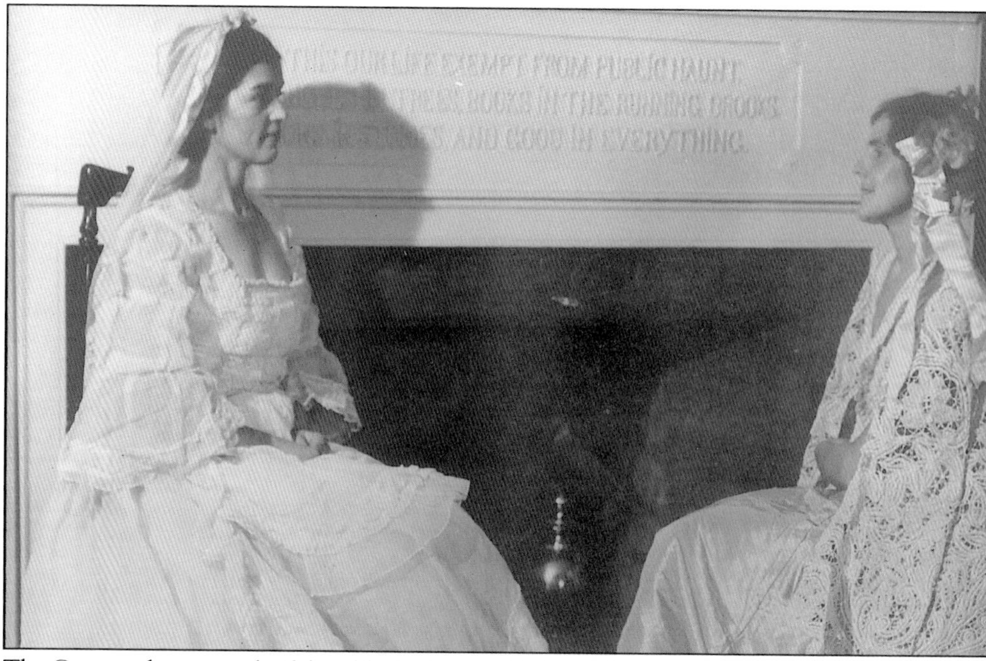

The Conover house south of the old Middletown Railroad Station was revered by the family and known publicly by its nickname, "The Homestead." J. Dey Conover nostalgically recalled the house as he wrote in a commemorative booklet (*c.* 1910), "The tired toiler in the trying school of modern endeavor years each day for a nightly haven of peaceful rest, and nowhere can this be found half so satisfying and complete as under the sheltering eaves of the old homestead." Ruth Mandeville (left) and Thelma Jelliffe (right) are pictured inside at a 1934 fund-raiser. The house burned in the early 1960s.

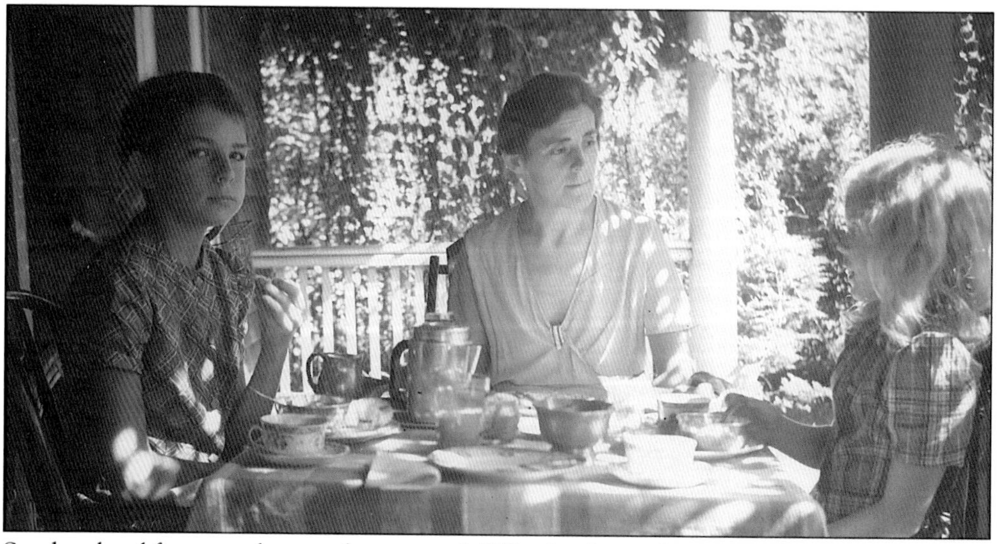

Sunday breakfast on the porch was a Jelliffe family tradition at their Liberty Street house. Pictured here in the 1940s are, from left to right, Arity, Thelma, and Lynn, who recalled that the setting permitted interaction with the village's modest street traffic. The practice is infrequently replicated as both casual walking and porches have declined at the end of the century.

Orson S. Fowler, a phrenologist, popularized a house style in his 1849 work, *The Octagon, A Home For All*, which claimed many virtues for this type of house, including increased ventilation and light (which would seemingly be marred by its division for rooms). The 19th-century origin of Middletown's example, Belford, is obscure, but long ownership is associated with the Lube family. The house, located at 26 Church Street, appeared tatty in this 1964 photograph; it was a burned shell following a 1975 fire.

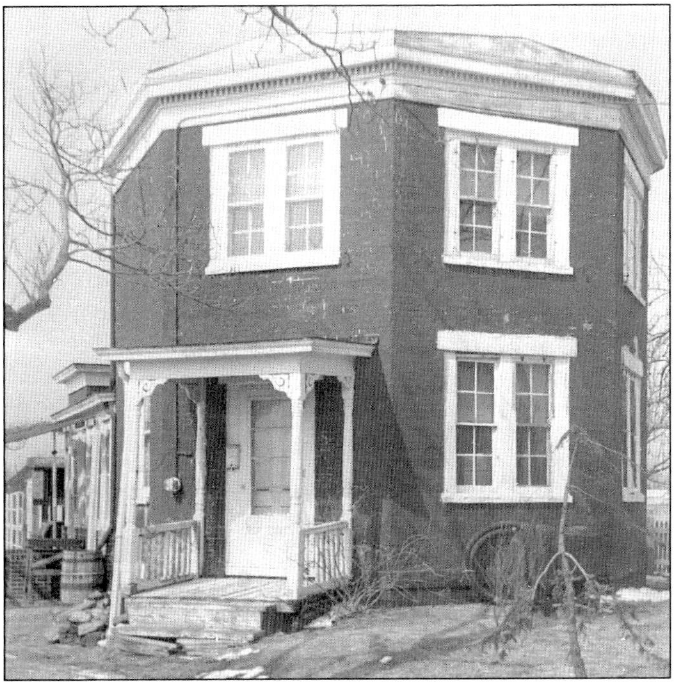

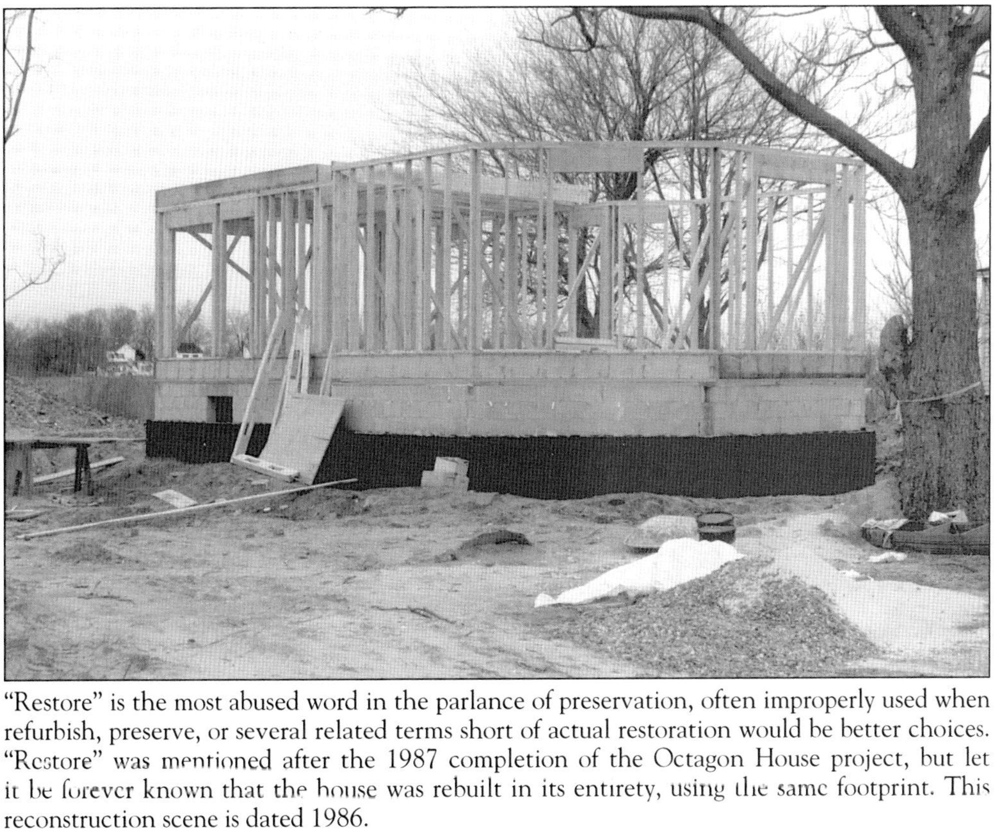

"Restore" is the most abused word in the parlance of preservation, often improperly used when refurbish, preserve, or several related terms short of actual restoration would be better choices. "Restore" was mentioned after the 1987 completion of the Octagon House project, but let it be forever known that the house was rebuilt in its entirety, using the same footprint. This reconstruction scene is dated 1986.

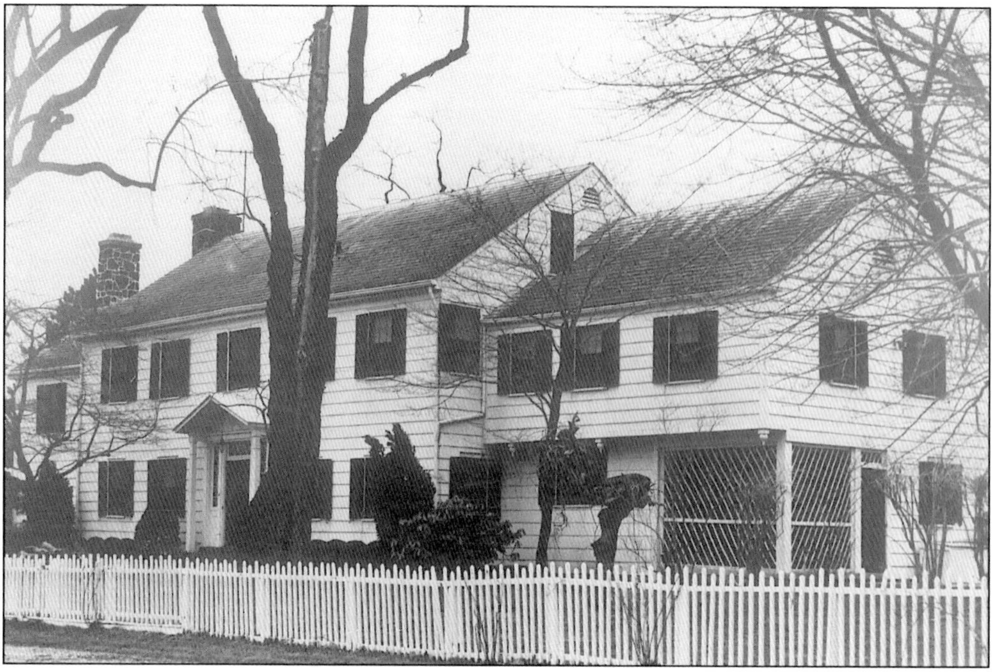

Gentlemen farmers buying old country places was an oft-repeated preservation process during the early decades of the 20th century. Harry H. and Katherine K. Neuberger's alterations to the Grover-Johnson farm (also known as Sunnyside) after their 1933 purchase included raising the old, typical one-and-a-half-story Georgian side hall section to two and a half stories. It is pictured at right in this 1970s photograph of what today is known as the Monmouth County Park System's Sunnyside Recreation Area, located at 600 Middletown-Lincroft Road. Interior changes and the major expansion of a single room to a two-story wing were other significant improvements.

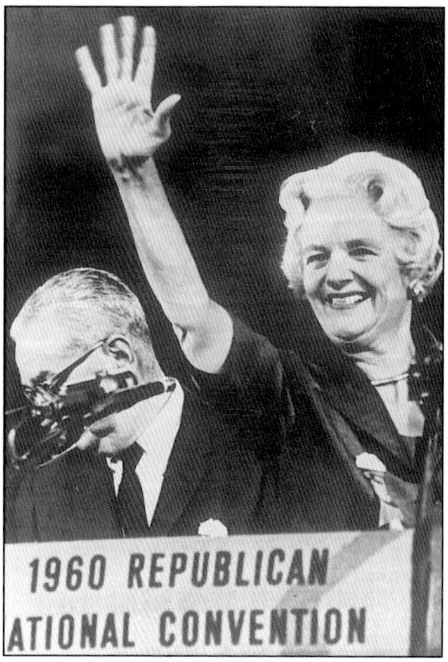

Katherine K. Neuberger entered Republican politics soon after the family's 1933 purchase of Sunnyside Farm at the behest of Geraldine L. Thompson. She rose higher than any Middletown woman in politics, beginning through the Federation of Republican Women. She succeeded Mrs. Thompson as Republican state committeewoman, joining the national committee in 1961 and serving on the party's executive committee from 1969 to 1972. Neuberger went to her first Republican national convention in 1952, attending four others as a delegate from 1960 to 1976, and making a nominating speech for Henry Cabot Lodge in 1960. She held numerous positions on public bodies, notably the state board of higher education, which she considered her "home base." Neuberger lost a reelection bid to the Republican National Committee in 1976, a time when the party was taking the conservative bent that still plagues it at the national level. She died in 1982.

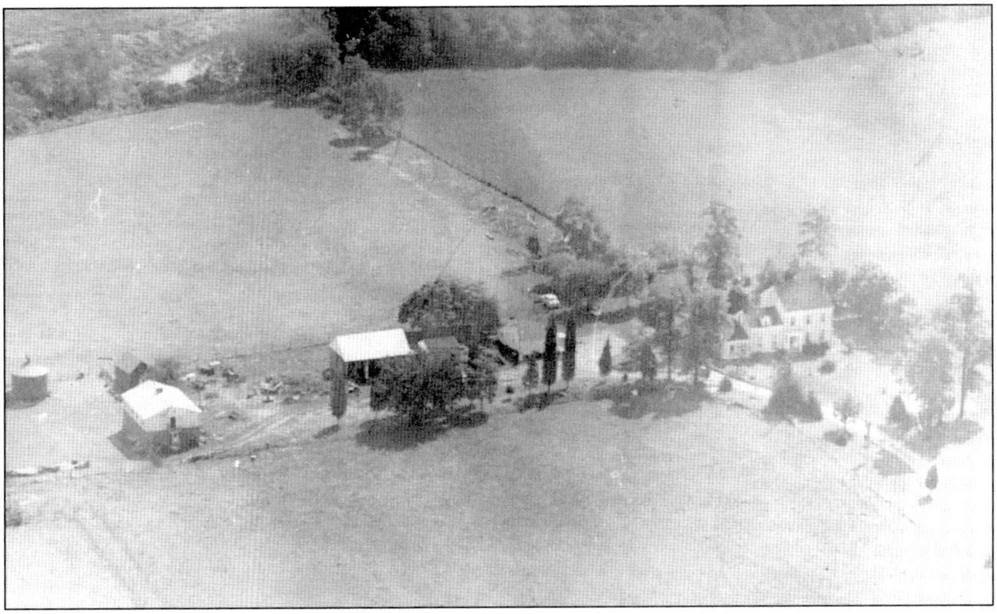

The Dr. Edward Taylor farm was a 170-acre expanse near the eastern reach of Kings Highway and adjacent to Chapel Hill. In 1937, it was purchased by H. Norman Hoyt. The house, which can be seen close up on p. 65 of Volume III, is pictured in this aerial view c. 1940s in a setting developed by new houses in 1993–94. By the 1930s it had become run down, but was restored by Robert W. Crawford after he purchased it in 1945.

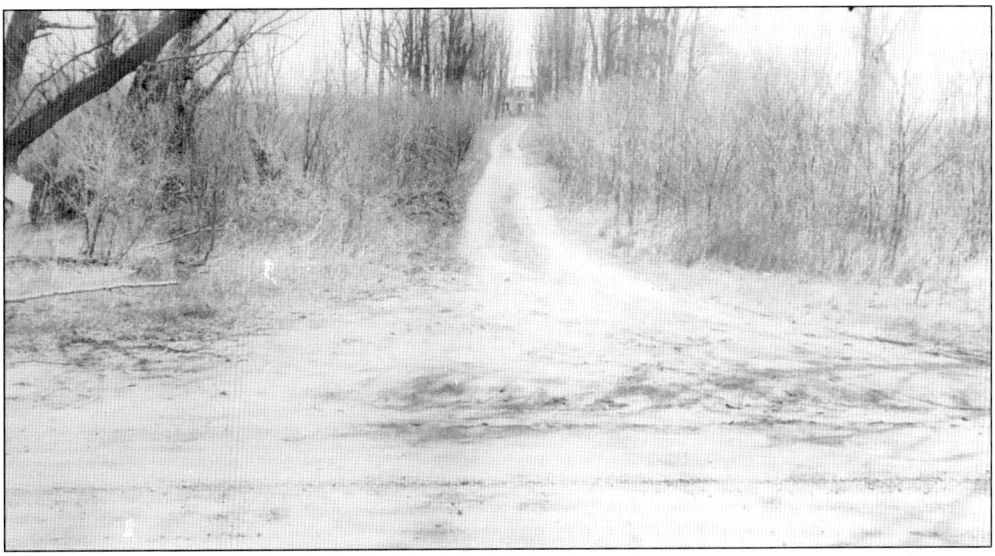

The entrance to Garryford Farm (Crawford's name for the Taylor farm) was a long driveway north from Sleepy Hollow Road. Although old farmhouses are usually closer to the street, this was at least on a main thoroughfare. Development terminated the house's access to Sleepy Hollow Road, placing it within a new street pattern on Garryford Drive. The first criterion of developing historic properties was met, building around the old structure and keeping it on its original site.

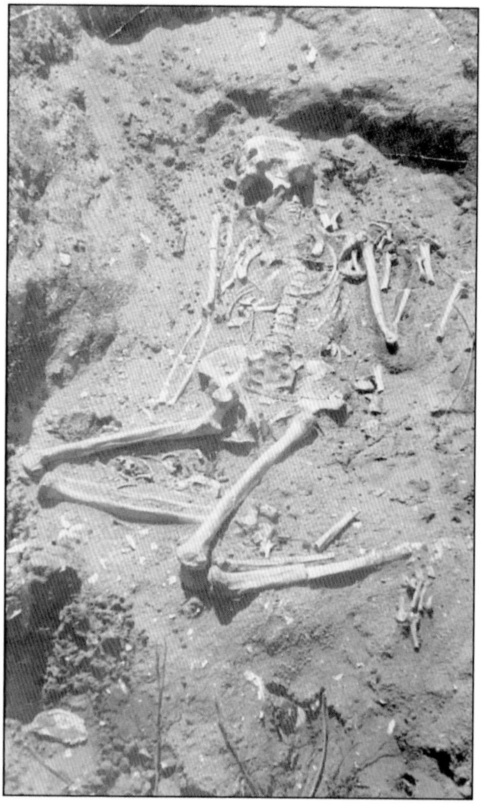

McClees Creek runs through Garryford Farm, the site of S. Burritt Boynton's discovery of a Native-American skeleton in 1937. He chose his digging site by imagining its desirability to our early native settlers. This area had easy access to the Navesink River, and was sheltered, while its light, sandy soil assured good drainage. He also noticed a large accumulation of shell fragments, presumably turned up by a farmer from a shell pit, as well as pottery shards and flint chips. Boynton wrote a lengthy account of his discovery, which contains beliefs of the day on burial practices and excavation techniques. The text was printed in the *Red Bank Register* on May 6, 1937.

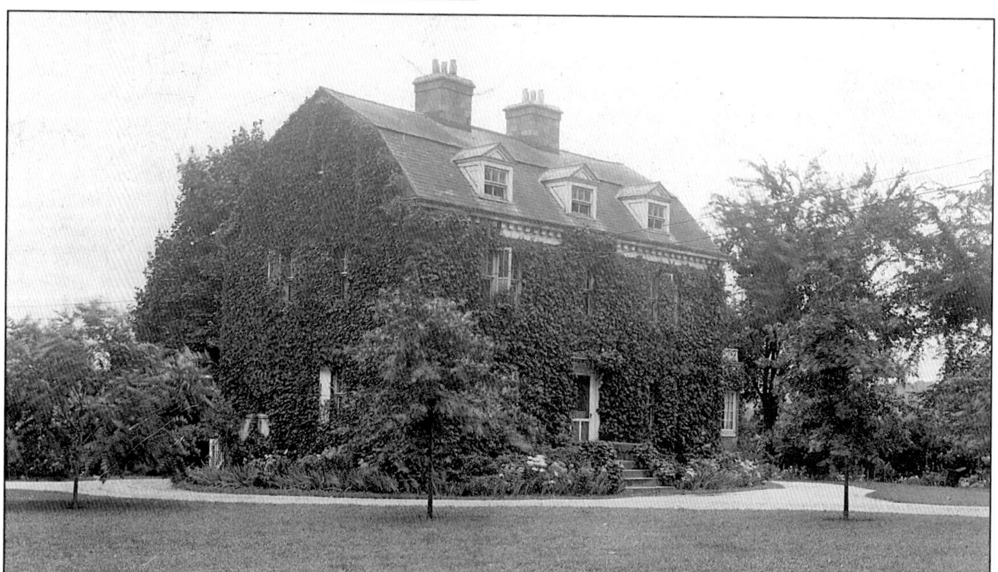

Emile French's residence, built of concrete and terra-cotta tile in 1908, was also pictured in Volume I (p. 58) when it was new. The latter material, now a brownish red, gave rise to its nickname, "The Pink House." In this picture, perhaps from the 1940s, it has an ivy covering that fell from its former grace as vegetative charm to its plain reality as a destroyer of building materials. The ivy is gone now, of course, highlighting the appeal of the original material.

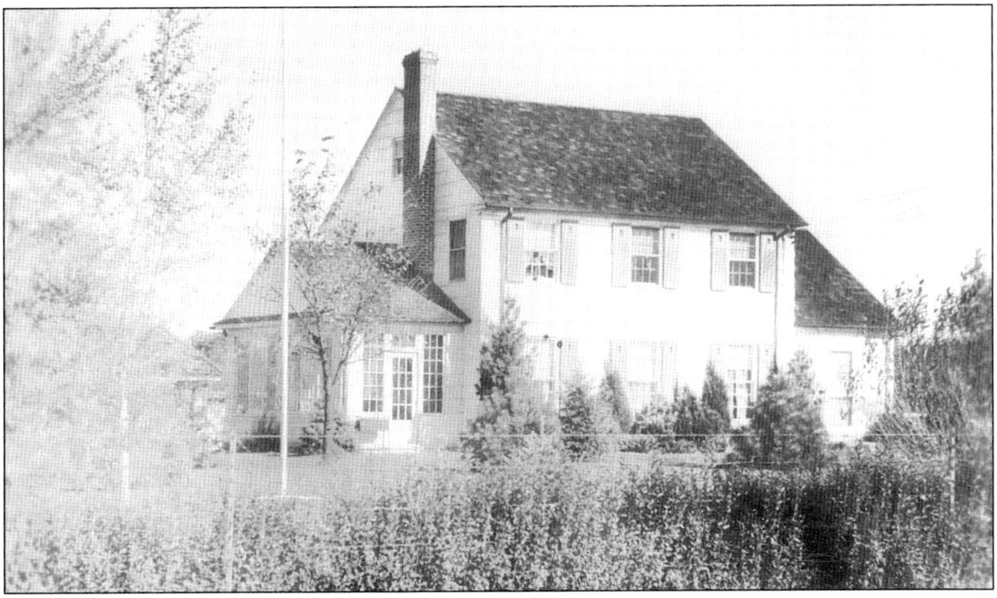

Leslie R. Stewart built this eight-room house on the north side of Newman Springs Road, Lincroft, in 1930 after selling the Langendorf farm. The house, erected by Quackenbush and Nevius, may have been designed by Frank Quackenbush, who drew the plans for much of their work. It reflects the prevalence of the Colonial Revival style in all sized housing.

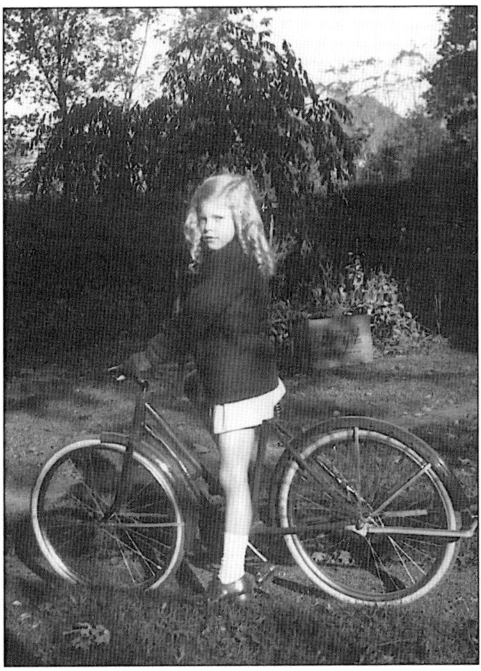

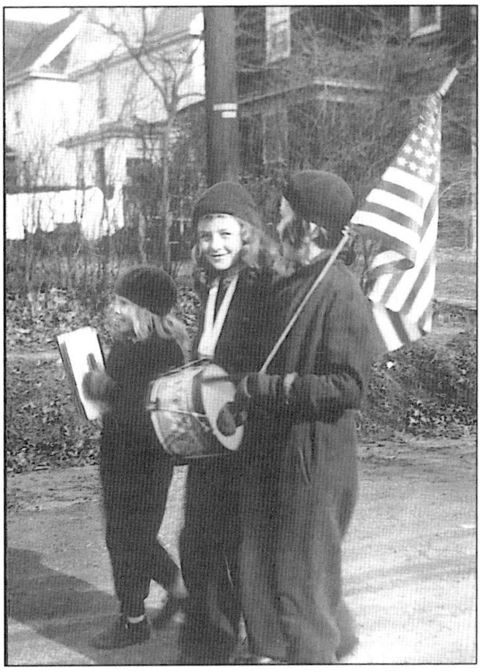

Lynn Jelliffe Friis' appealing pose on a bicycle reminds one that 1940s Middletown traffic may have been more conducive to cycling. Pictured at right, drummer Audrey Smith has an eye for the camera, while the Jelliffe girls, Lynn with the pad and Arity with the flag, fill out a trio practicing for the next summer's Fourth of July parade. The site is Liberty Street, near the alley that had been behind the houses fronting the west side of Church Street.

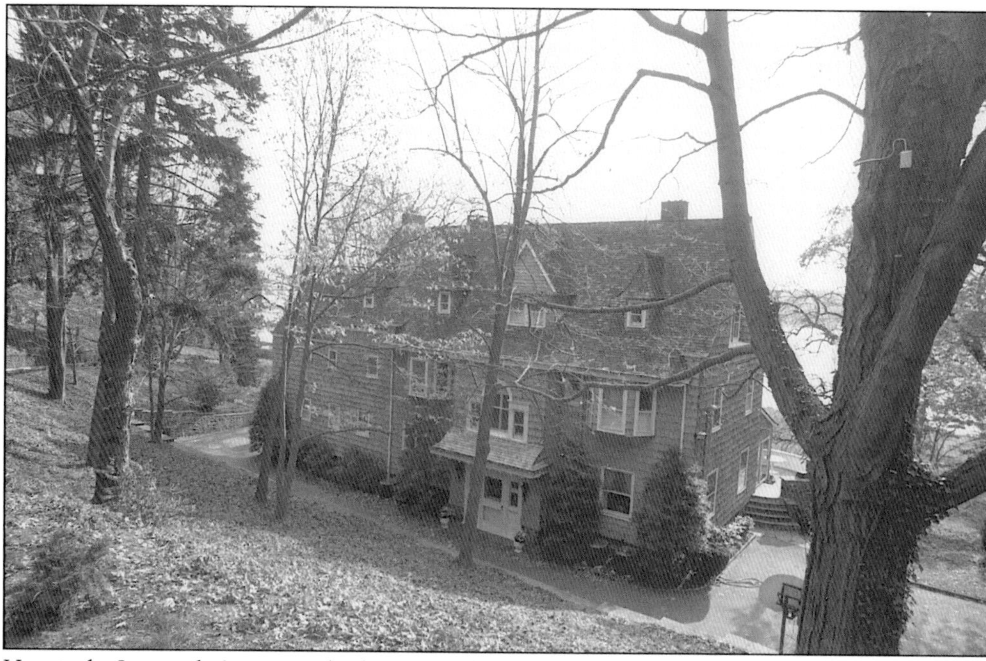

Hyacinthe Lamarche's six sons built summer houses east of their father's place at 820 Navesink River Road following the 1891 death of his widow.

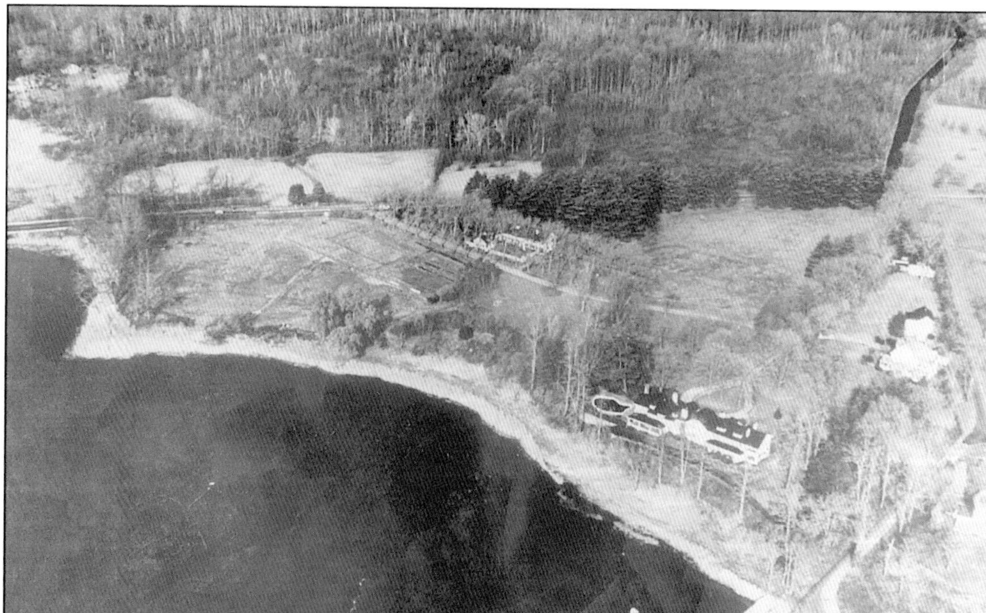

The re-erection of the Connecticut Building from the 1876 Centennial Exposition in Philadelphia in Sea Bright and its move to 700 Navesink River Road was illustrated in Volume III (p. 124). The same house is pictured in this aerial view, perhaps from the 1950s, at the McClees Creek juncture with the Navesink River. At the time of this book's initial printing, the house was nearing the completion of extensive reconstruction and preservation, a process that helped reveal the joining of a number of buildings, including the discovery of one on the site previous to the 1915 move from Sea Bright.

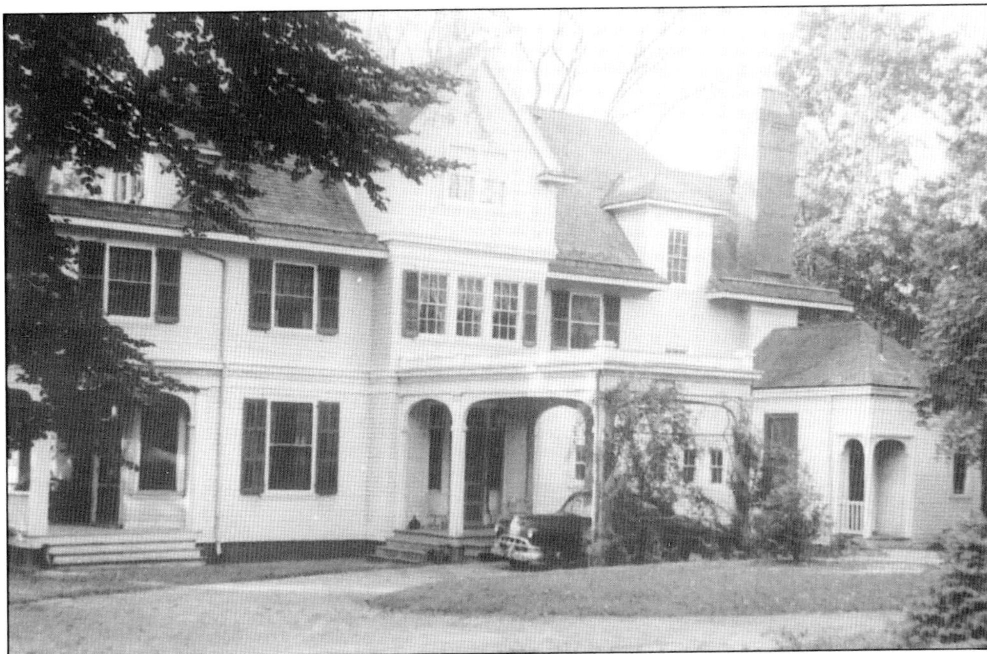

The Louis H. Amy house, built in 1901 at 928 Navesink River Road, is frequently pictured on its south facade. This photograph shows the north elevation in the early 1950s.

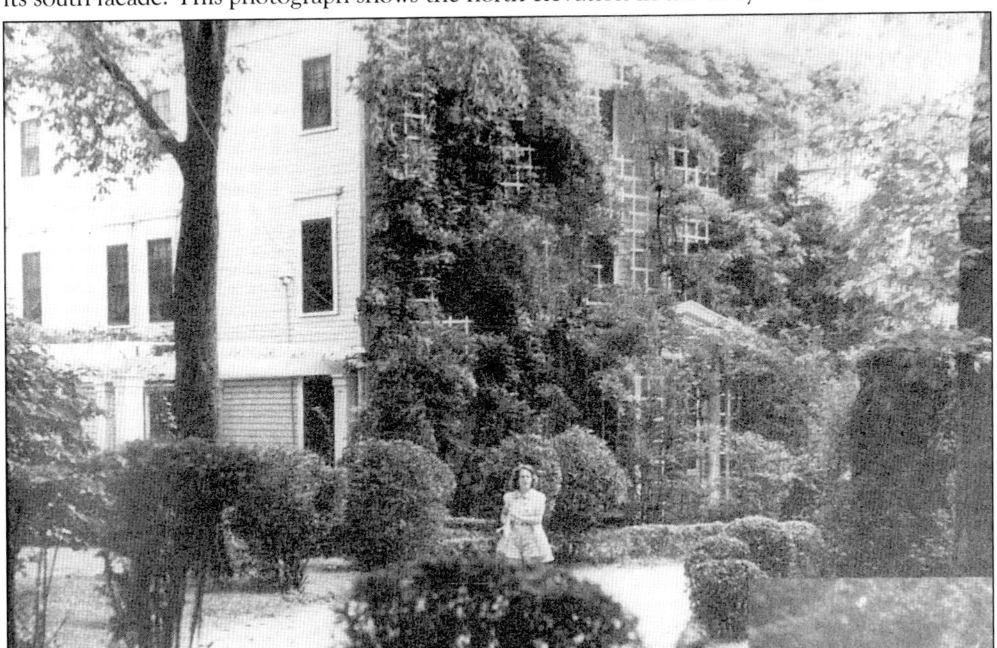

Isaac B. Hosford bought and enlarged the Downes house in 1903, making it one of the area's showplaces. His property of about 150 acres was located north of Kings Highway East and south of Leonardville Road, near the former Chapel Hill Lighthouse. Occupied by a daughter after his death, the house was converted to the hotel Red Oaks in 1932. Its operator, Mrs. Albert Strumsky, attracted a New York entertainment clientele. This picture, with an unidentified subject, was previously published in the 1937 *Jersey Shore Pictorial*.

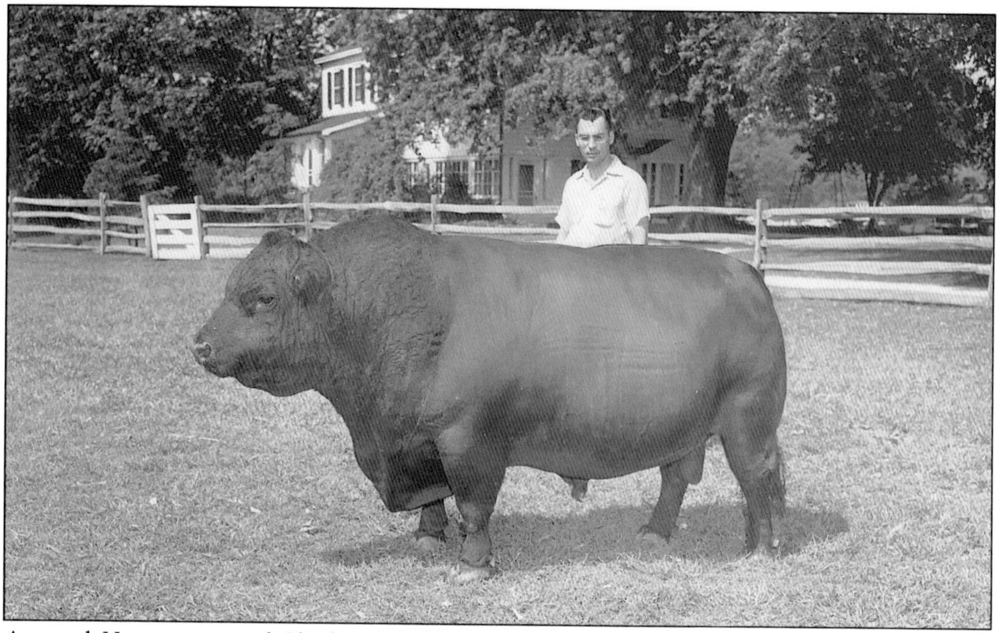

Armand Hammer owned Shadow Isle Farm in River Plaza, where he maintained a famed American Angus beef cattle breeding operation. Prince Eric of Sunbeam, pictured in 1952, was his finest sire. The prize bull unexpectedly died on August 13, 1953, of a burst lung vessel, but his bloodline maintained his fame and high prices. Today, the former farm embraces much of the land of the Shady Oaks and Shadow Lake Village communities. (The Dorn's Collection.)

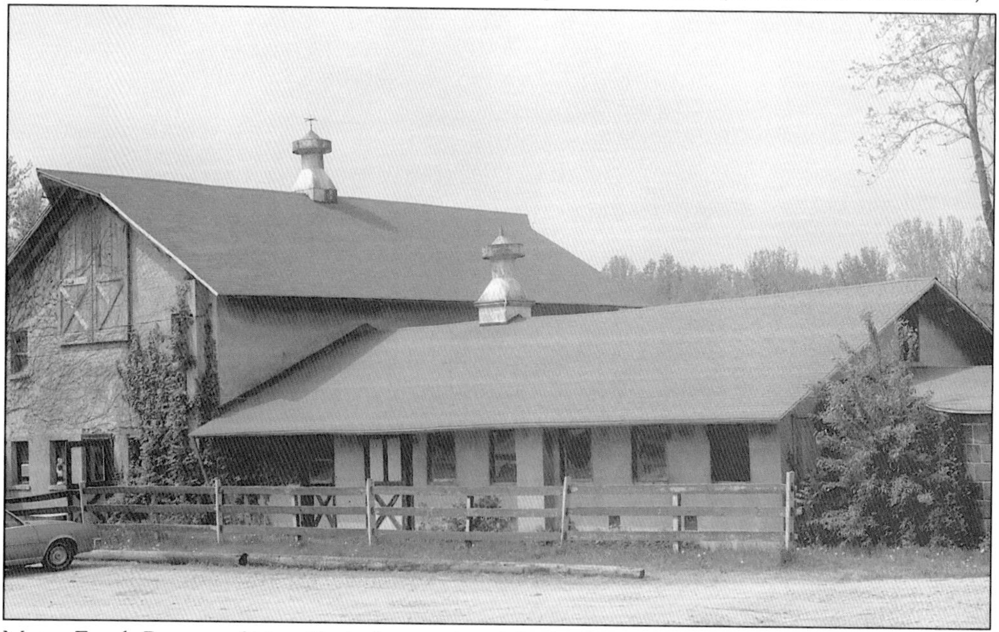

Major Frank Barrett of New York designed and built these stucco-clad barns in 1916 on the former Joseph C. Patterson property on Cooper Road, part of the vast James Patterson estate that was divided among his five sons after his 1867 death. The two-story barn housed horses, while the one-story building was a dairy. Barrett owned a herd of costly pure-bred Guernseys of the high-ranking Ne Plus Ultra strain.

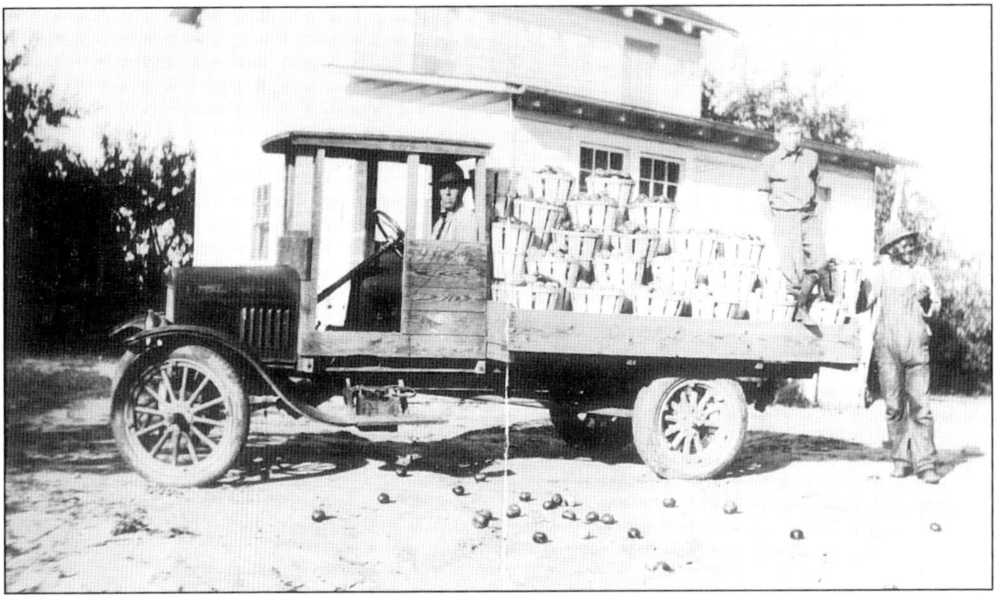

Henry Vining is pictured behind the wheel, while Sherman Vining is standing on the body with an unidentified worker at left in this photo from October 1928. If that many apples hit the ground in the loading process, what would a few bumps in the road have done?

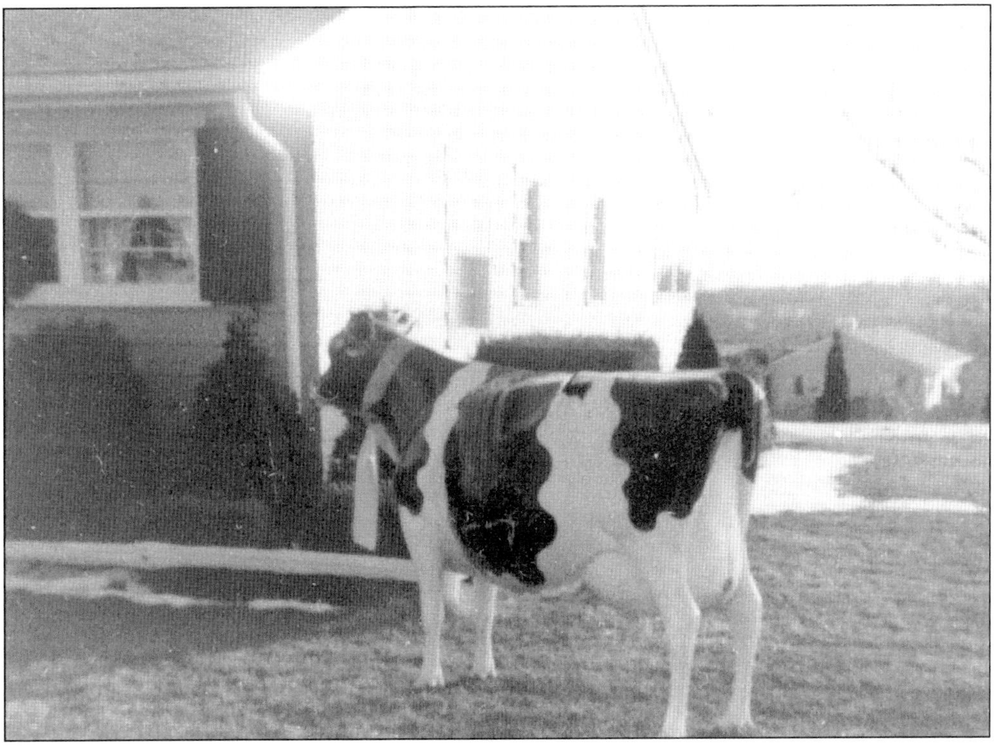

An unidentified practical joker left this model cow on the Hemlock Court lawn of dairyman Frank Van Nortwick. It remained there for one day in February 1967, just long enough for this image to be preserved for posterity. The prankster, never identified, made quite a mark, and his joke turned into historical lore.

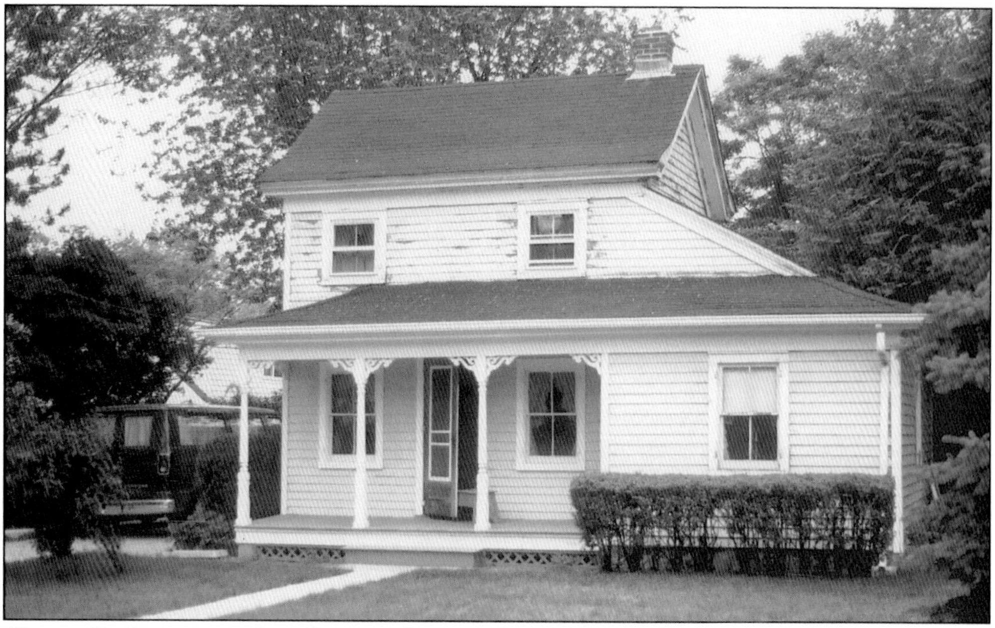

The smaller house is worthy of historical note and preservation. The simple Vernacular Victorian style and well-preserved state of 414 Main Street, Belford, merited its listing in the Monmouth County Historic Sites Inventory. Such houses may present space constraints for contemporary lifestyles; however, in this instance, a large addition was made on the west without marring the original's exterior. This 1987 view predates expansion.

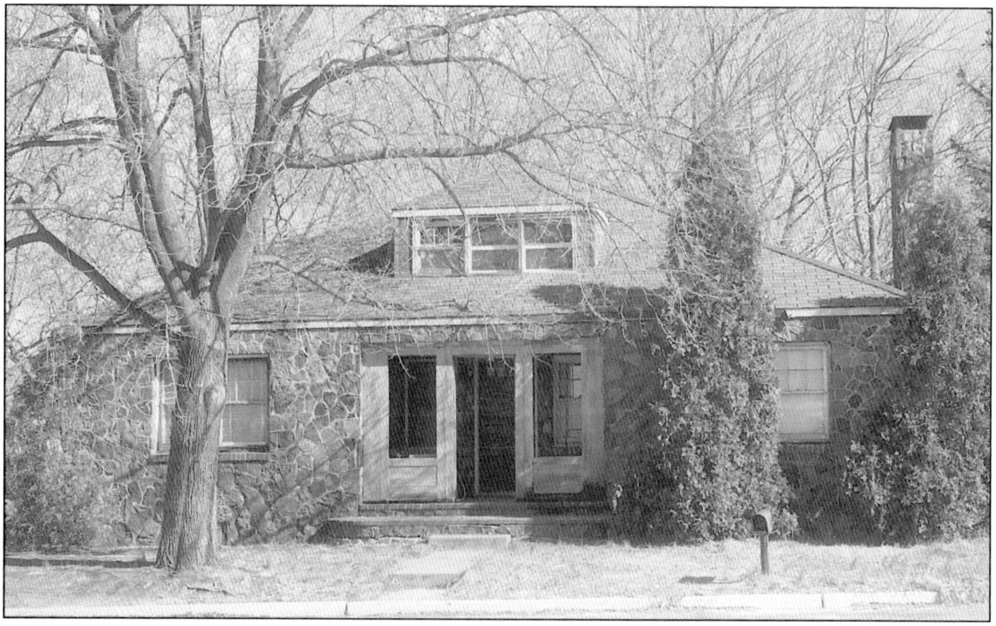

The once-considerable local deposits of peanut stone were used in many ways, typically in foundations, fireplaces, fences, gate posts, and even for a local pond. One infrequently encounters entire buildings of peanut stone, but this one stands on the east side of Avenue D, north of Leonardville Road, Leonardo. It was photographed in 1990 and is still in shabby condition, meriting needed refurbishment.

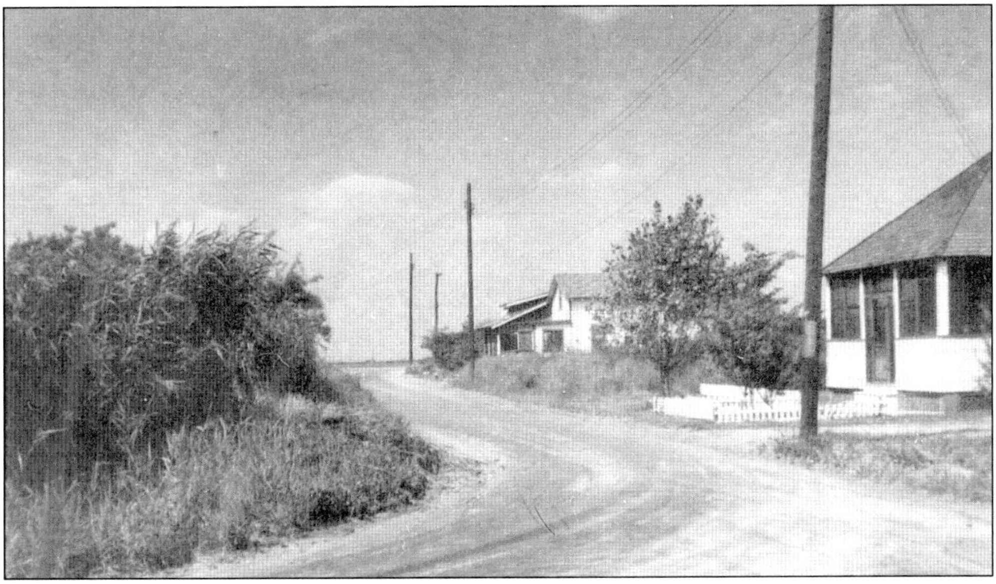

Many small seasonal cabins were built in the bayshore communities during the first three decades of this century, including this example on Benton Avenue, Leonardo, bought by Augusta and George Sotz c. 1926. It was remodeled beyond recognition, while the nearby marina was expanded toward the opposite side of the street. Gail Gannon, a Sotz granddaughter and lender of the picture, recalls World War II blackout conditions on the shore here, a process that was "scary to a kid."

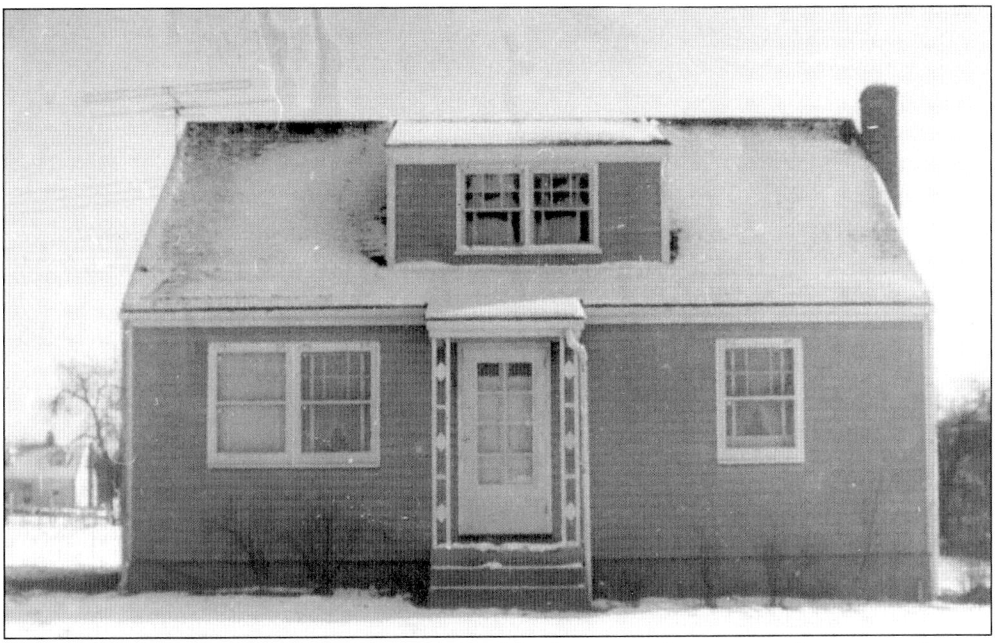

Zoning regulations and the barring of look-alike housing often come after an unpleasant experience. The area around Swartzel Drive was developed in the late 1940s in "secrecy." Access to the site was cut off as contractors quickly built many foundations, leaving the landscape with a massive number of tiny boxes. They were expandable, and most were, including 49 Swartzel Drive, photographed in 1948 and expanded in 1953–54. Tighter land use regulations followed.

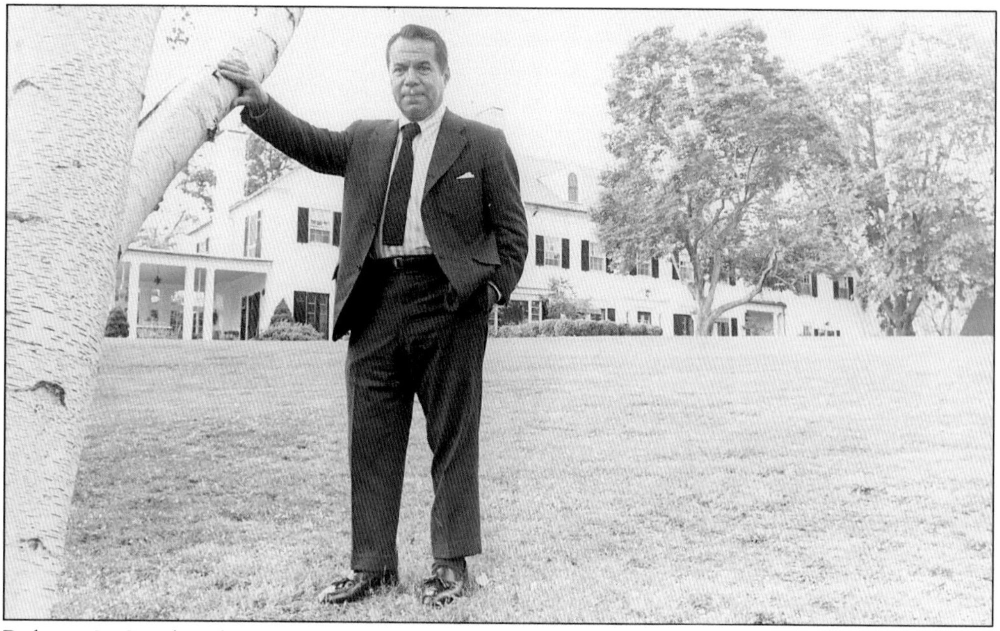

Robert C. Stanley, born on Staten Island, was a decorated veteran of World War II and a key executive of various precious metal mining firms. He was a major figure in the New Jersey Republican Party and delegate to four Republican national conventions. Stanley was a substantial Monmouth County philanthropist, holding positions with numerous organizations, including Monmouth Medical Center, Monmouth College, the Monmouth County Council of the Boy Scouts of America, the Monmouth Conservation Foundation, MCOSS (now the Visiting Nurse Association of Central Jersey), and the New Jersey Hospital Association. Stanley, pictured here in front of his Navesink River home, died in 1985 at age 67.

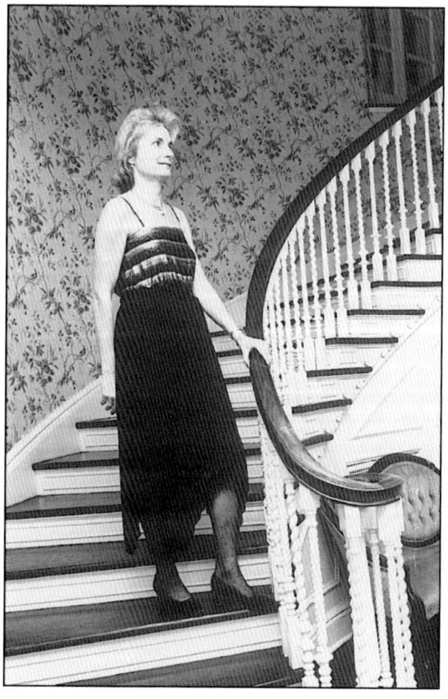

Judith Stanley, pictured here in 1981 in her Navesink River Road home in a gown she planned to wear to the presidential inaugural ball, has made a profession of community activism and public service. The former chairman of the New Jersey Highway Authority has long-headed the Middletown Planning Board and the Monmouth Conservation Foundation, groups that impact and reflect her concern for our environment and surroundings. Her concern for public health is reflected in her board chair of the Visiting Nurse Association of Central Jersey (formerly MCOSS), which has named their Red Bank office building in her honor, and her board chair of Monmouth Medical Center. The history major graduate of Smith College is also a trustee and co-president of the Monmouth County Historical Association. Ms. Stanley is determined to see her goals accomplished, and is a hands-on executive who works tirelessly to make her town a better place.

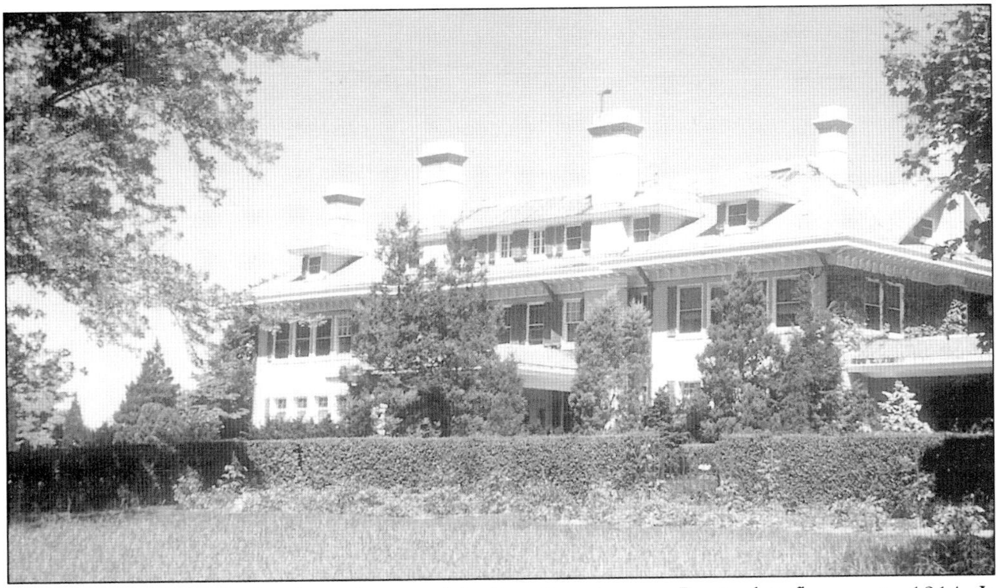

Samuel J. Riker built this large house of Italian Renaissance Revival influence in 1914. It was designed by Long Branch architect Leon Cubberley and located on his "Overlook Farm" on Navesink River Road. Riker, a New York lawyer with extensive business interests, was a descendant of a family that settled in America in the first half of the 17th century. He died in 1936, and his widow sold the property in 1945. The site, considered for development and as a possible home for a private school, remained a residence when photographed in the 1960s. It was sold in 1963 for the foundation of the Navesink County Club, which modified the building for club use, its present occupancy.

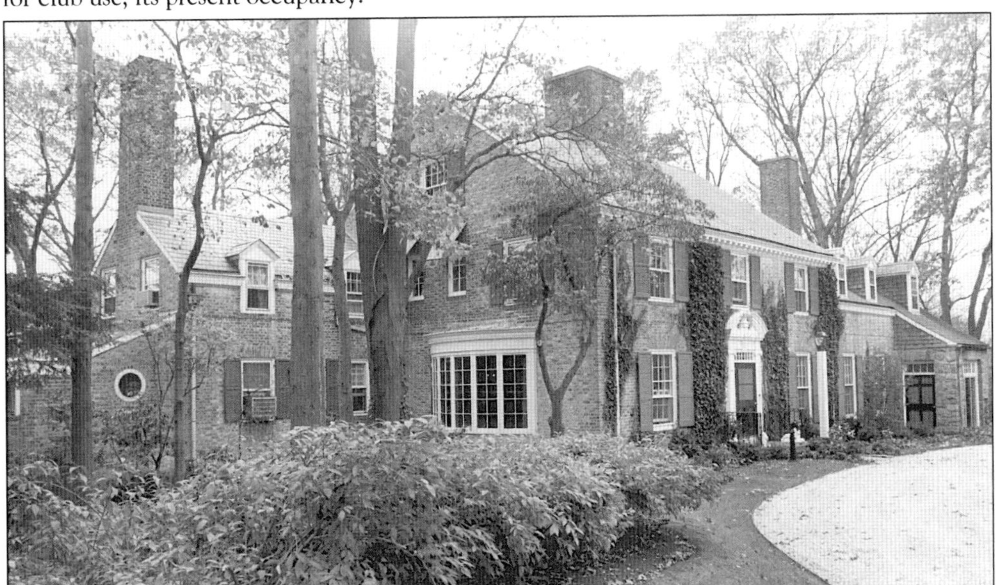

Wilbur Barlow Ruthrauff was a founder of the New York advertising agency of Ruthrauff & Ryan in 1912. He built this 34-by-106-foot Colonial Revival house on his McClees Road "Highlow Farm" in 1929. The house, pictured here in the late 1970s, still stands well preserved at number 203.

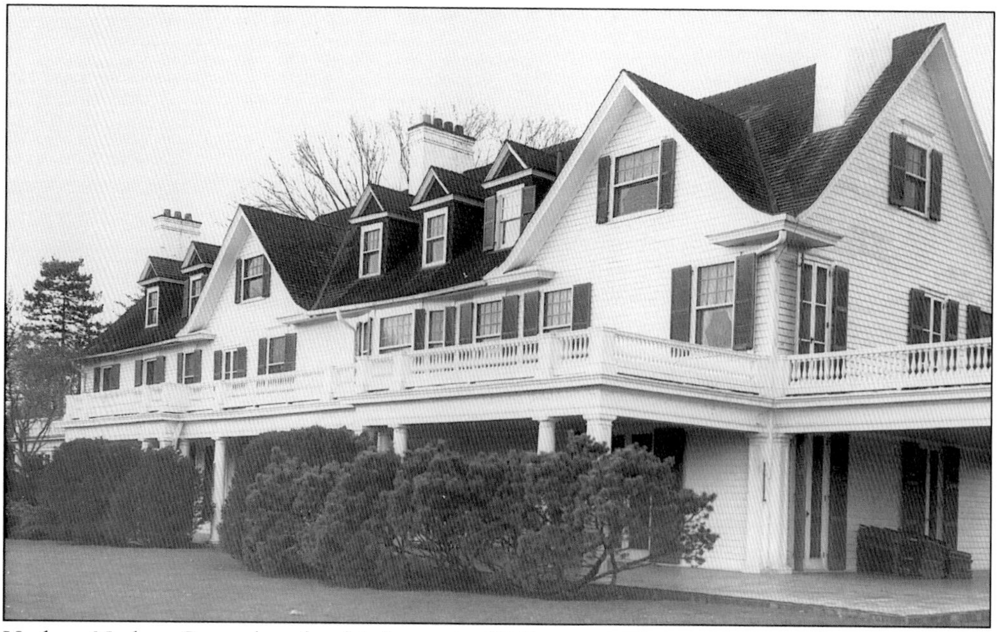

Herbert Nathan Straus bought this house in 1908 as part of an approximately 70-acre estate (at the time of its sale in 1949). It was likely built by Duncan D. Parmley after he lost the old Gordon farmhouse to fire in 1895. Local lore claims the Strauses planned to replace the house with one in an elaborate French-influenced style following completion of their two farm groups. The plans had to be canceled due to Straus' untimely death in 1933. This picture of the well-preserved house was taken *c.* 1951. (The Dorn's Collection.)

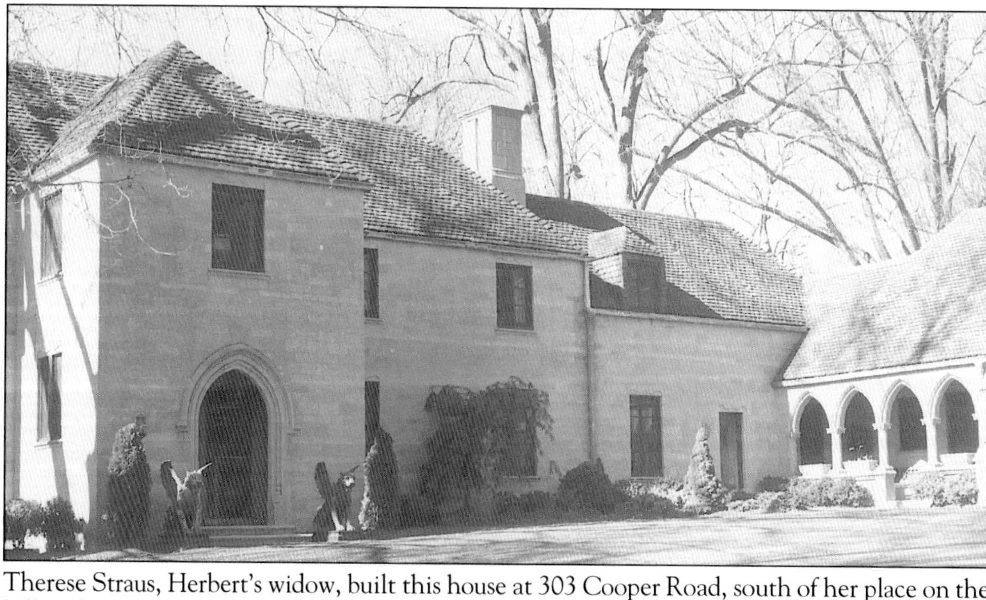

Therese Straus, Herbert's widow, built this house at 303 Cooper Road, south of her place on the hill and nearer the street, for her Middletown Farm superintendent, Thomas Head. Its architect is unknown, but the place bears a strong stylistic resemblance to Cobble Close (opposite). The house, then situated on a 2.9-acre lot, brought a higher price at Straus' 1949 sale than did the three other parcels, including each farm group on 20 acres! This recent courtyard view shows the main block at left and a service corridor at right.

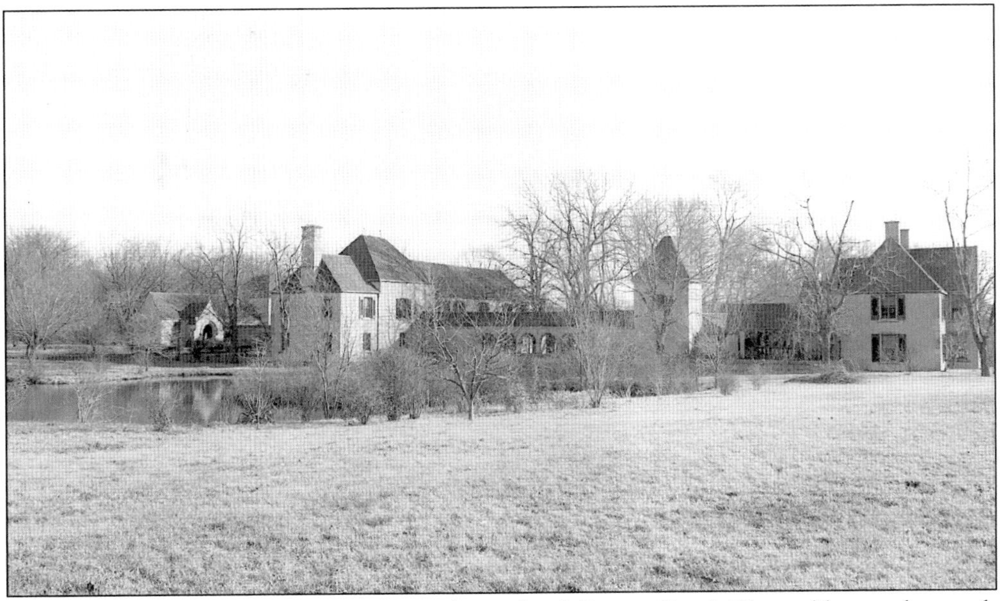

The Strauses built two farm groups on either side of Cooper Road. The stables on the north side behind the house were built first around 1930 (see Volume I, p. 128), and designed in the French Norman style by Alfred Hopkins. Away from the street, they are less visible than the dairy complex on the south side of Cooper, also designed by Hopkins in a southern French style. The arcade in the center and the pond in front of this 1951 photograph are key design features. (The Dorn's Collection.)

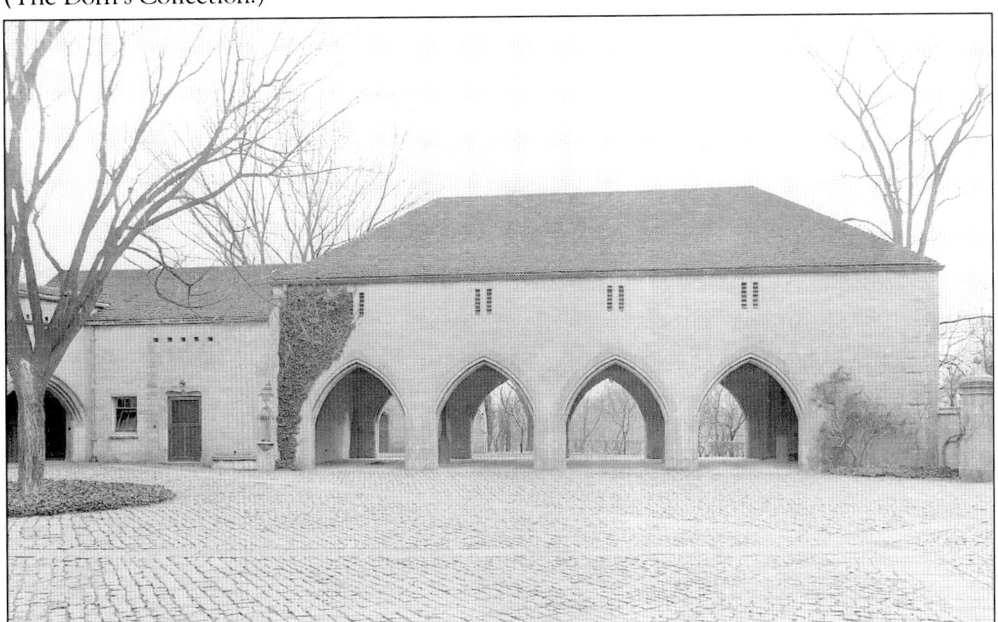

The dairy complex was named Cobble Close, reflecting its walled enclosure. This courtyard view c. 1951 overlooks the open farm vehicle storage shed, a structure with a hay storage loft on the second floor. Doors now make this space enclosed garages. Although the property was divided into condominiumnized residential units in the 1960s, it still retains a high degree of integrity as much of the structure is unchanged. (The Dorn's Collection.)

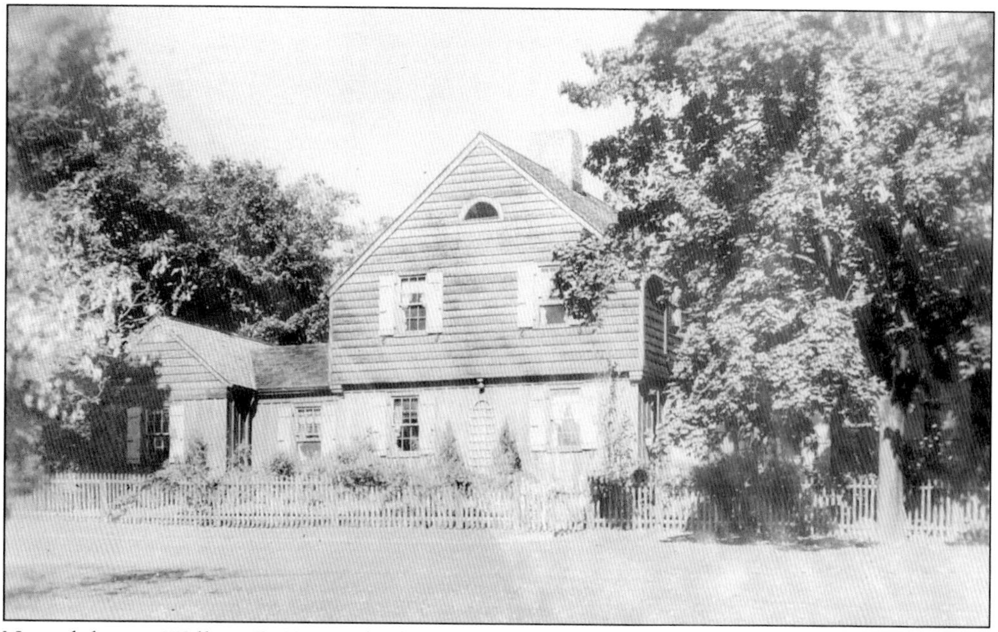

Newark lawyer William B. Kinney built "Distant Shore," a fine, large, brick house on Navesink River Road, in 1917. Researching the demolished house can be elusive. This photograph, marked "Mrs. William B. Kinney 1931" in the album of builders Quackenbush & Nevius, may be one of the estate's outbuildings located near the present street of Sailors Way.

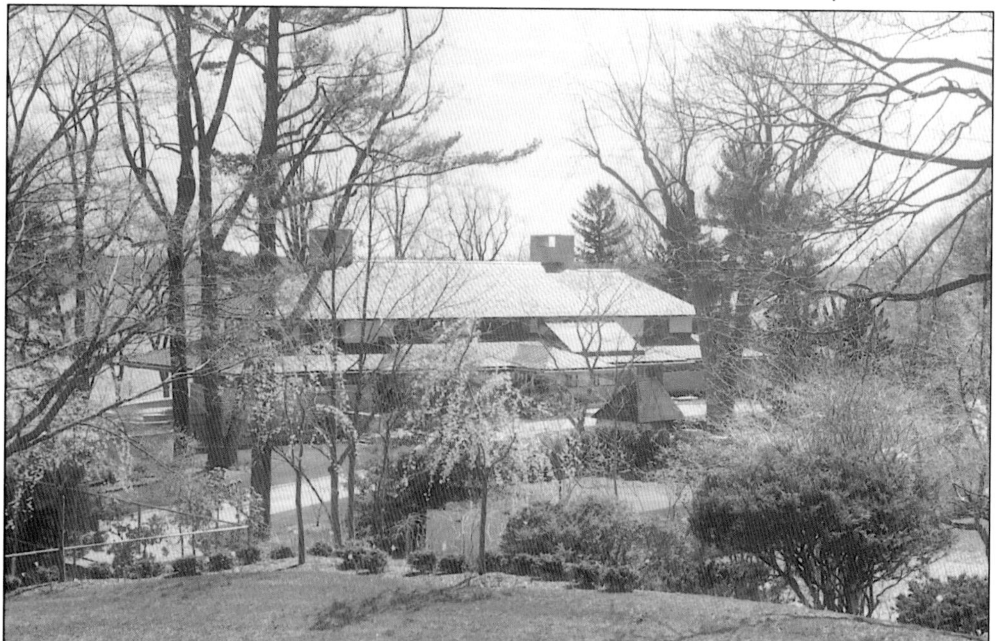

Donald Mallow designed this 10,000-square-foot house at 546 Navesink River Road, built 1987–90. The symmetrical house has a cantilevered copper roof and is known for the richness of its materials. They include walls of briar sandstone from Ohio, floors of bluestone from Pennsylvania, and countertops of granite from Brazil. The wood floors are white oak, while Honduran mahogany was used for the doors and cabinets.

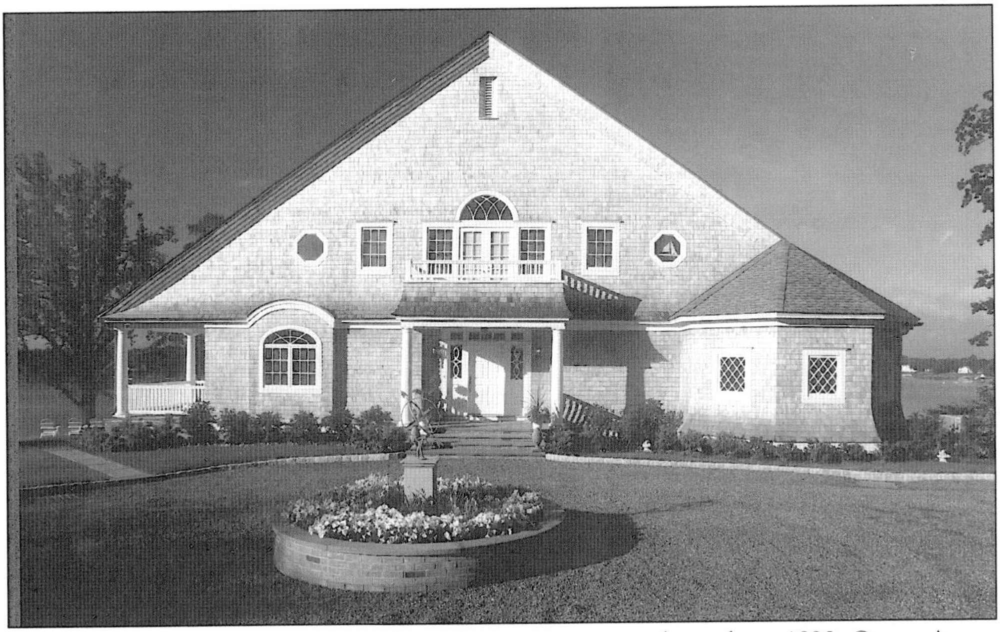

The proposed development of "Northover," an estate surrounding a large 1890s Queen Anne-style house (see Volume I, p. 49), was a critical planning issue in the 1950s. The 12 houses built there did not change the area's character, but the undistinguished two-level shore front ranch on the west side of Northover Place was a marginal use of what had become valuable property, and was eventually demolished. George Rudolph designed this house for the Fahmie family on that site, inspired by the Shingle Style that was in vogue during the late 19th century. The east elevation is pictured here.

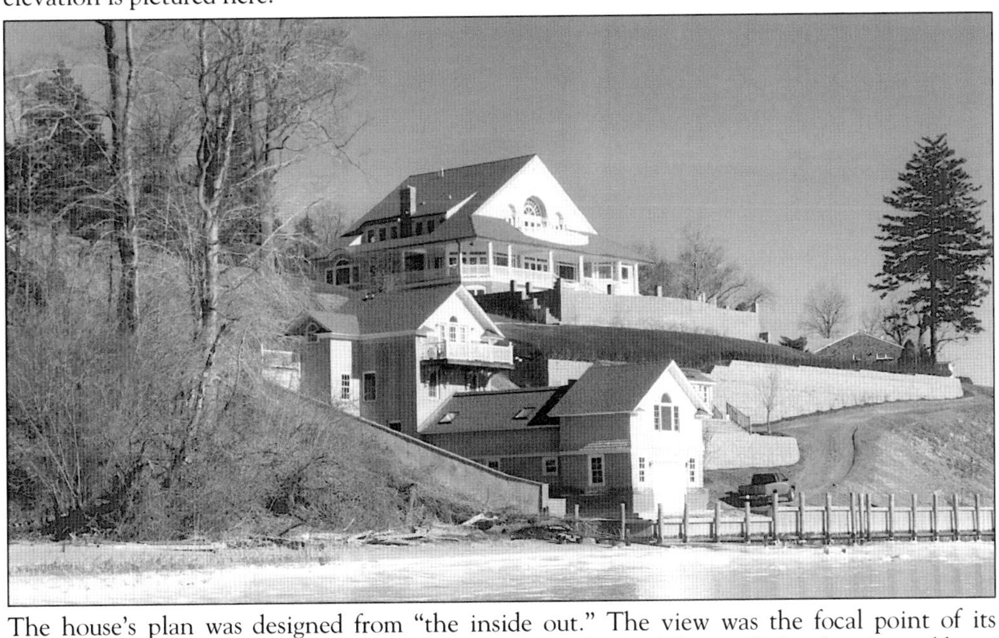

The house's plan was designed from "the inside out." The view was the focal point of its orientation, which was also designed to maximize ventilation. The south facade, pictured here, faces the river. The residence was completed in 1996; the project included the expansion and remodelling of an existing boathouse.

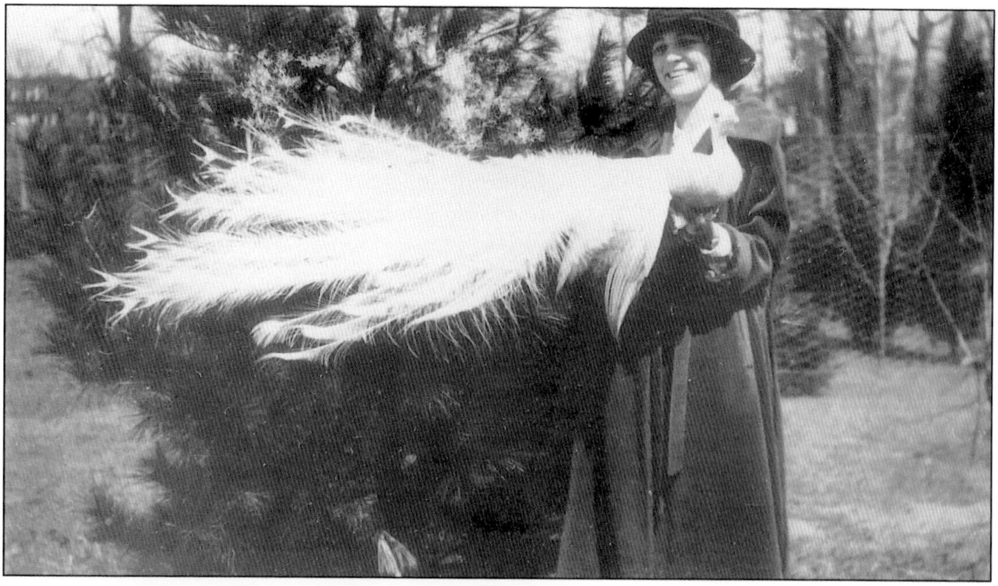

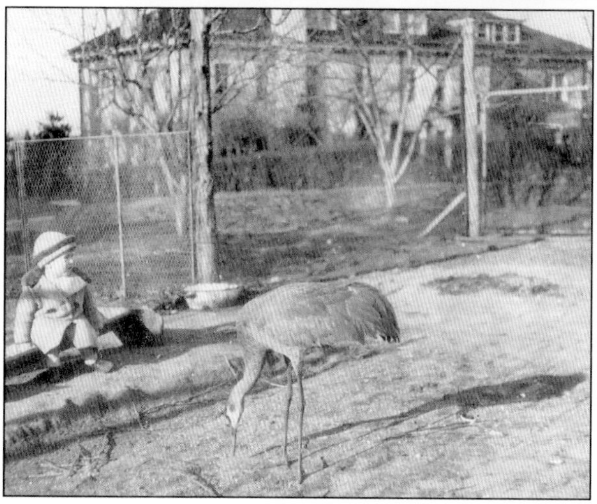

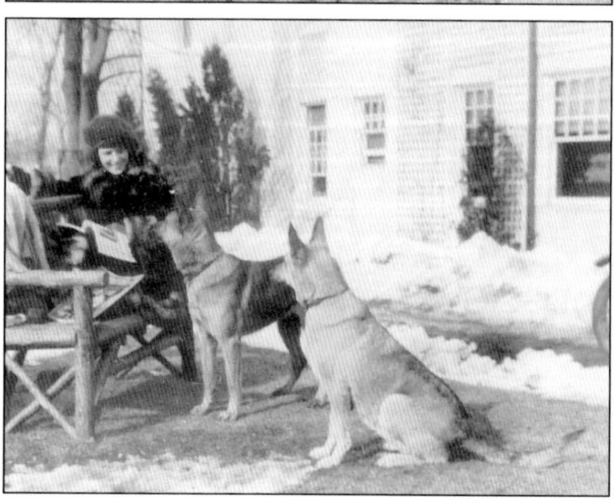

Oliver Holton's Twin Brook Zoo opened in 1925 on the south side of Highway 35, between today's Twin Brook Avenue and Woodland Drive. He began his operation earlier in that decade by trading in exotic birds, including emus, pheasants, and decorative waterfowls. He lived in the large Italian Renaissance Revival house at Spruce and Crest Roads (in the background of the middle image) with his wife, Mildred, and their two sons. A lobo wolf escaped from the zoo on July 24, 1927, and entered the Holton home, where it met the Holton's large "police dog" Trix, perhaps one of the pictured dogs. The two joined in attacking the younger Holton son, who died of his injuries. The attack effectively closed the zoo, although it remained open until the end of the season. The Holtons divorced, and Mildred found a strong attraction to her spiritual counselor, the Reverend Ernest Mandeville of Middletown's Christ Church.

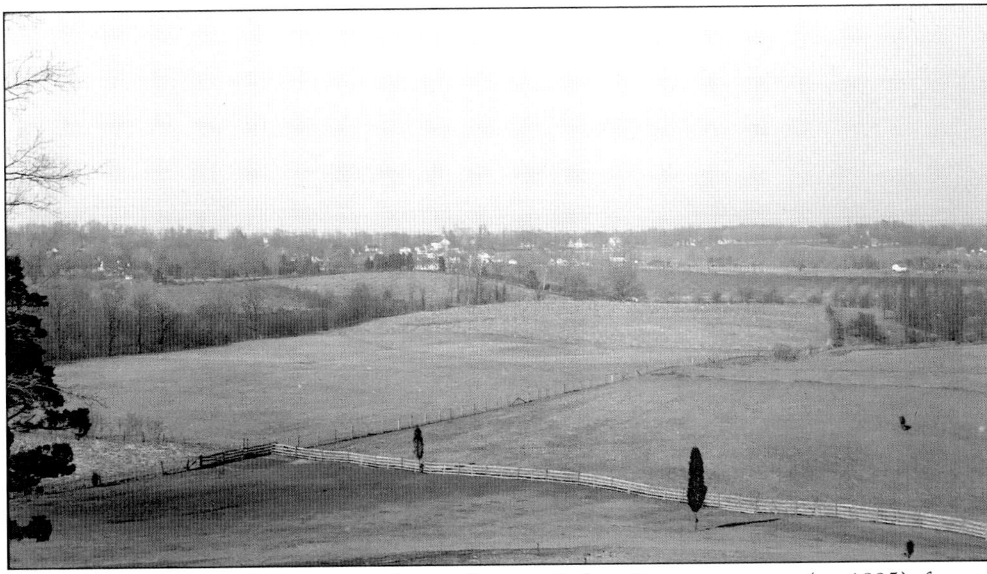

The Charles Gibson Bennett purchase of part of the Conover estate (*c.* 1895) formed a sizable farm embracing a rolling landscape east of Red Hill Road in the direction of Middletown-Lincroft Road, the perspective of this photograph *c.* 1940. The latter street is visible in the background. Much of this landscape was covered in the 1970s by the Fox Hill housing development.

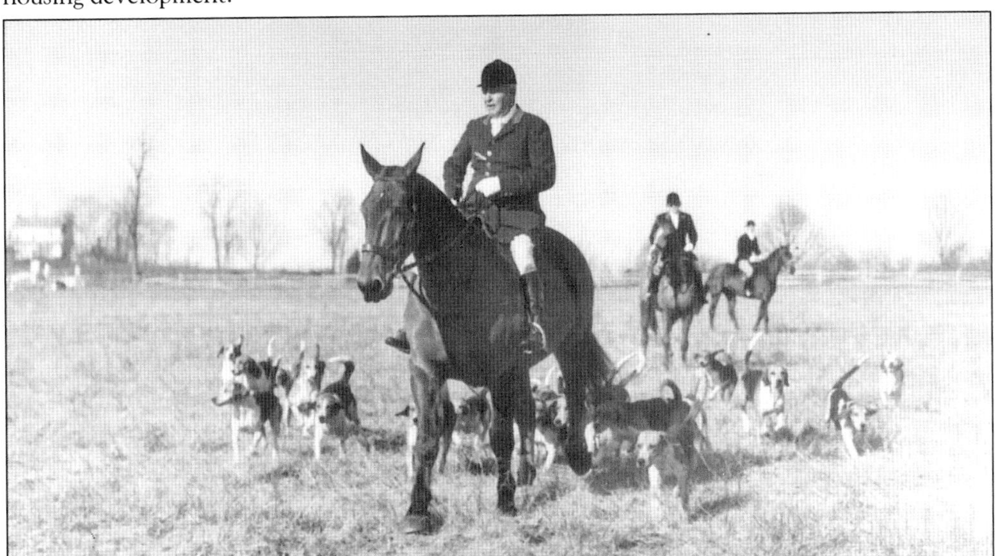

Amory L. Haskell acquired Woodland Farm in the hills north of Cooper Road, adjacent to Oak Hill Farm, which was owned by his father, J. Amory Haskell. The younger Haskell was an accomplished rider in his early youth, and continued his lifelong interest in equestrian activities. A World War I aviator, he held several business positions, including a vice-presidency of General Motors, a firm he left to found an automobile glass company that he sold to the Pittsburgh Plate Glass Company and the Libby-Owens-Ford Glass Company. He is pictured in the fox hunting pose for which he may be best remembered, as founder of the widely attended annual Hunt (or Race) Meet, an event not held since 1996. (Collection of the Monmouth County Historical Association.)

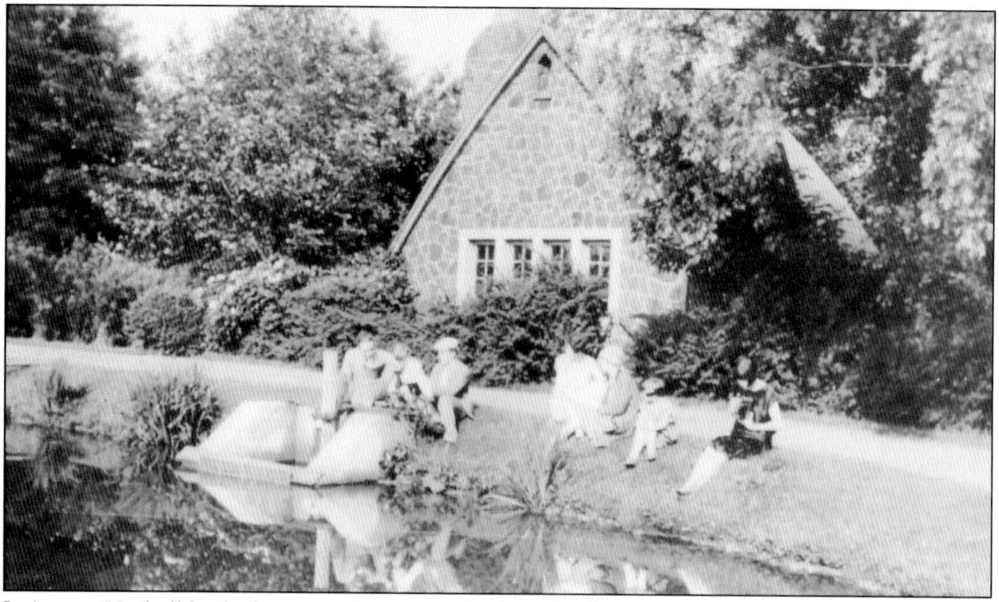

J. Amory Haskell built this pump house in 1916 on the former Lufburrow Mill property, which he bought from Oscar Hesse in 1915. Close to the Whippoorwill Valley Road, it has appealed to visitors for many years, including youths who treated it unkindly as a hang-out in the early 1980s. The pump house was preserved by incorporation into a new residence built c. 1984 for Ara Hovnanian and designed by Red Bank architect Robert De Santis of Kaplan Gaunt De Santis.

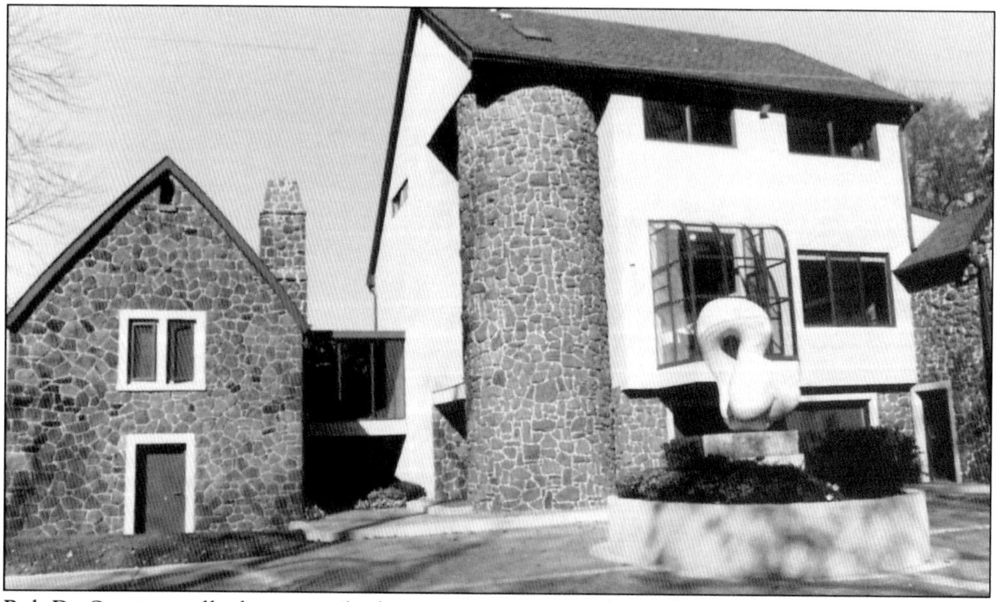

Bob De Santis recalls that an early design concept was to keep the pump house separate, using the main structure as a backdrop and connecting the two with a transparent hall. The upper story was initially the owner's bedroom, but it was later converted to a guest suite. Some pump machinery was placed in working order, and the peanut stone for the new house was found on the site. The three-story round tower contains spiral stairs. This 1985 view shows the east elevation; the pond is on the west.

This record provides evidence of what Stephen Sondheim did before writing hit Broadway musicals. He did advertising work, such as this piece, a "bright miniature musical about a family like yours in search of a new home," done for Jacob Lefferts' Oak Hill Farm c. 1960. The author lives in one of these houses and it is not new any longer. One question frequently asked of this historic house specialist is, "Do you live in an old house?" His cheerful, but not happy, response is always, "Yes. It's about 40 years old and showing signs of age."

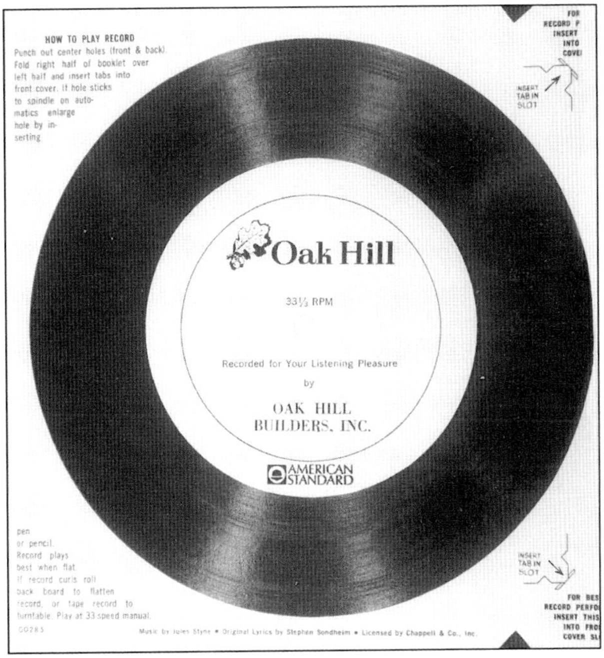

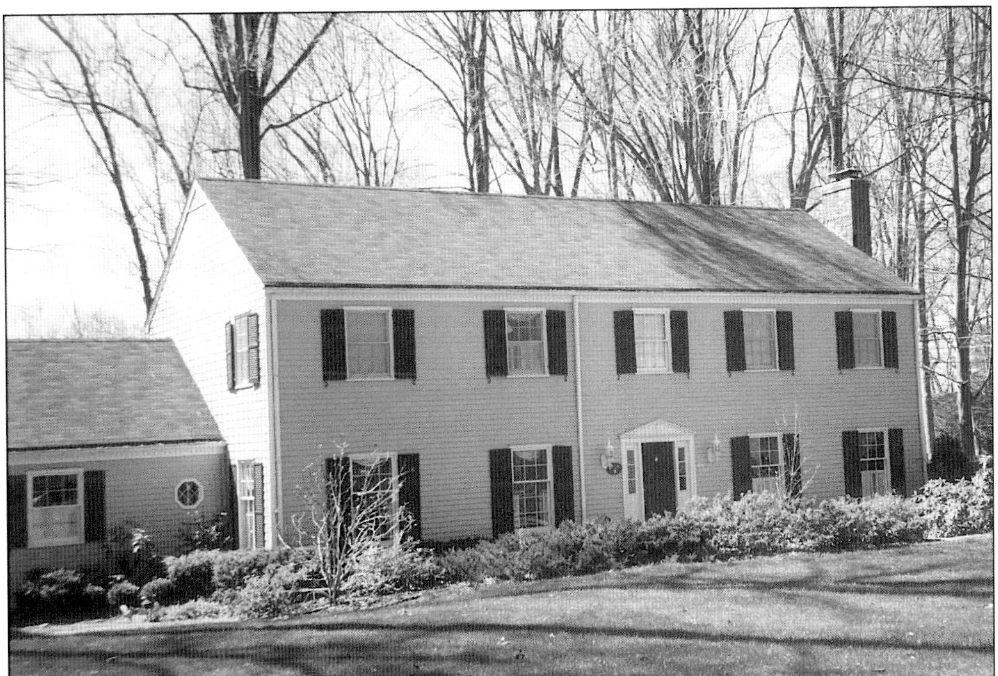

The New Jersey Natural Gas Company sponsored a tercentenary home, built by Oak Hill Builders at 65 Townsend Drive, as a commercial tie-in to New Jersey's 300th anniversary celebration. The house, designed by Noboru Kobayashi of Red Bank (Lefferts' principal architect in the development), combined "colonial" motifs and modern gas appliances, including central air conditioning. Middletown's claim as the first settlement in the state and the company's prior builder's awards prompted the Oak Hill site selection. The unchanged house is pictured here in this recent photo.

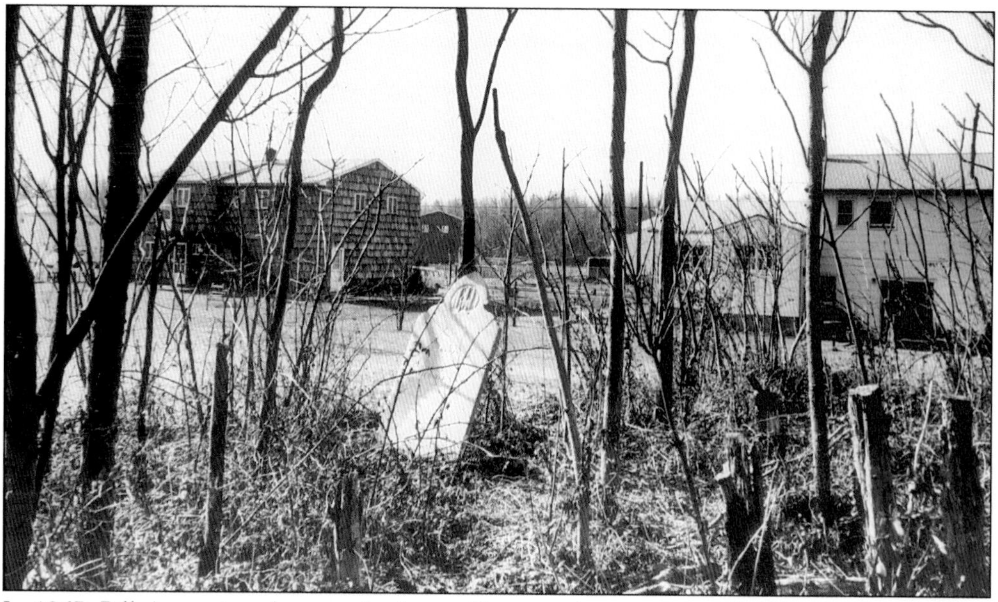

In 1967, Bill Augustine photographed a small private burying ground off Harmony Road in a project in which he searched for houses that were advertised for sale in the 1750s. The premises, containing graves primarily of the Wood and Dennis families, illustrate a virtually unregulated preservation problem—the protection of old, abandoned cemeteries. The deficiency of legal constraints against their destruction necessitates respect by owners that is too often lacking. (Special Collections and Archives, Rutgers University Libraries.)

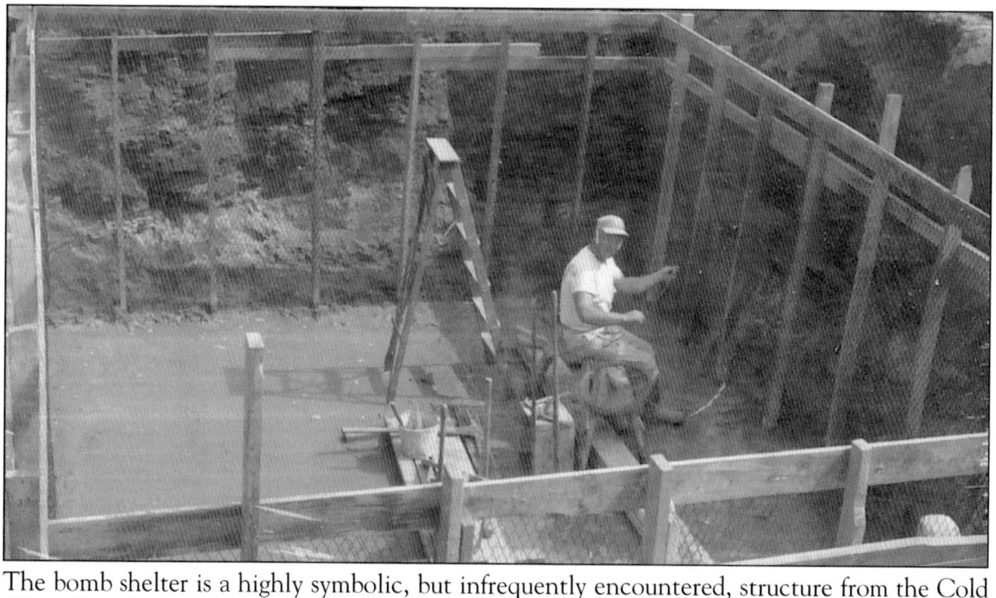

The bomb shelter is a highly symbolic, but infrequently encountered, structure from the Cold War. This photograph taken in 1961 shows one under construction at the 707 Park Avenue home of Dr. Peter and Virginia Brady. Virginia recalled recently that its building was prompted by her husband's concerns for their children. The room was stocked with the anticipated necessary supplies and its bunk-type sleeping facilities contained space for a number of neighbors, too. Its entrance is built into a slight elevation now covered by vines, and the facility is no longer maintained.

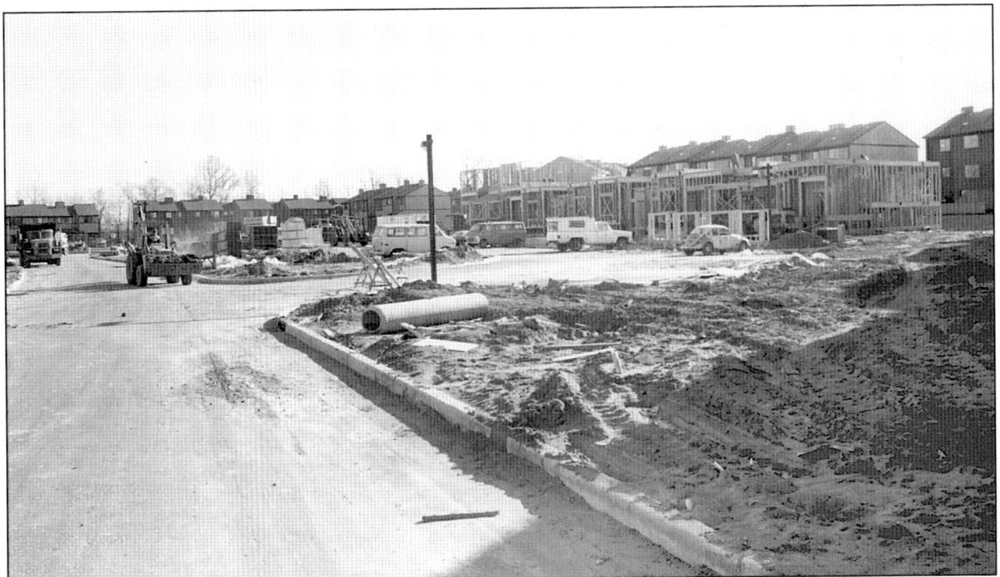

Building density and the residential mix are issues that impact any developing town. While single-family, stand-alone housing characterized the township, a large condominium townhouse complex was built in the late 1970s in the vicinity of Harmony and Cherry Tree Farm Roads. This late construction scene was photographed in January 1990.

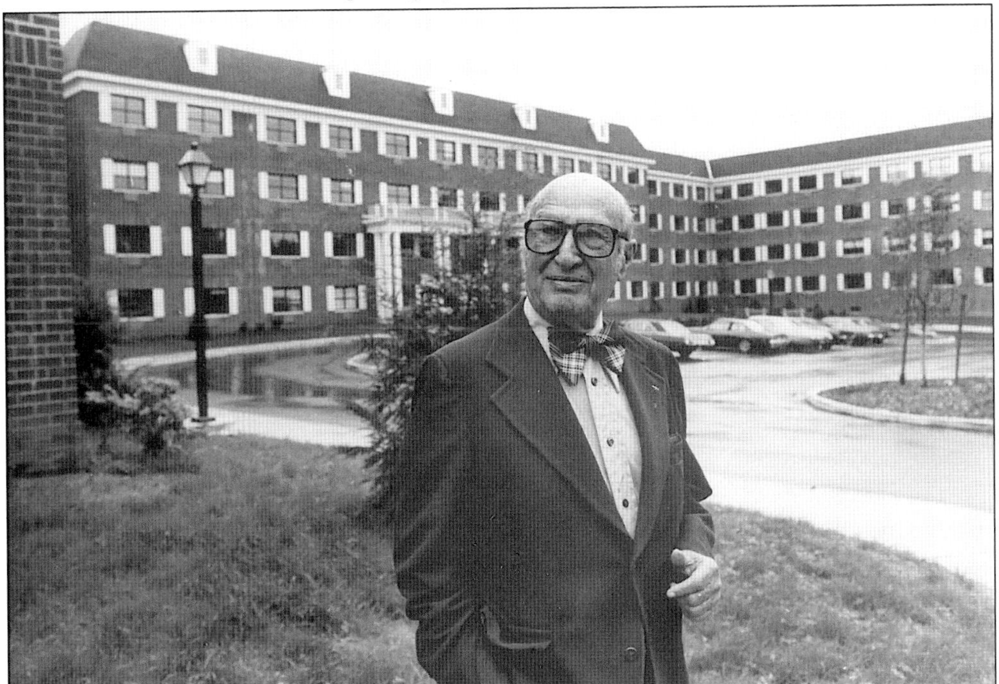

Colonel Harry J. Luftman is pictured here in 1979 in front of the new Luftman Towers, a senior citizens apartment building on Hurleys Lane, Lincroft. Luftman was the first director of the New Jersey Housing Authority in 1937 and served in a number of housing positions, including the chair of the Lincroft Senior Citizens Housing Corporation. The complex was named for his deceased wife, Adele Braelow Luftman.

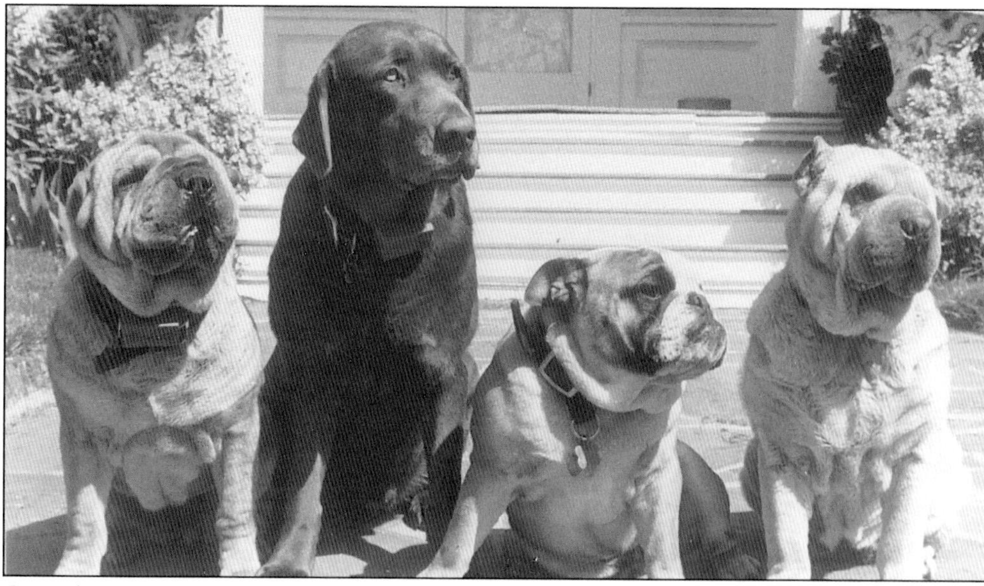

Over the past century, the dog has been elevated from a working animal to a full-fledged member of the American family. C.C. Dyer has fond memories of growing up with dogs; her mother bred English cocker spaniels. When she and her husband, Geraldo Rivera, were contemplating moving from New York to the "country" (such is Middletown from a New York City perspective), the opportunity to live with dogs was a key factor. They started with one black lab, who preceded their children into the family. Their canine members now number four, including, from left to right, Gabby, Clay, Toto, and Connie (Gabby's mother), who are pictured here on the porch of "Rough Point." The household also includes 5 birds and 27 fish. (Photograph by Scott Longfield.)

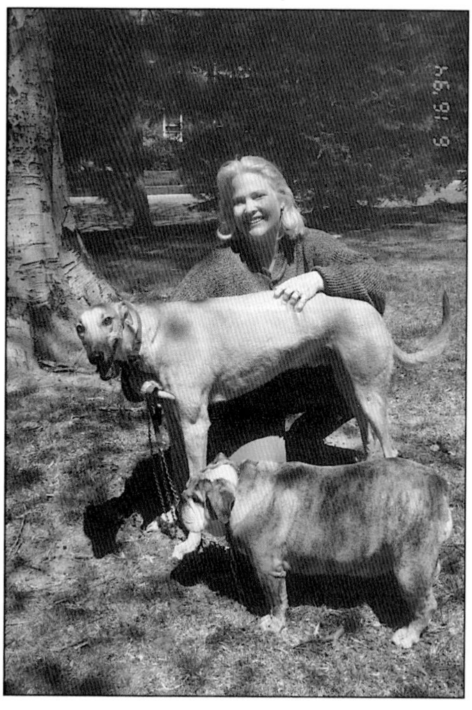

Margaret Lundrigan has owned purebred dogs, including Ginger, the bulldog in the foreground; however, she recently discovered that many fine prospective pets are already born, but are unwanted, such as greyhound racers, whose longevity is nil if their racing careers are not successful. Al, adopted at age two and a half, has proved to be gentle and quite suitable as a pet. Some older greyhounds also become available, but whatever the age, the supply is greater than the demand. Greyhound Friends has a New Jersey chapter to help give these deserving dogs a second chance. (Photograph by Tova Navarra.)

Two

Roads of Commerce

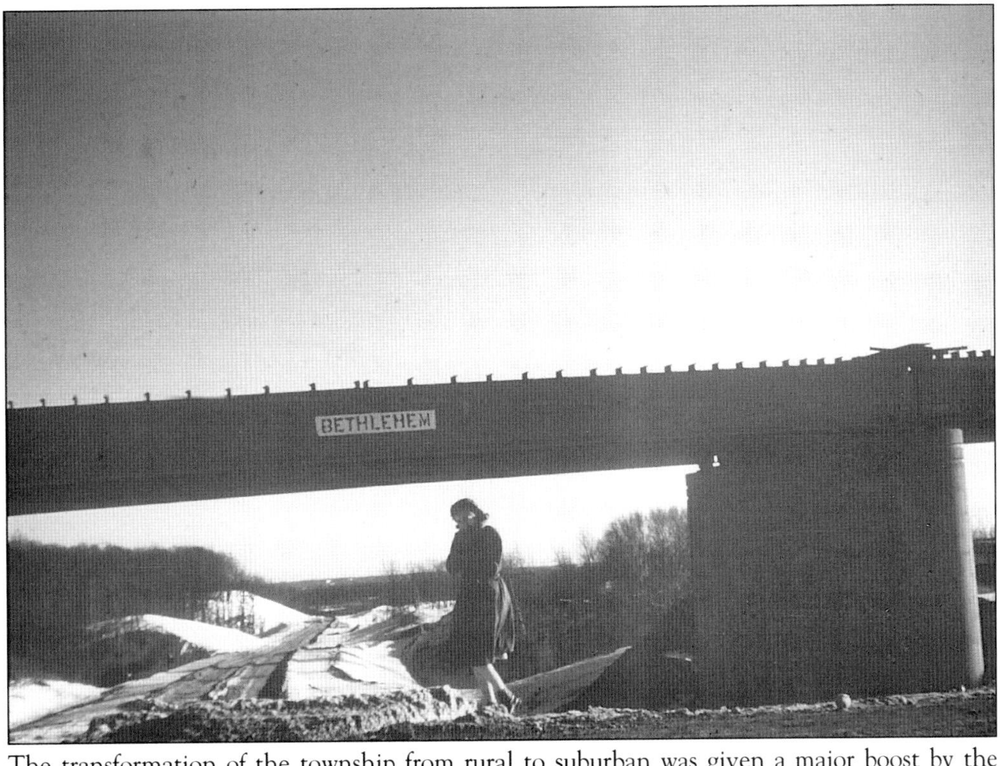

The transformation of the township from rural to suburban was given a major boost by the 1954 opening of the Garden State Parkway, which accelerated a building boom that had been ongoing since shortly after the end of World War II. This construction scene of the Red Hill Road overpass was taken in February 1954. It shows a girder manufactured by the Bethlehem Steel Company, a reminder of an era when a vibrant steel industry regularly produced around 100 million tons per year. Exit 114 at this road was not opened until 1964.

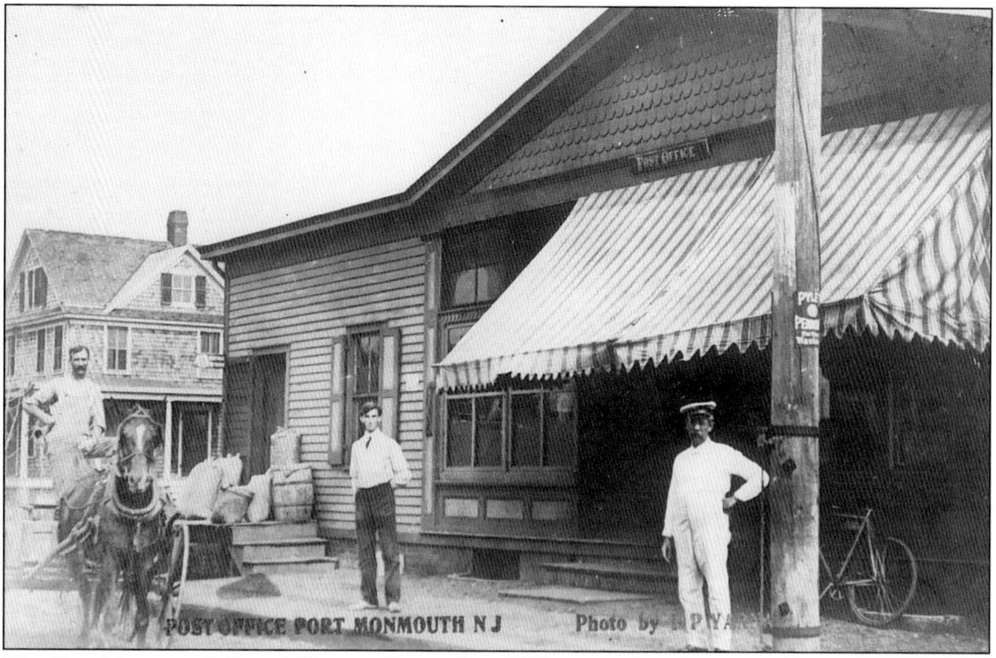

The Port Monmouth Post Office was located in William Seeley's store on the east side of Main Street when this image was taken c. 1907 by Frank Yarnall for a photographic postcard. The building does not appear to be extant. Post offices of the time were often relocated with a party change of the presidency. Port Monmouth's was later located on the west side of Main in Walling's store (see Volume I, p. 82).

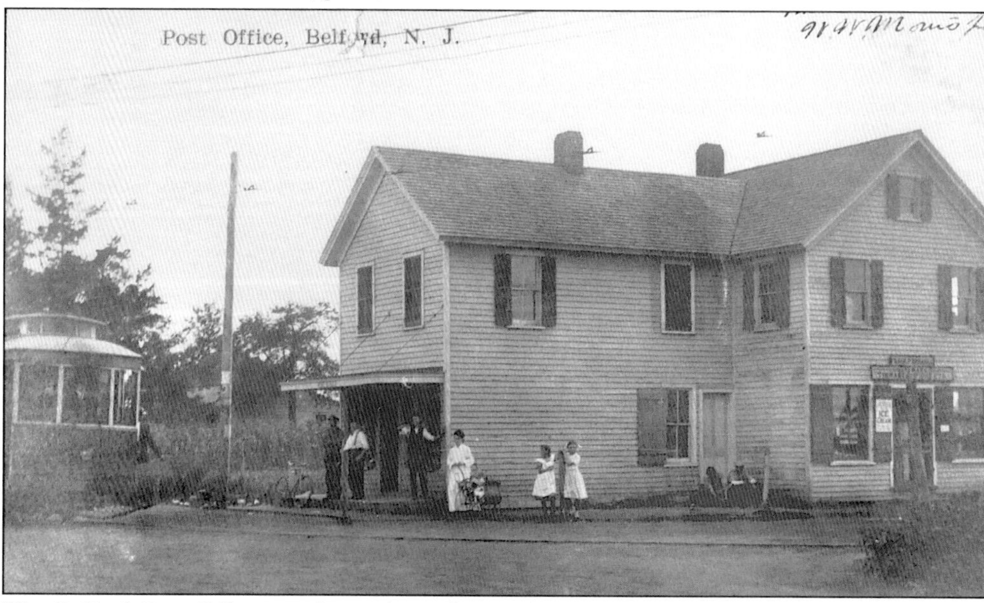

The Belford Post Office was located on the southwest corner of Main Street and Railroad Avenue when Frank Yarnall, who had a store at the side, took this photograph c. 1907 for a postcard. At times the office was located at Bennett's nearby store (see Volume II, p. 96). The pictured building, now 744 Main Street, has been enlarged on both its front and sides, but the two gables make the place, still a store and dwelling, recognizable today.

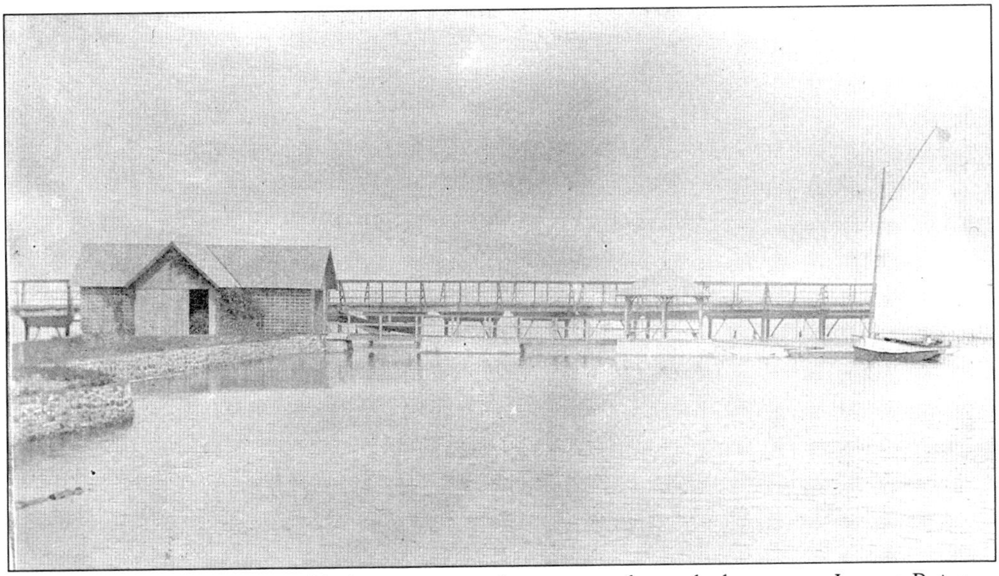

Early area roads were more likely waterways. Locust was formerly known as Locust Point, a reliable indicator of the presence of a dock. Locust's Mounts Dock, seen here in a late 1890s photograph, was located just west of the Oceanic Bridge. Locust Point and Browns Dock, situated farther west on the Middletown shore, served an extensive local farming network in the 19th century, but their activity diminished after the turn of the 20th century. The shallow Navesink River had its main channel near the south bank in the early decades of the 20th century. (Collection of Richard C. Winters.)

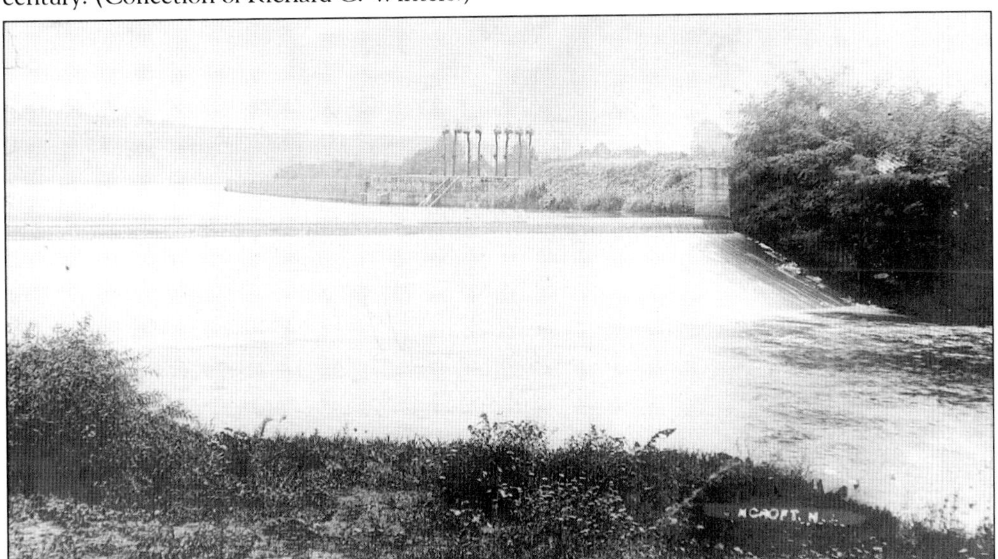

This dam at Swimming River was likely built near the turn of the 20th century by the Tintern Water Company, a firm later absorbed by the Monmouth Consolidated Water Company. Its overflow line of 15.4 feet was flooded in 1955 (see Volume I, p. 34). Replacement by the present dam began in 1958. The unidentified poles in the background appear to contain nests for ospreys. Land upstream on the Middletown side (right) was part of the large farm formerly owned by Christ Church. The image is a c. 1910 Alick Merriman photographic postcard. (Collection of Harold Solomon.)

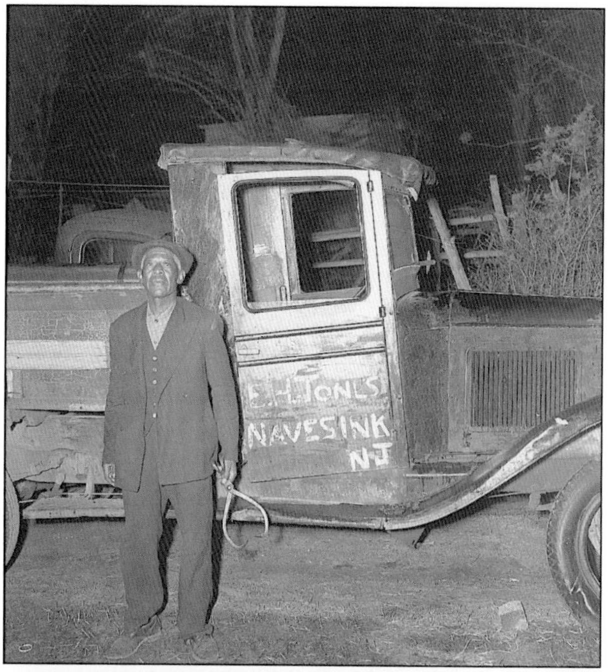

The iceman cameth into the mid-20th century, serving domestic needs when ice was the principal form of refrigeration. Some oldtimers called the electric refrigerator an "ice-box" long after power replaced frozen water. E.H. Jones, who had a Navesink-area route, presents a certain dignity attired in a three-piece suit, tongs in hand, in this undated photograph.

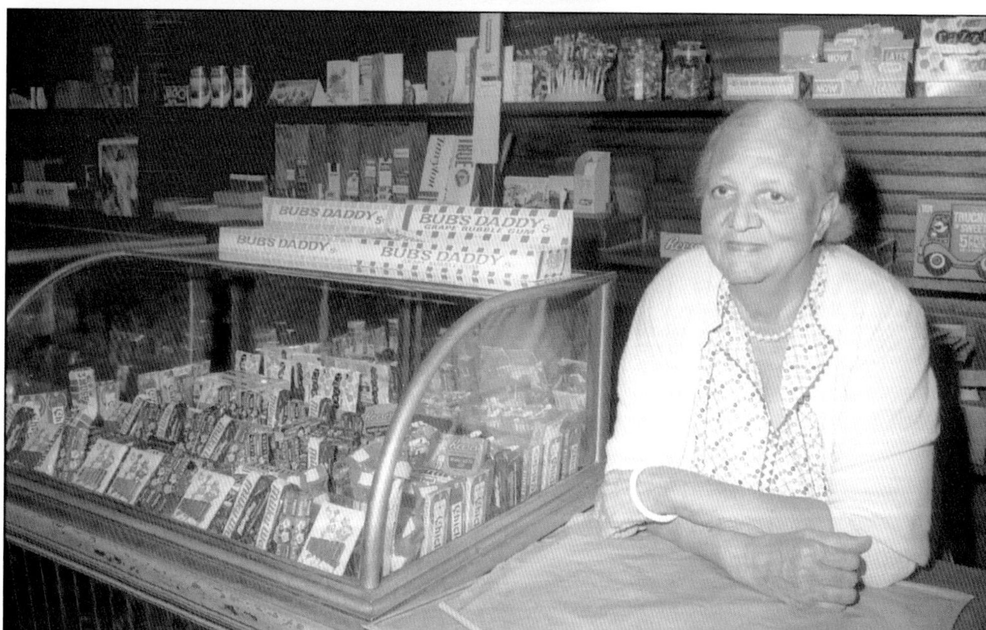

Rebecca Alston is pictured here inside her general store on Red Hill Road in 1972, a business founded by Hilliard Alston and his brother in 1902. Rebecca, who was their niece, operated the store from 1963 until it closed in the 1970s. It served the needs of a local clientele at a time when one may have left his neighborhood infrequently, lasting into the modern suburban era as a vestige of another world. The few remaining reminders of Red Hill as an early African-American community include two churches, the Clinton Chapel, the AME Zion Church, and the Union Baptist Church. Alston was a longtime activist with the Middletown Republican organization, serving 30 years on the local election board. The store is now a private residence.

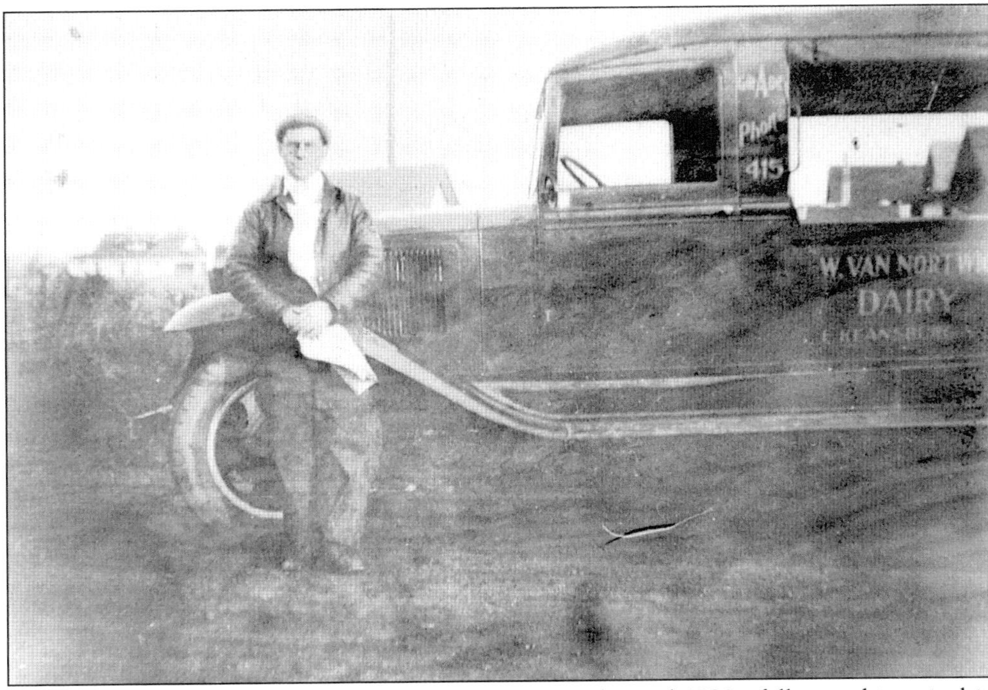

Walter Van Nortwick opened a milk delivery route in the mid-1930s, following his arrival in Middletown from Newark. Walter, pictured here with an early delivery truck, died in the 1930s.

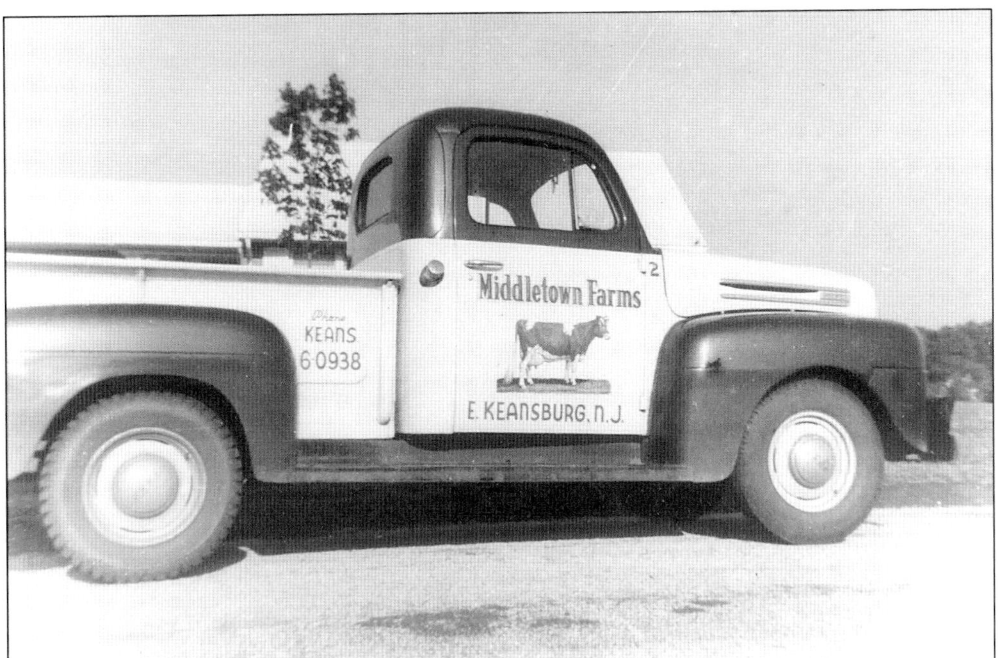

The Van Nortwicks adopted the Middletown Farms trade name in the late 1950s after the family name became publicly identified with their bus line. Frank and Walter maintained a delivery and vending machine operation—the latter was a forerunner of the convenience store—until supermarket competition caused them to close the business in about 1970.

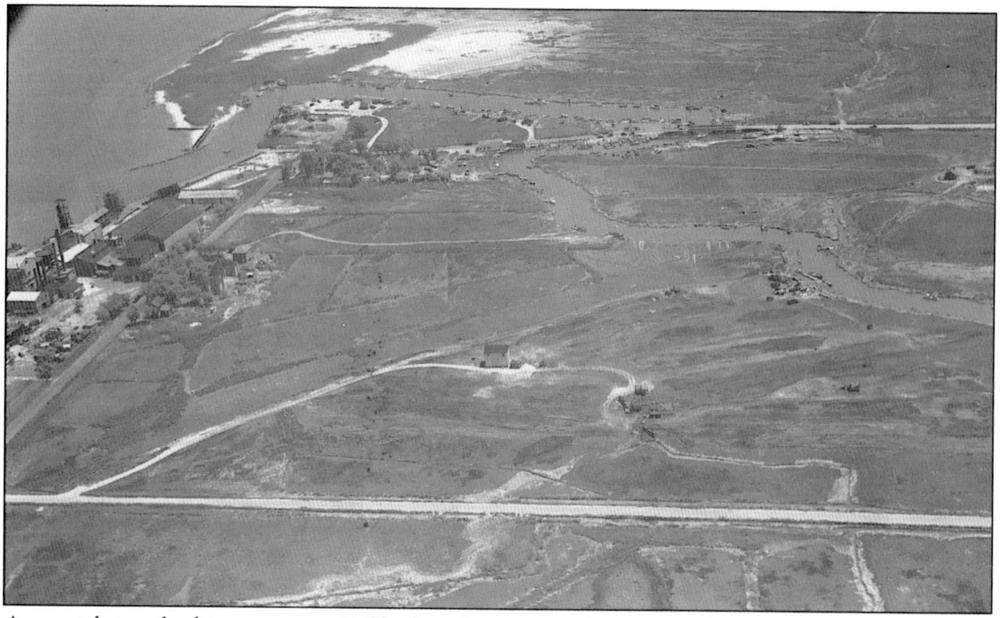

An aerial view looking east over Belford, perhaps in the late 1940s, shows the former J. Howard Smith fish processing plant at left in a predominately marshland landscape. Church and Main Streets are the two north-south streets visible at bottom and center respectively, while Comptons Creek is the stream with the undulating course. The township sewage treatment plant was built east of Main in the late 1960s, while the "fish factory," its popular name, was demolished in 1989. (The Dorn's Collection.)

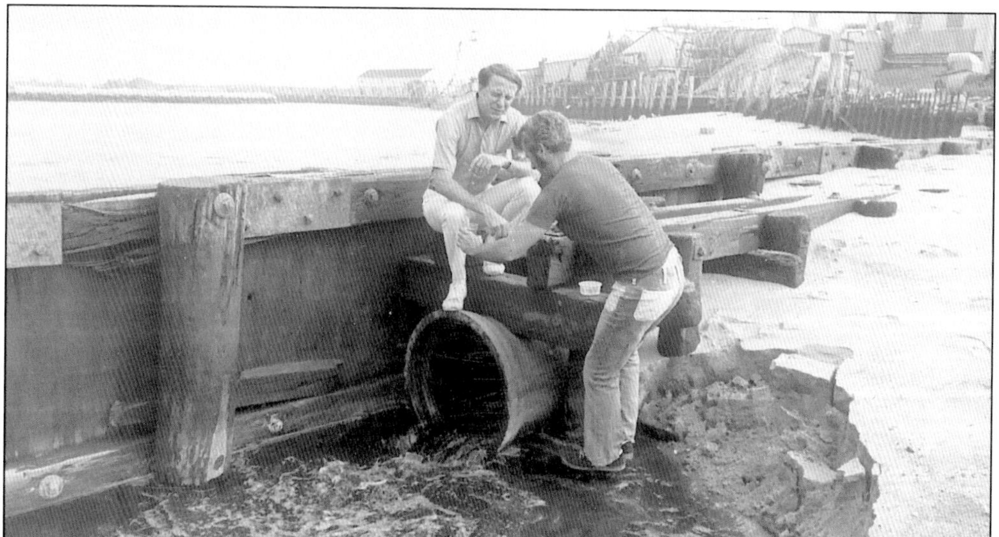

Although it may be tempting to wax nostalgic about menhaden fish processing, a quintessential shore industry and once Middletown's largest employer, it was a foul, smelly business that was an environmental fright long before concerns about clean air and water were heightened in the 1960s. In this photo from 1976, local resident James Quick shows Frank Self (left), township committee candidate, a 20-inch discharge pipe at a low tide. The pipe carried effluent from the air cleaning system of the plant, then owned by Seacoast Products, Inc. The cleared site is the subject of ongoing development proposals.

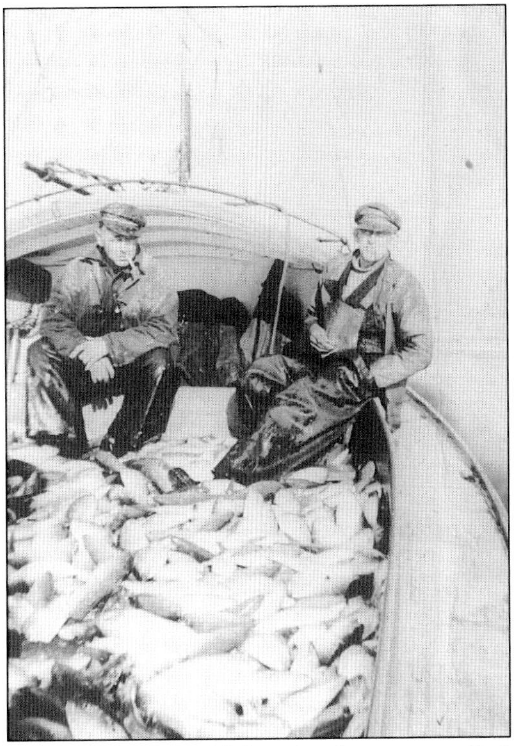

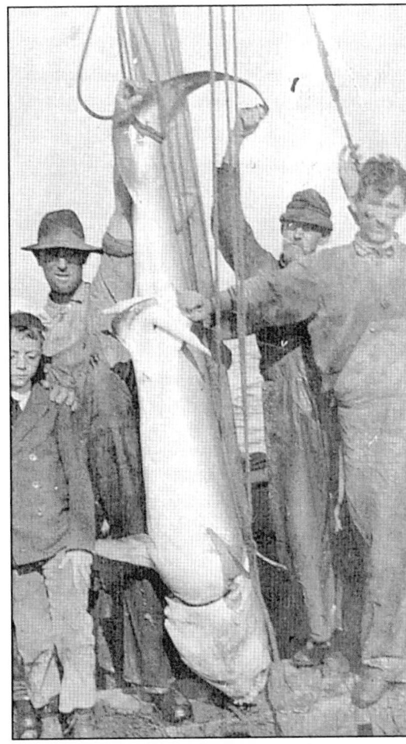

The wide variety of fish in local waters usually has market value. In the photo at left, Captain William Thompson (right) is surrounded by bluefish in his boat. The shark in the photo at right might be less marketable, but it made for an interesting image. Carsten Bade appears second from the right.

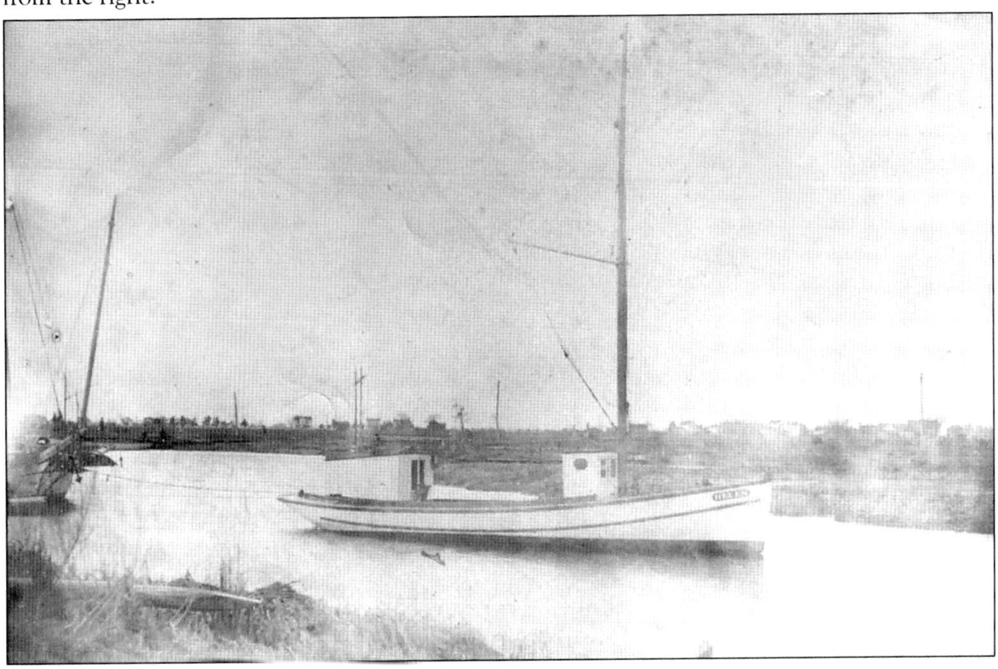

The *Helen* is pictured *c.* 1910 in Comptons Creek.

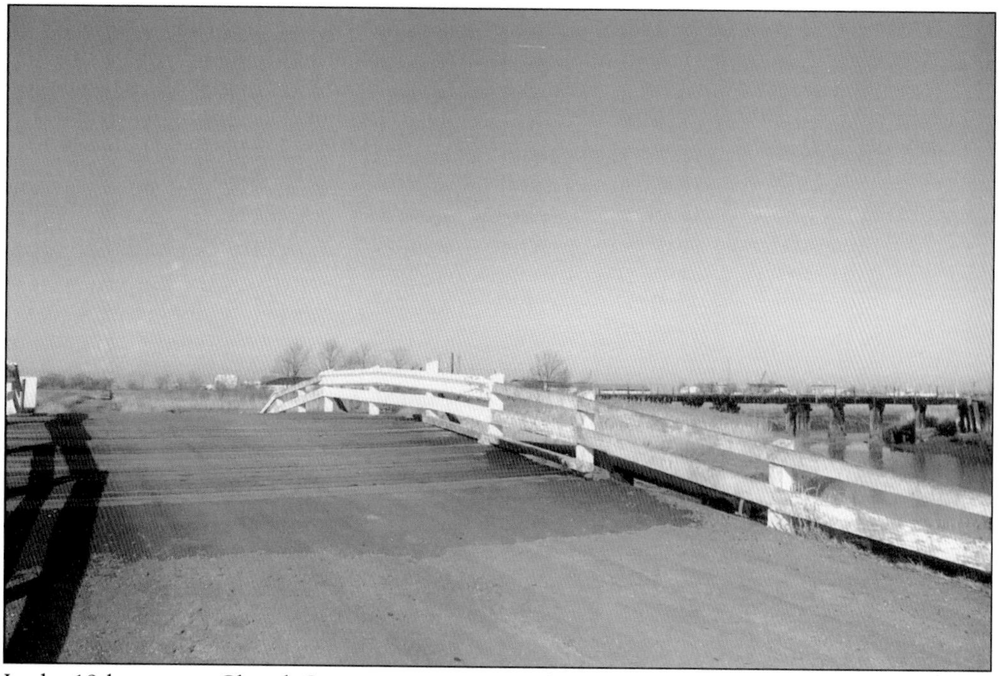

In the 19th century, Church Street was a major north-south thoroughfare in Belford. However, the dualization of Highway 36 in the 1960s impaired its utility as a through street, while its unpaved northern stem and the rickety bridge over Compton's Creek, seen here in 1983, minimized its use for travel to the shore. Church Street was cut off at Broadway to facilitate travel by the replacement bridge pictured at bottom, which opened in 1997 and was accessed via Broadway. Note at top the bridge in the right background, containing the tracks of the area's original railroad, the Raritan & Delaware Bay, which opened in 1861.

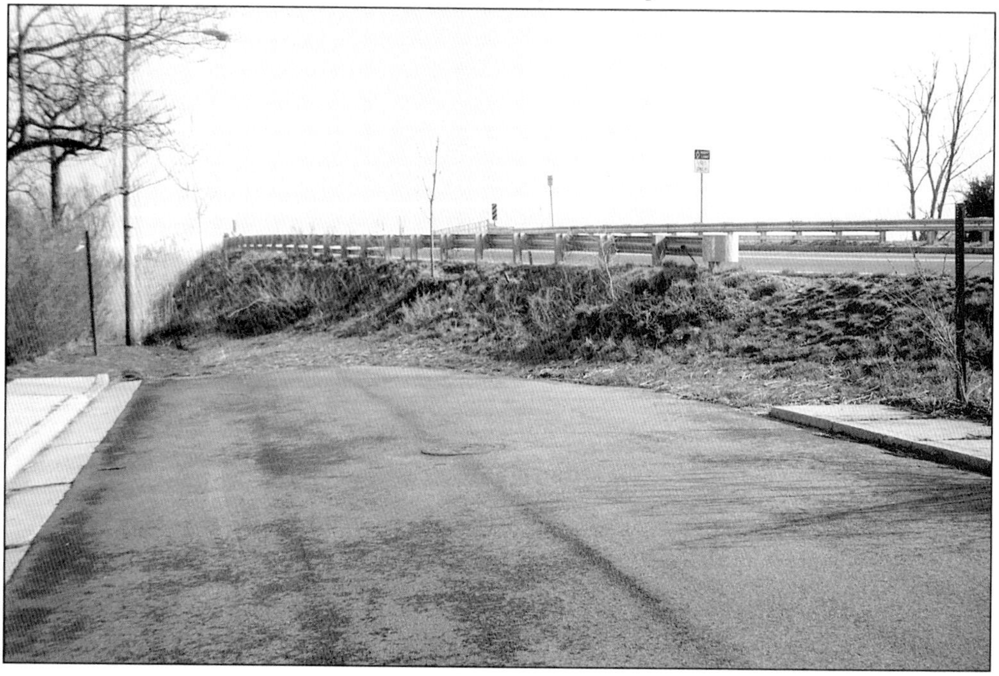

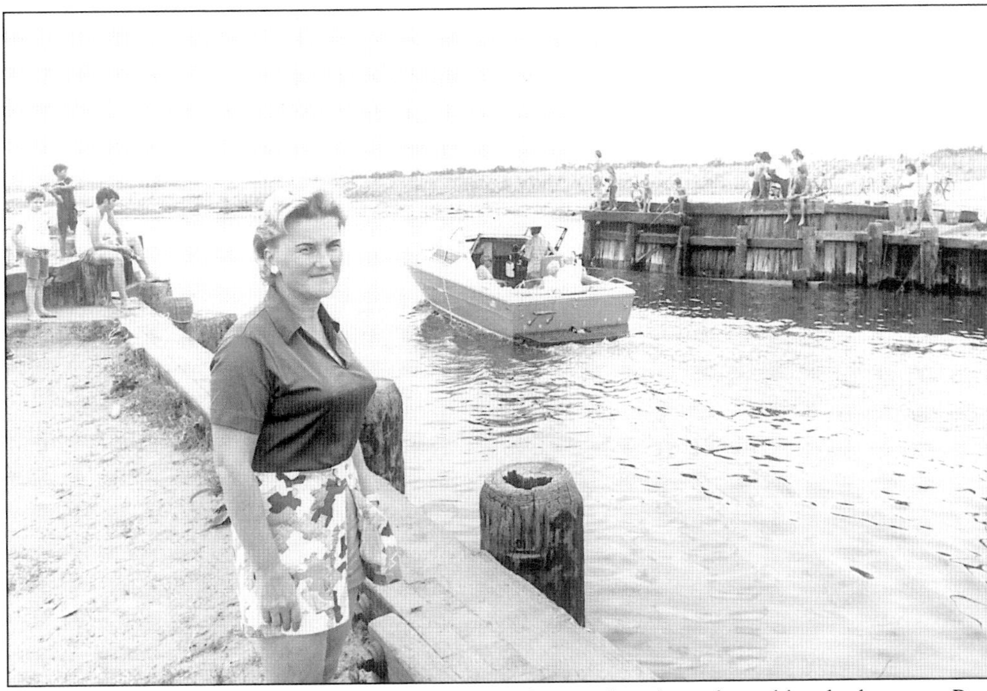

The Port Monmouth Road Bridge over Pews Creek served as the informal border between Port Monmouth and East Keansburg, or North Middletown. This section was damaged by Hurricane Donna in 1960 and removed as unsafe in 1964. Ruth Lopomo, who became "the conscience of the Pews Creek Bridge project," was photographed there in 1974 when the communities wondered what would motivate the authorities to reconstruct. Their wait was much longer; the replacement bridge, located slightly to the south of this still-present break in the old road, did not open until 1997. Thus, replacing the bridge took about four times longer than sending a man to the moon. The new span is a fine structure; the first crossing by this driver inspired the thought, "Wow! Am I really here!"

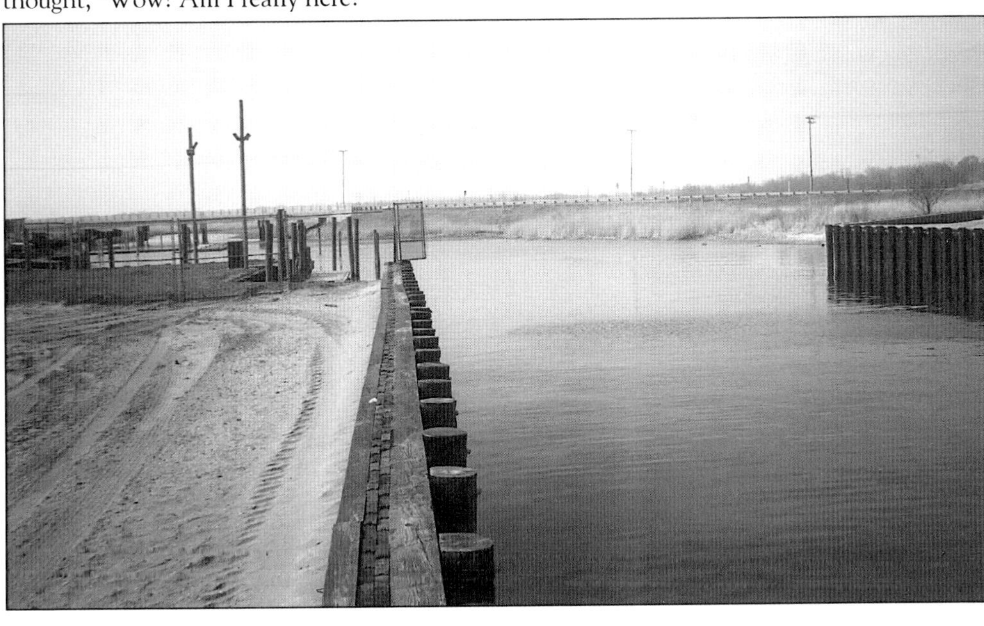

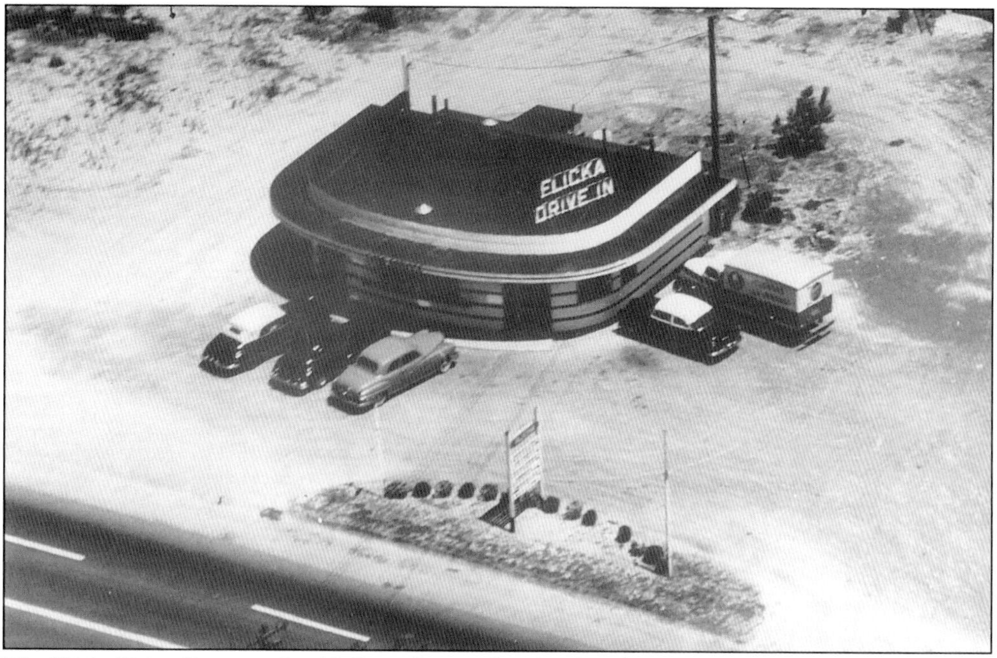

The Flicka Drive-In opened *c.* 1948 on the north side of Highway 35, almost opposite Township Hall. This aerial view, taken when the place was new, shows an undivided highway; the parking near the road and the Moderne-influenced building reflect an uncrowded roadway and the place's singular character. "Flicka" means "girl" in Swedish.

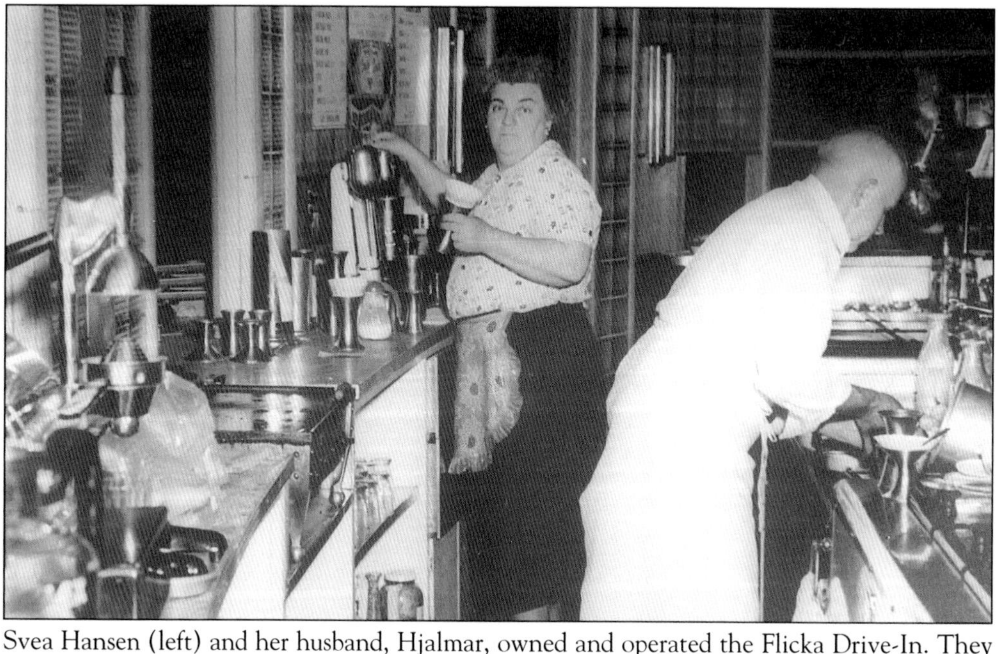

Svea Hansen (left) and her husband, Hjalmar, owned and operated the Flicka Drive-In. They sold it *c.* 1961, shortly before her death. The building later became a dry cleaners, and now the site is the office at 923 Highway 35. Seeing Svea at the mixer reminds one of times when the malted milk was the classic fountain drink, made with malt and milk, as opposed to today's "shake" made from who-knows-what.

Service to your car window characterized the 1950s drive-in, in this instance provided by Rose Marie Hansen Coyle. Today the drive-through window provides the essential character of roadside fast food. It is so important that towns wishing to avoid fast food eateries zone against drive-through windows rather than this type of establishment. Rose Marie later worked for Dorn's and assisted her husband William in the surveying business.

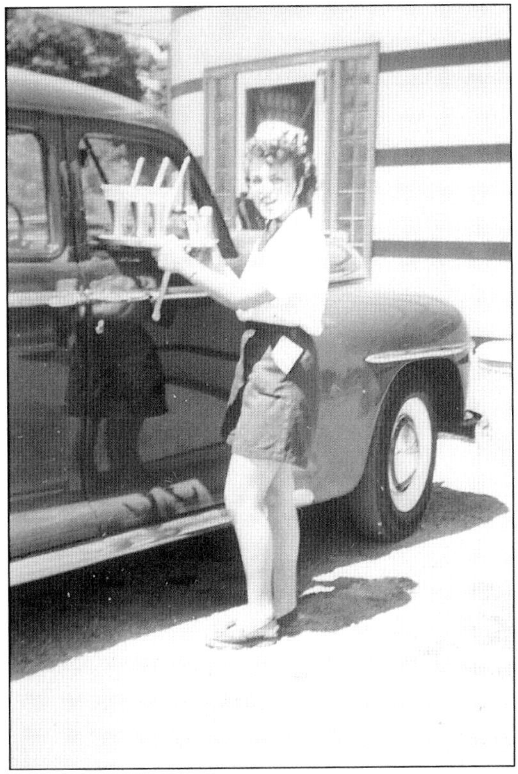

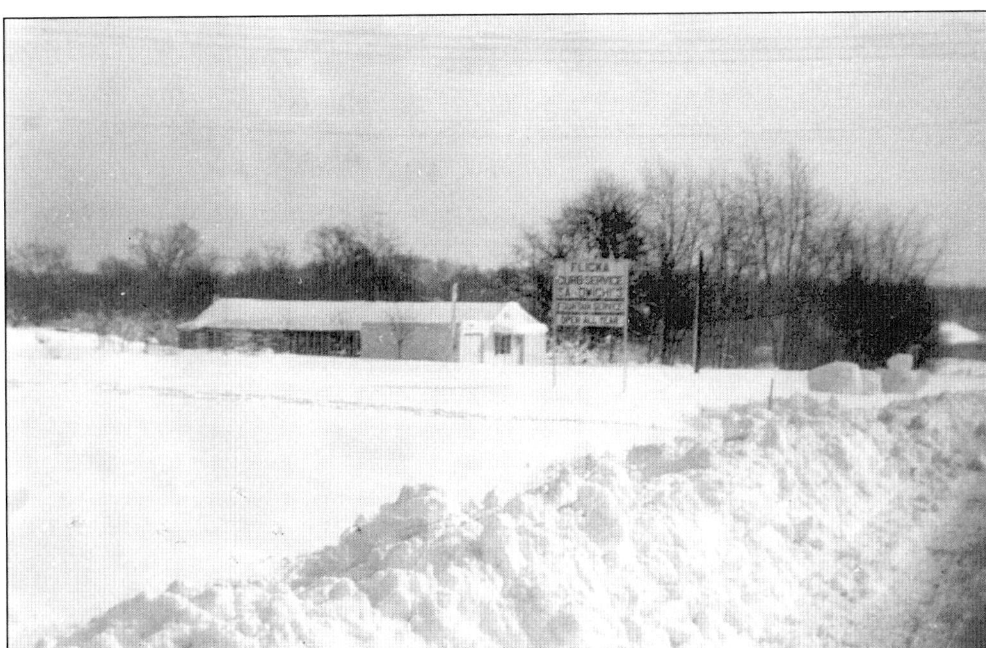

This c. 1947 view of the north side of Highway 35 looking east toward Tindall Road shows the kennels then on the site occupied for many years by the R & S Strauss store. German shepherds were raised there. It was located east of Flicka's, which accounts for the presence of the sign.

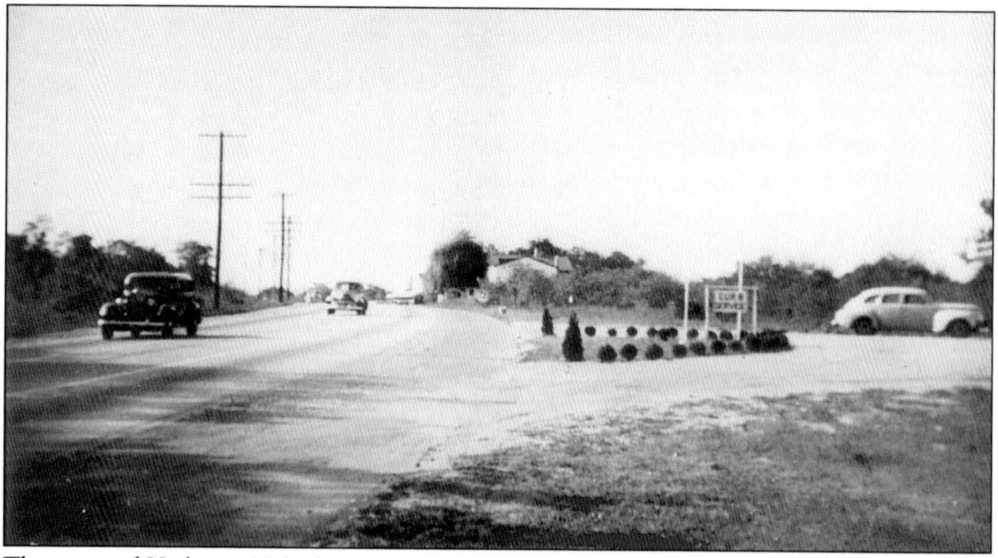

This view of Highway 35 looking west opposite Township Hall in the late 1940s captures a corner of Flicka's and a since-changed country highway. Today this stem is one of the busiest in the township. A McDonald's is now in the background, prompting the author to offer one of his motoring tips: try not to drive in lanes where other cars can turn into, or out from, popular fast food places.

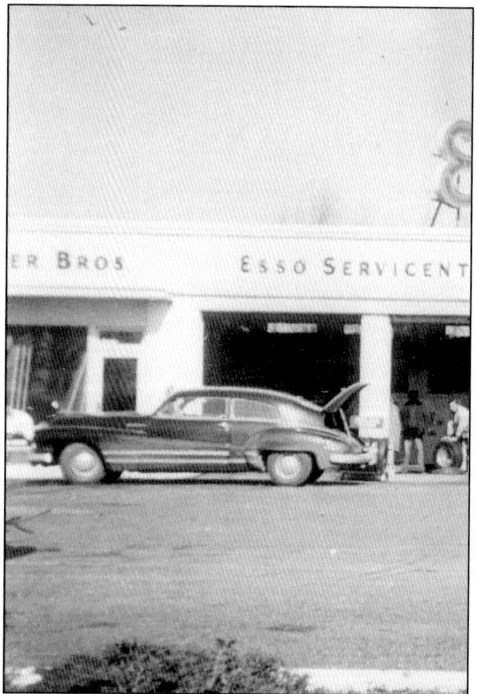

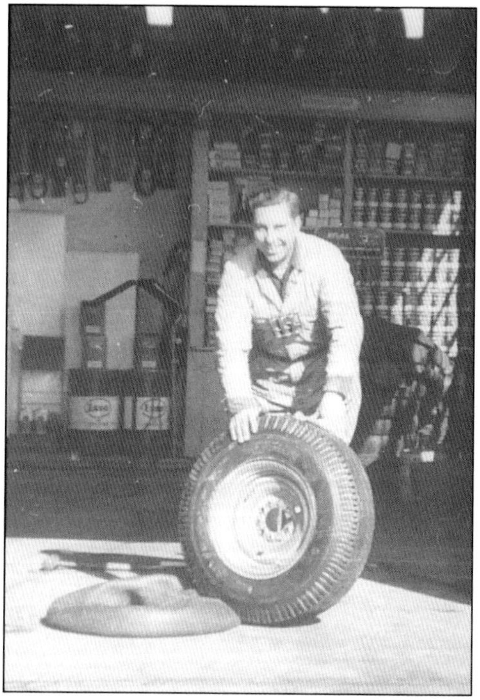

The late 20th century saw many petroleum refiners transform their service stations to gas only stations, or gas with a convenience store. Exxon, the current name of Esso, still sells gas at the northwest corner of Highway 35 and Tindall Road, but there are no repairs made there now. One of the Millers is seen here repairing a tire around 1949. One current improvement is a large canopy over the pumps.

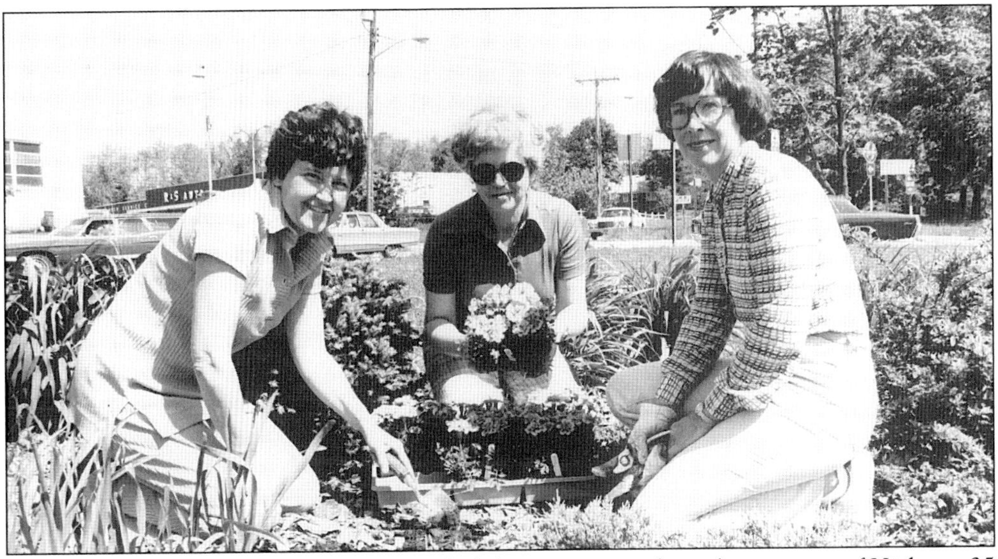

The Village Garden Club has long-beautified the grassy triangle at the juncture of Highway 35 and Tindall Road (one of the township's most dangerous intersections). Seen here planting in May 1978 are, from left to right, Mrs. Raymond Boyce, Mrs. Raymond Misch (president of the Village Garden Club), and Mrs. John Chappell (president of Garden Club RFD). Boyce and Misch shared chairmanship of the Highway Beautification Committee. The photo's background shows the eastern stem of highway illustrated in several preceding pictures.

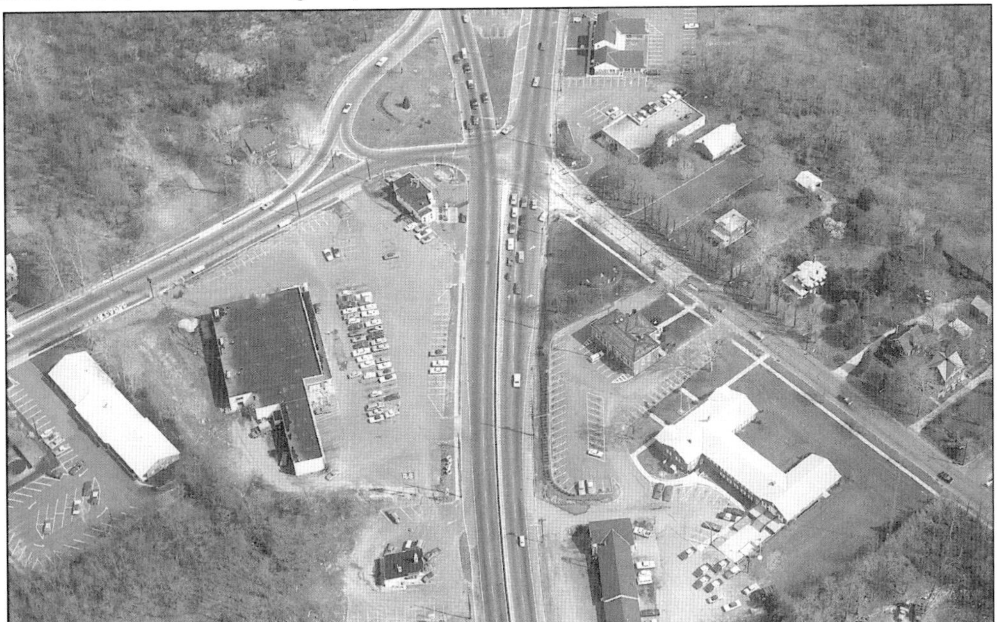

This aerial view c. 1980 of Highway 35 looking east shows a stem (at left center) that is pictured on the preceding three pages. The plot pictured above is the triangle with rounded point at top left. The road visible at the bottom is part of a .7-mile cut off built around 1920 to relieve traffic on the historic section of Kings Highway (right). The road at top right is part of the roadbed of the trolley that was discontinued in 1923. When paved for street traffic, it formed the awful, awful island at top, so dangerous with modern traffic volumes, as is the intersection below it.

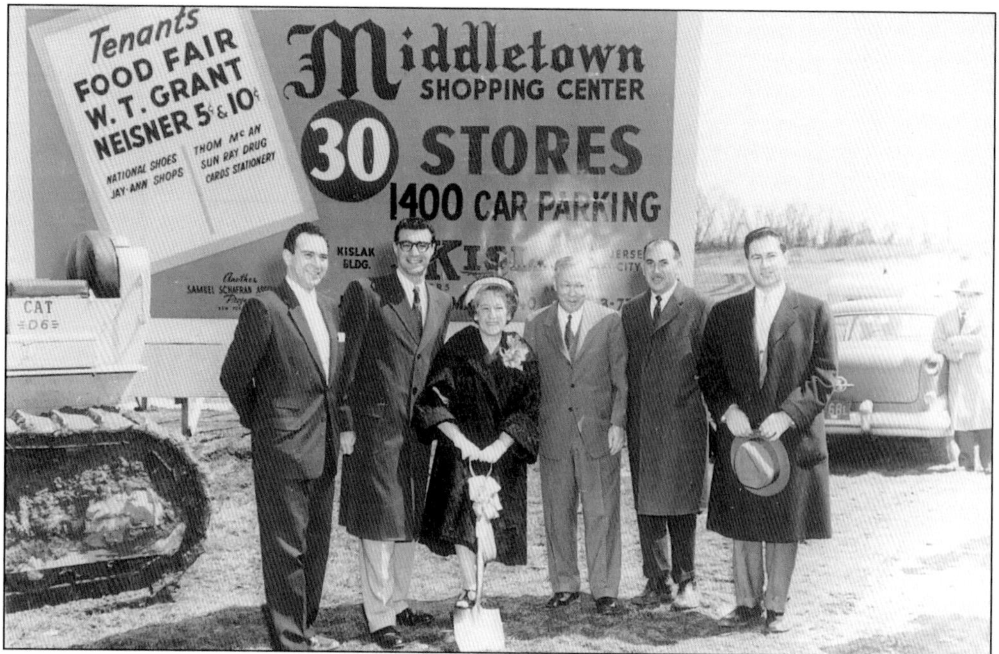

The post-1950 retail presence in Middletown and much of suburbia was the strip shopping center. Officials gathered for the 1956 groundbreaking of the 100,000-square-foot Middletown Shopping Center, located on a 10-acre site on the northwest corner of Highway 35 and New Monmouth Road, pose under a sign indicating who was who in 1950s retailing. The anchor stores are long gone, but one of the others remains, Sun Ray Drugs. Howard W. Roberts, the key township figure, is the fourth person from the left. The others likely include representatives of the real estate and construction interests.

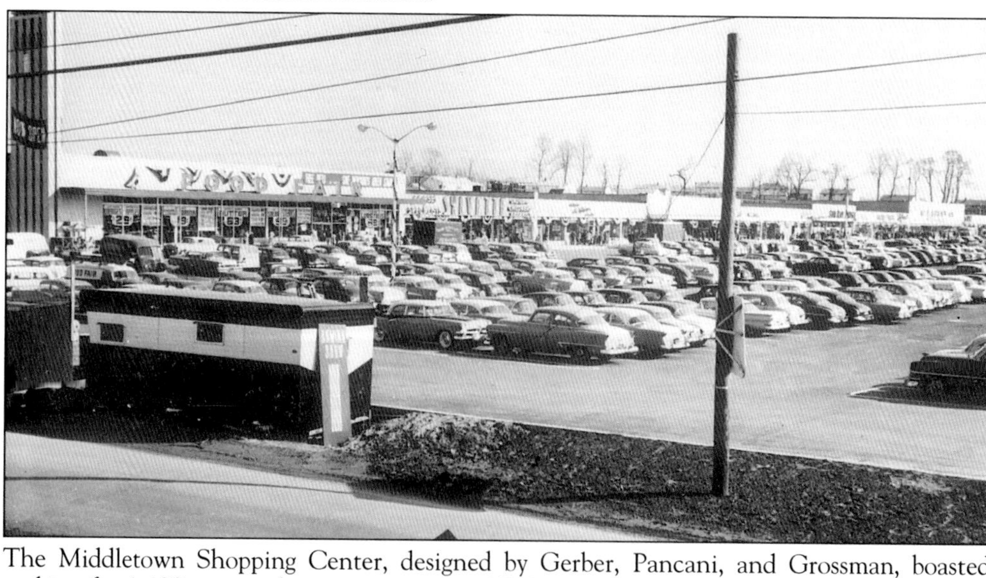

The Middletown Shopping Center, designed by Gerber, Pancani, and Grossman, boasted parking for 1,400 cars, and most spaces seem filled at its November 1957 opening. New York contractor Samuel Schafran built the center for Food Fair Properties, Inc., while J.L. Kislak was the renting agent. In the 1980s, the strip was expanded on the east and its front remodeled, while all but one of its original tenants have changed.

Ronald I. Cohen, a 1956 graduate of Rutgers University College of Pharmacy, is pictured here in 1961, the year he bought Sun Ray Drugs. The colored globe then provided a link with the past, but the store is now modern and up-to-date. It has also moved several doors from its first location as part of an expansion. Sun Ray, the Middletown Shopping Center's only original tenant, has an affiliated medical supply organization and an extensive line of gifts and stationery. They also serve as Middletown Township's headquarters for the Arcadia book line.

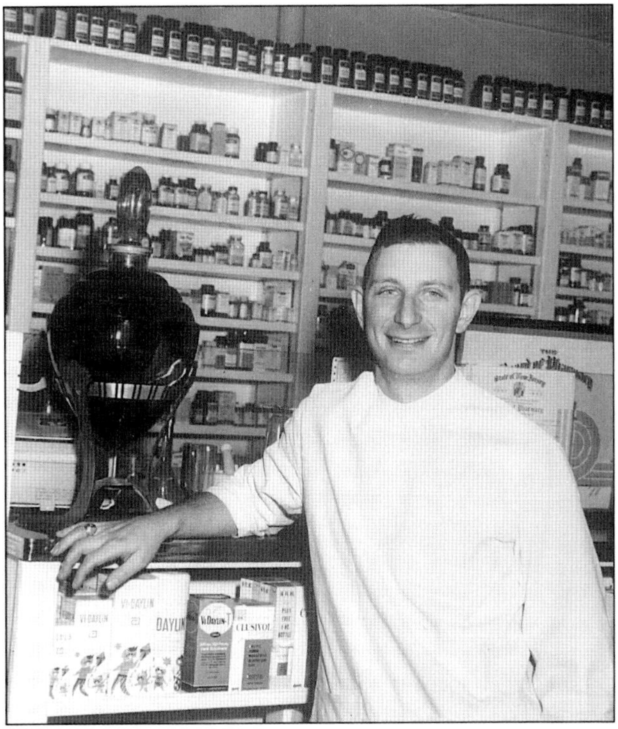

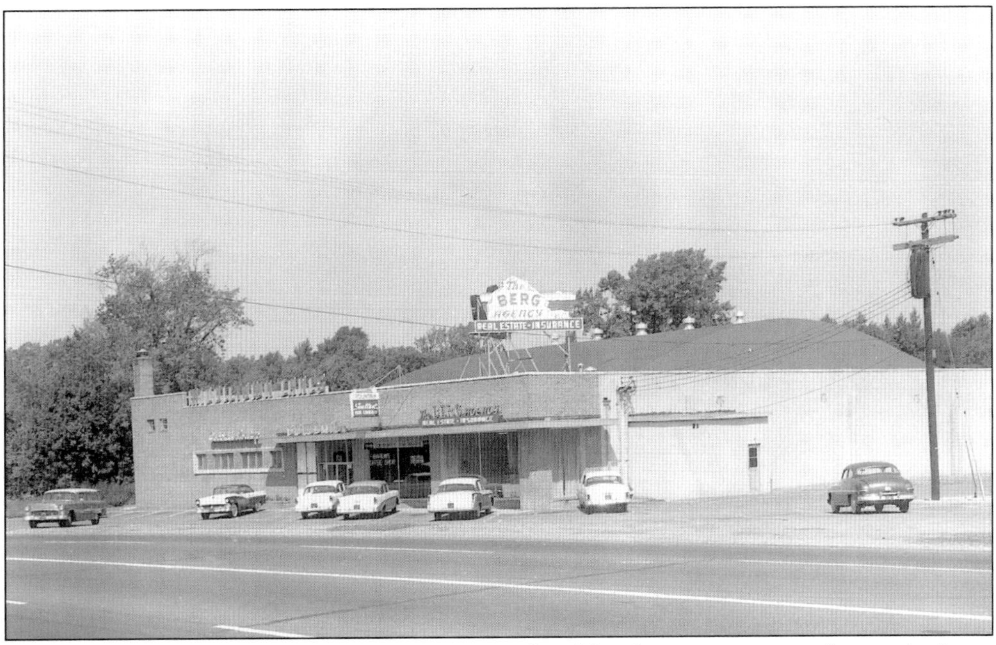

Bowling's popularity in the 1950s was accommodated by the construction of many highway alleys, or lanes, to use the more dignified term. Middletown Lanes, located at 1281–85 Highway 35, on the north side between New Monmouth and Harmony Roads, was typical, and like many, fell victim to the game's decline in popularity. The building, pictured *c.* 1956, still stands, its front resurfaced, now occupied by as Chinese restaurant and Asian food store. (The Dorn's Collection.)

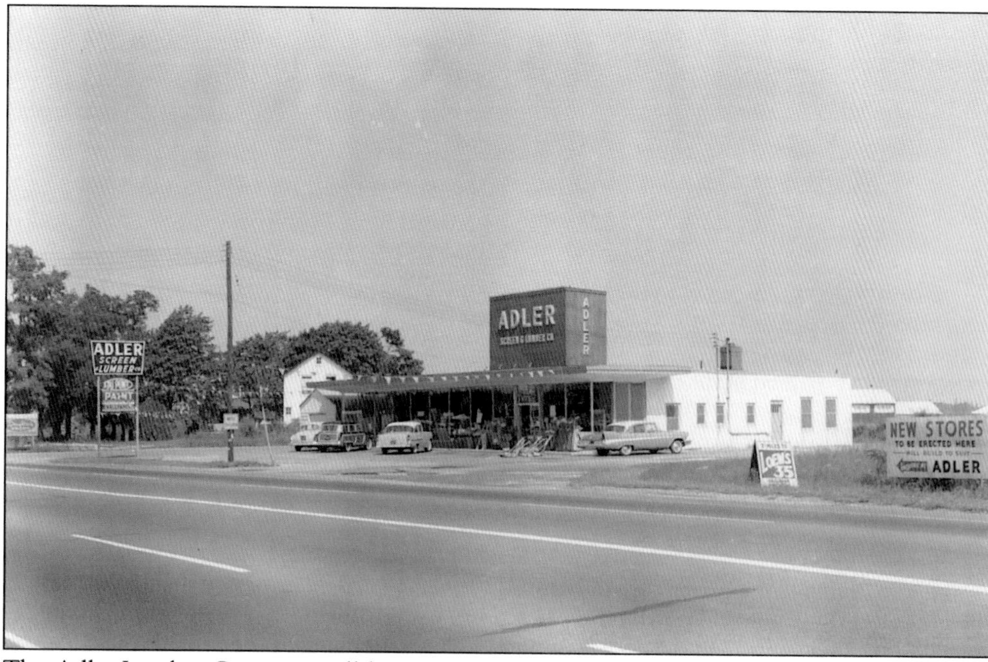

The Adler Lumber Company still has a store at 1837 Highway 35, but the building pictured here was destroyed by fire. Notice the house at left. Commercial buildings were often built amidst well-spaced residences, but few of the latter remain. (The Dorn's Collection.)

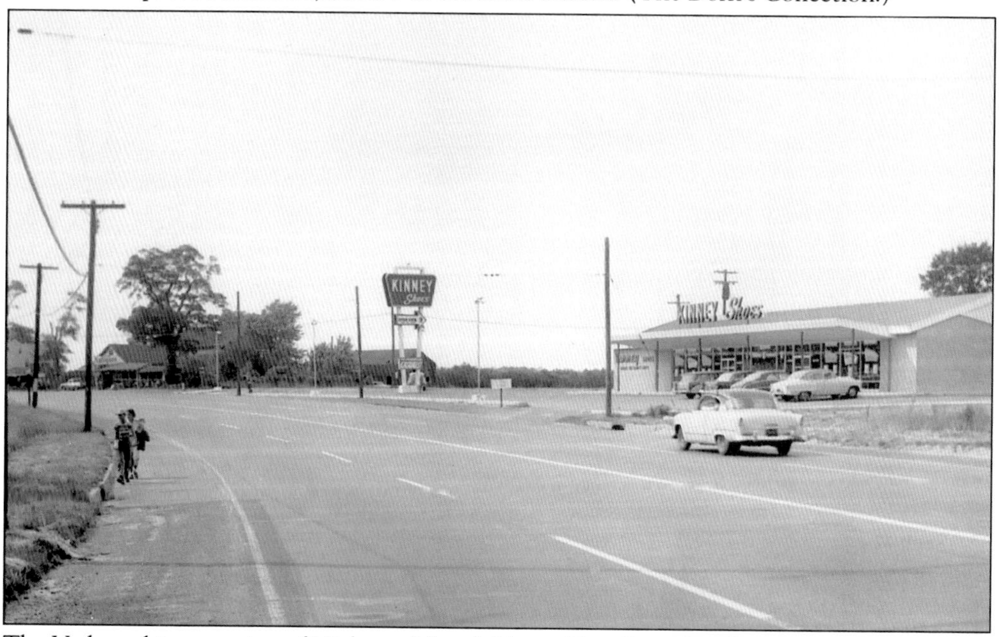

The V-shaped intersection of Highway 35 and Cherry Tree Farm Road was once the site of one of the township's most valuable business locations. Prior to the 1950s construction of this store, the location was occupied by a gas station. Seen here in 1958, the store still stands, but with a new front, located at 2009–11 Highway 35. The John T. Hendrickson house (Volume II, p. 45), barely visible at the left edge, was later the site of a large furniture store, and where a larger variety store is reaching completion at publication time. (The Dorn's Collection.)

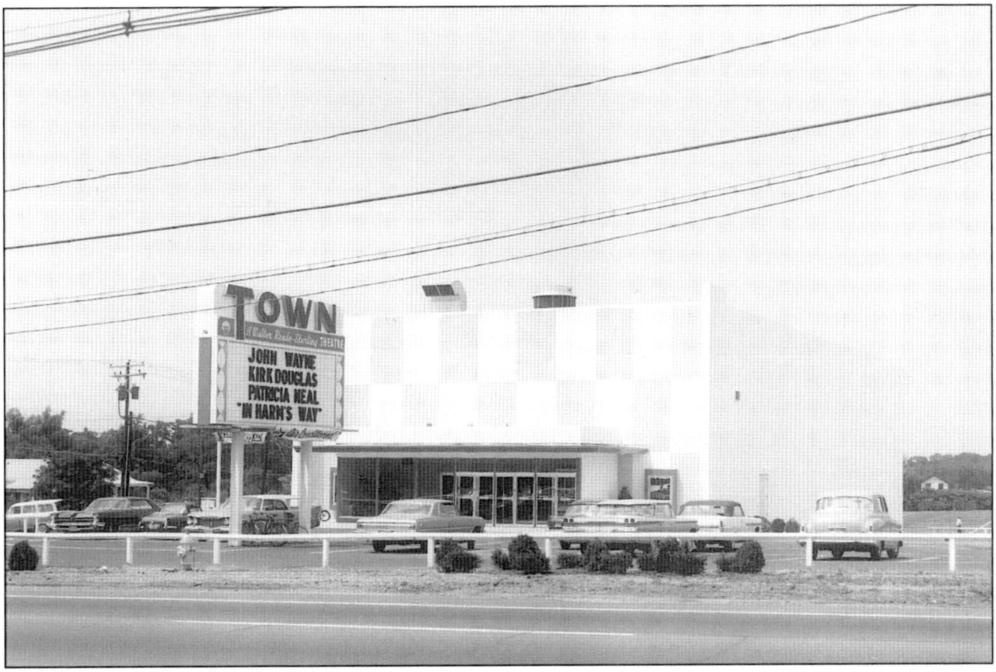

The Towne Theater, built around the mid-1960s and seen in this 1965 photograph as it occupied the northeast corner of Highway 35 and Palmer Avenue, thrived for years, expanding its number of screens to reflect ongoing trends of larger-scaled movie complexes. It succumbed in 1998 and was demolished, effectively losing its business to an even larger facility in nearby Hazlet. (The Dorn's Collection.)

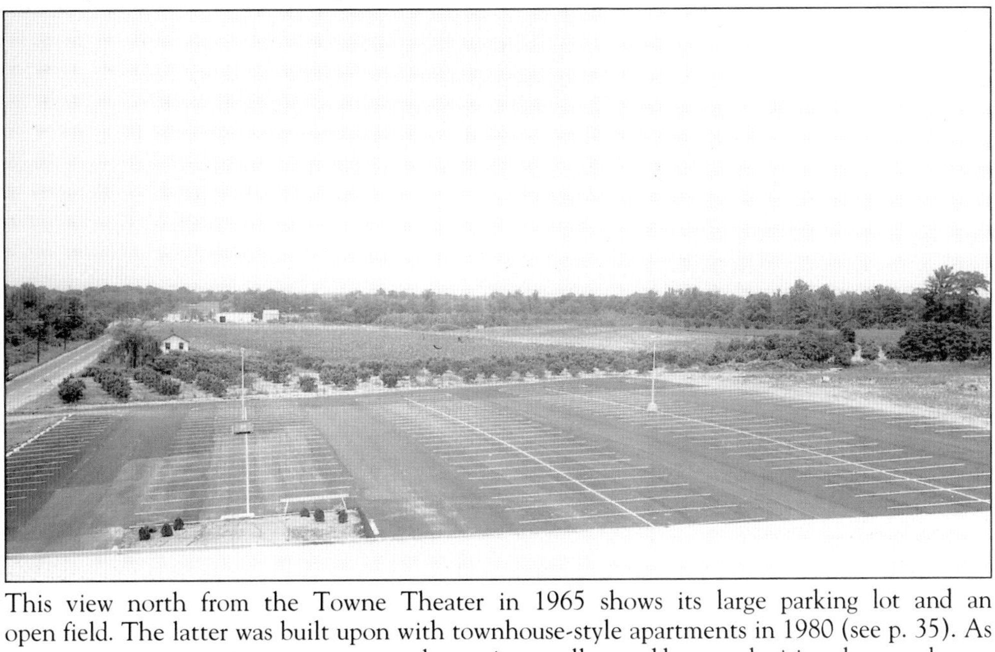

This view north from the Towne Theater in 1965 shows its large parking lot and an open field. The latter was built upon with townhouse-style apartments in 1980 (see p. 35). As motion picture screening rooms seem to be getting smaller, and home televisions become larger, we can expect the sizes of shrinking movie screens and expanding television screens to meet soon. (The Dorn's Collection.)

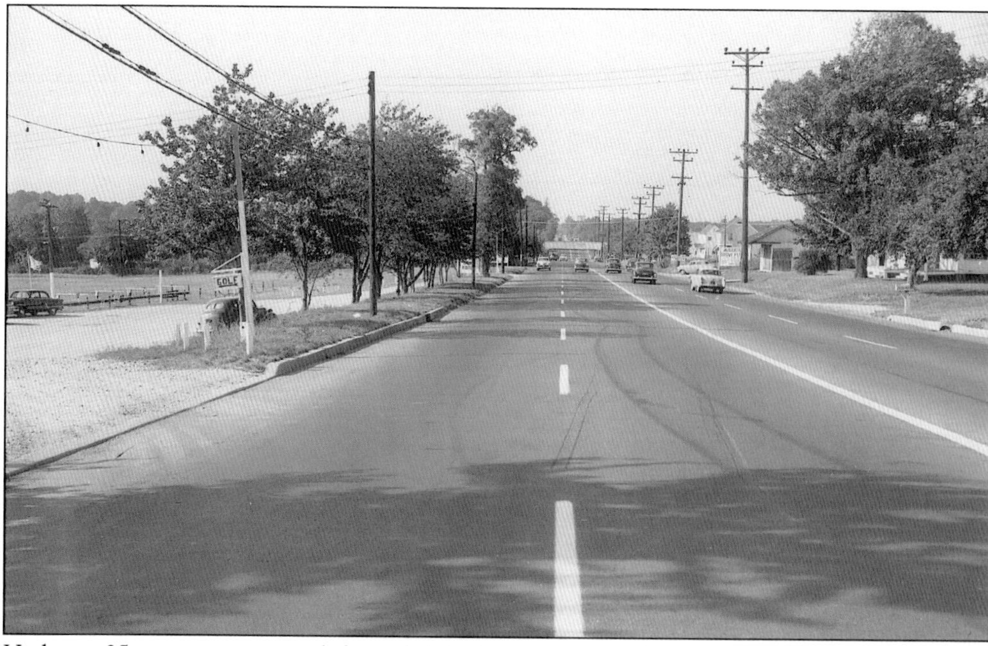

Highway 35, an east-west road through Middletown, is visible looking west toward the Navy overpass in this photo *c.* 1951. It had four lanes without a center divider and attained the dubious distinction as one of the area's most dangerous roads. Some longtime residents will remember the bumper sticker "Stay Alive On 35." The road was once lined with houses, with many later converted to commercial use, as illustrated at right. (The Dorn's Collection.)

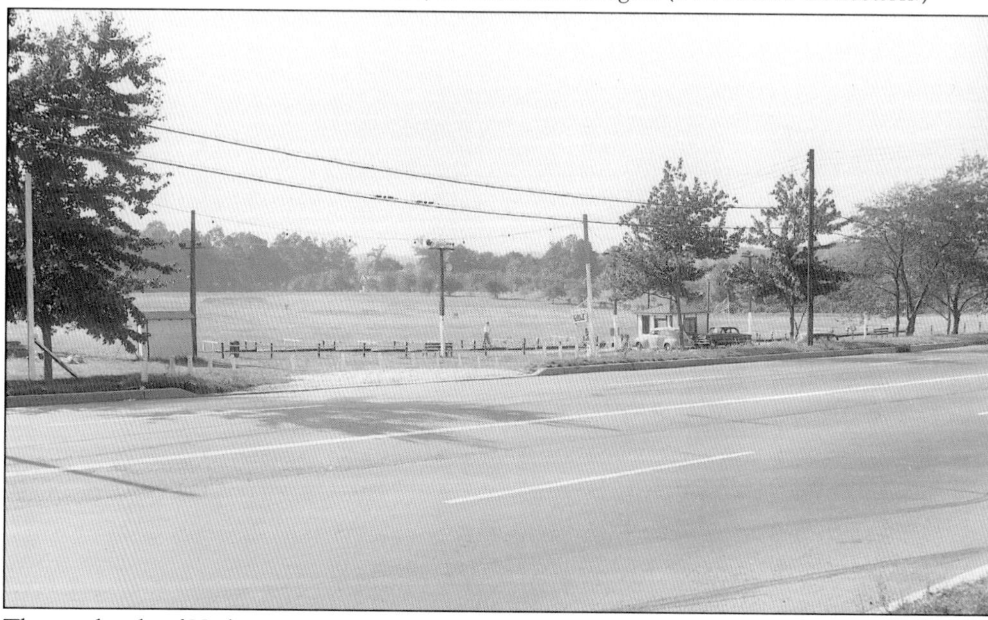

The south side of Highway 35 is visible from the point pictured at top, providing a partial view of the Jackpot Golf Driving Range that was replaced by the Union Square Shopping Center in the early 1980s. This is a good example of the succession of an early motoring-age recreational spot by a higher and better use in a mature town by a retail establishment that aimed for an upscale market. (The Dorn's Collection.)

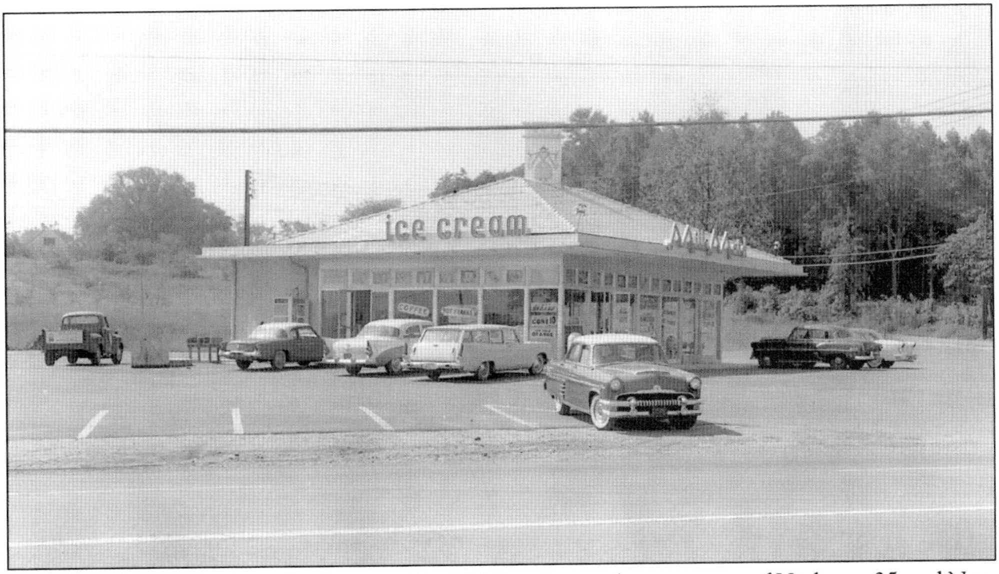

The Milk Maid Drive-In, which opened in 1956 at the southeast corner of Highway 35 and New Monmouth Road, suggests that this major intersection (and current traffic bottleneck) had not reached its potential by the mid-1950s. The place was merely a simple box, but is nostalgic of a time when roadside eateries had individual character rather than franchise chain sameness. The painted chimney of the Milk Maid is appealing, but you are getting old if you recall cones for a dime (a memory to which the author confesses). (The Dorn's Collection.)

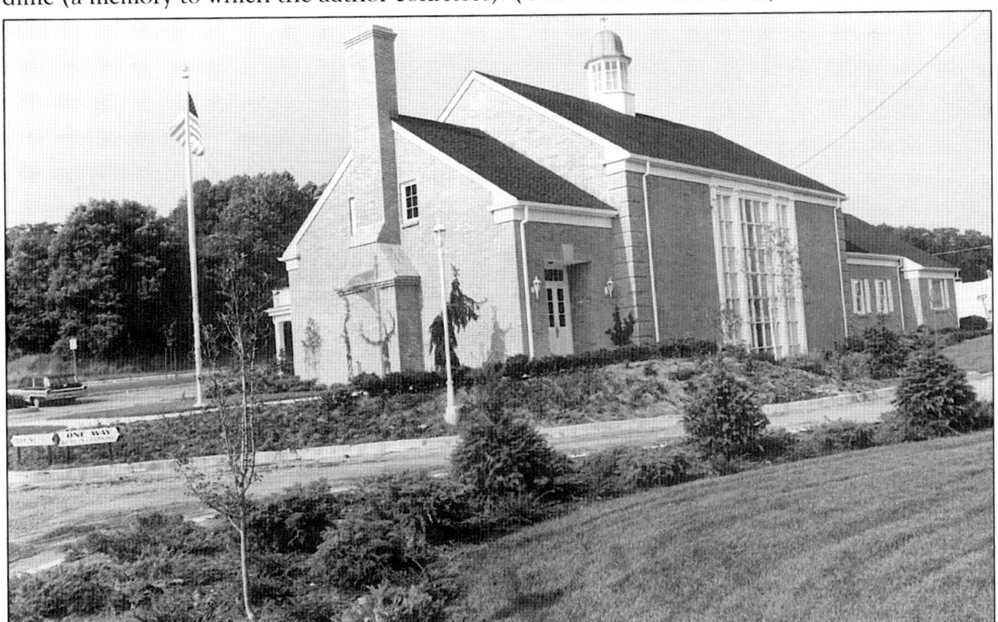

The Marine View Savings & Loan Association, successor to the Atlantic Highlands Building & Loan Association, built this new headquarters building in 1972 on the site of the Milk Maid Drive-In. Pictured when new, the building was designed by Bernard Kellenyi, its Colonial-inspired motifs reflecting age and stability. Marine View was taken over by regulatory authorities in the late 1980s. It business was later absorbed by Summit Bank, which still occupies the site in an unchanged building.

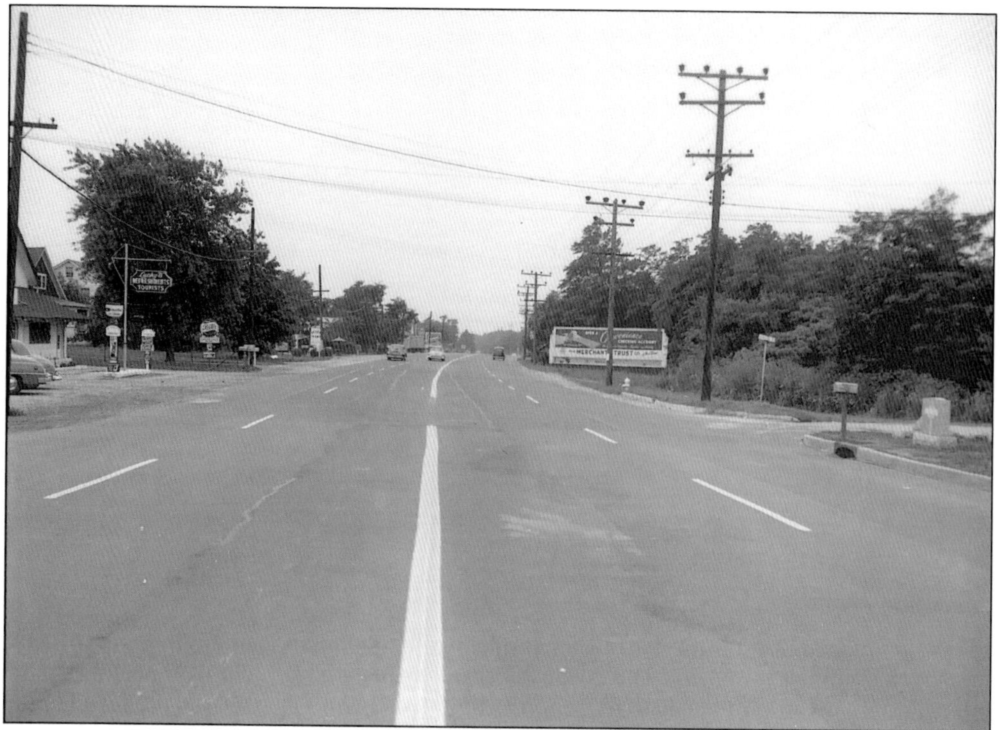

This early 1950s view of Highway 35 looking east from Harvard Street shows a corner of Barclay Hendrickson's monument yard at right. The wooded corner on Harvard's east side is now occupied by the Stafford Tire Center. (The Dorn's Collection.)

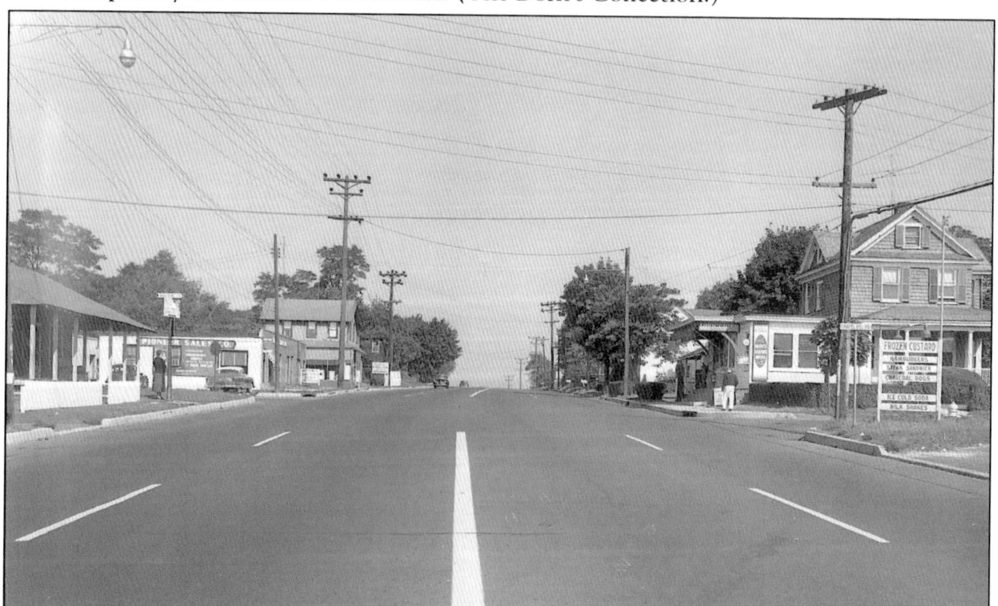

There was an offset of several feet at the juncture of Oak Hill and Chapel Hill Roads at the time of this 1953 photograph, detectable today if one notices the latter's pavement's curve, which was needed for the two to intersect. O'Flaherty's store on the northwest side of the "intersection" was lost when the jug-handle turning lane was built. (The Dorn's Collection.)

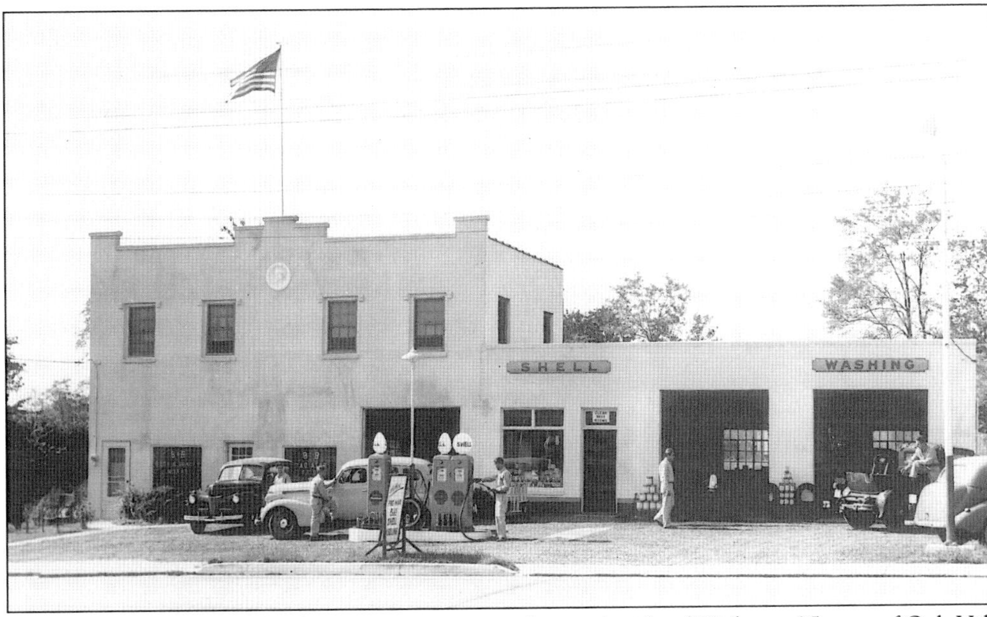

The medallion crest on the former gas station on the south side of Highway 35, east of Oak Hill Road, gives it a dignity one rarely finds on a stucco-clad building. Notice the old Shell gas pump globes, fine collectibles now. The bays at right appear to be later additions. The structure is still allied to the automotive business, as are so many former gas stations, now housing a car wash. (The Dorn's Collection.)

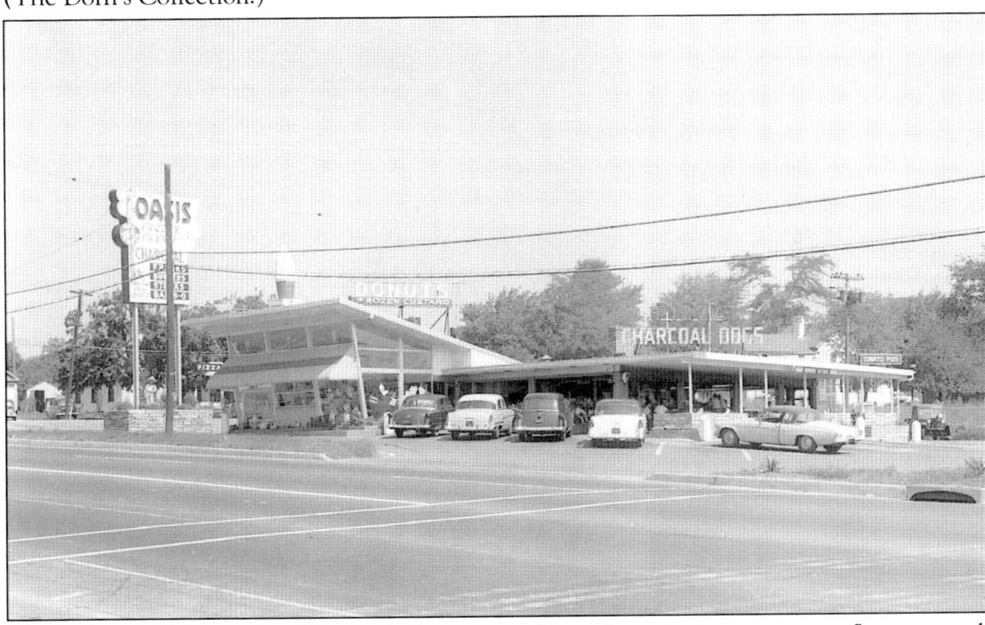

The Oasis was a typical 1950s roadside eatery, although their signage may reflect a couple singular or dated products. Was a charcoal dog made to resemble the inadvertent result of one left too long on a backyard barbecue? And surely the tomato pie could not have been dessert. The site at the northeast corner of Highway 35 and Chapel Hill Road later housed a burger joint, but was vacant for many years prior to construction of the Chapel Hill Dental Arts building nearing completion at press time. (The Dorn's Collection.)

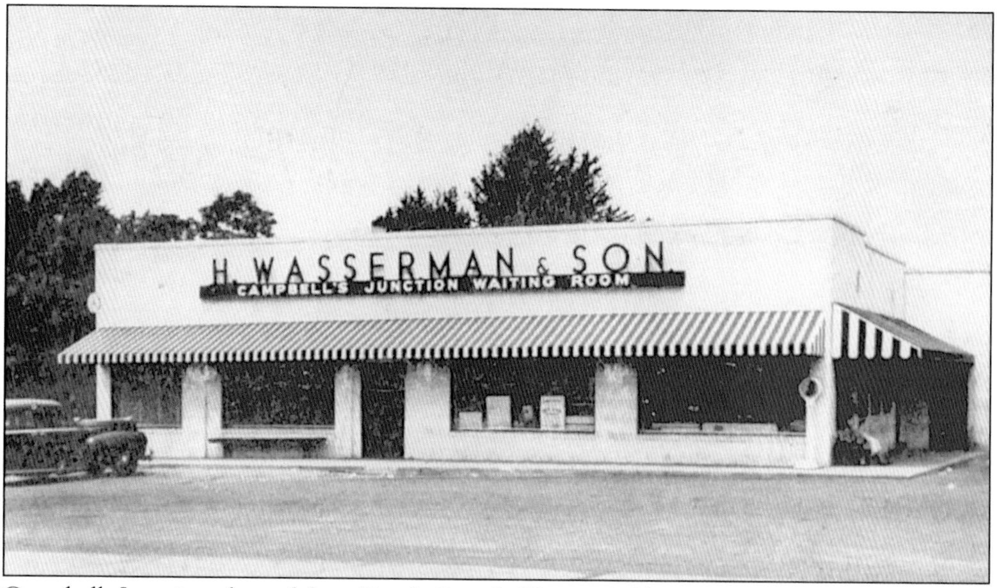

Campbells Junction, formed from Derek Campbell's cornfield around 1904 as a transfer point for Jersey Central Traction Company trolleys, was the closest thing the rural township had, or has, to a central business district. Henry Wasserman opened this store in 1949 adjacent to the former waiting room (Volume III, p. 90) on land leased from the township. His ridiculously low rent would become a public sore point years later. A general store remained on the site until about 1990, when the place was divided and remodeled for its present multi-tenanted state. The image is from a 1949 postcard, which claimed 6,000 items were for sale. (Collection of John Rhody.)

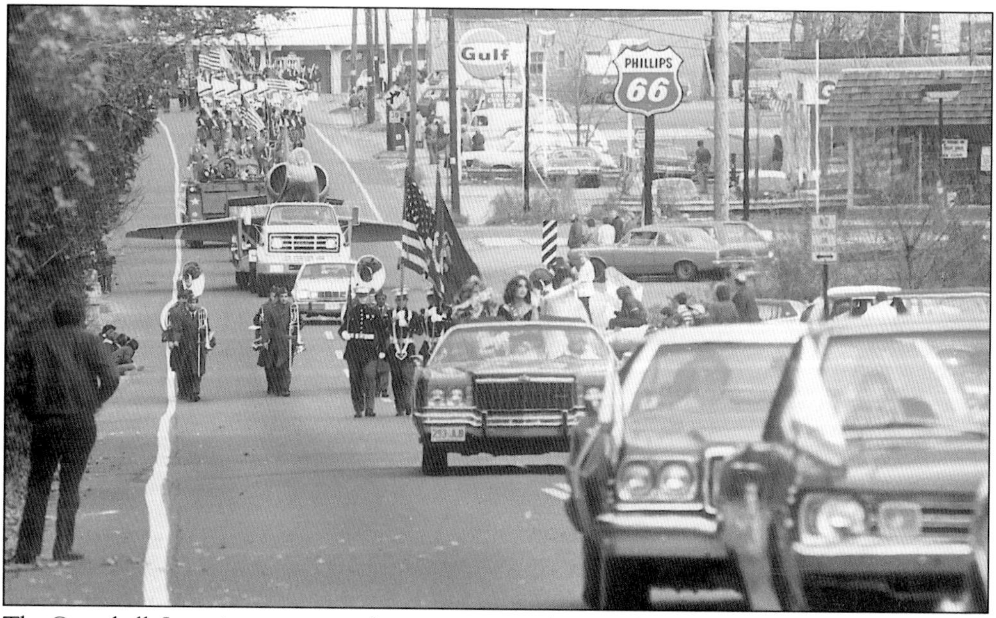

The Campbells Junction commercial strip appears in this view looking southwest on Leonardville Road during the November 12, 1978 procession of the Veteran's Day parade. The marchers were on their way to the VFW home in Port Monmouth with an unusual display: a Navy F-14 fighter on a float.

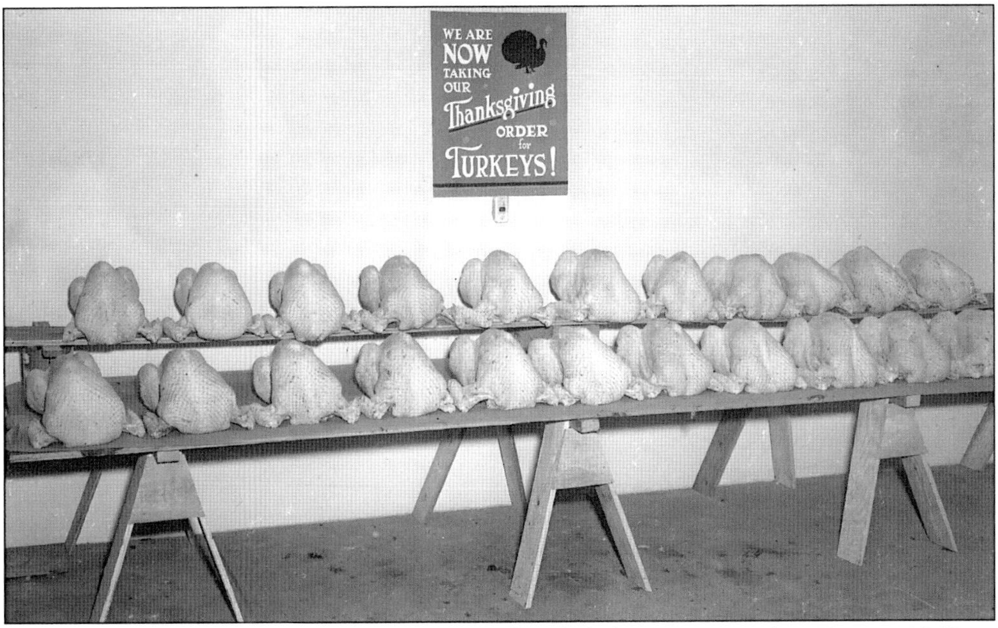

Barth Hocken, a former automobile salesman, founded the Sunrise Turkey Farm c. 1945 on about 85 acres in Belford. He acquired newly hatched poults, flown from California to Newark, and raised them in brooders and the outdoors. Sunrise also had a killing and freezing operation, although these birds, seen here in the 1950s, appear to be marketed fresh. Hockin's was known for creating a market for large birds. The farm, developed for housing in the 1960s, is remembered by the street names Sunrise Road and Hockin Street. (The Dorn's Collection.)

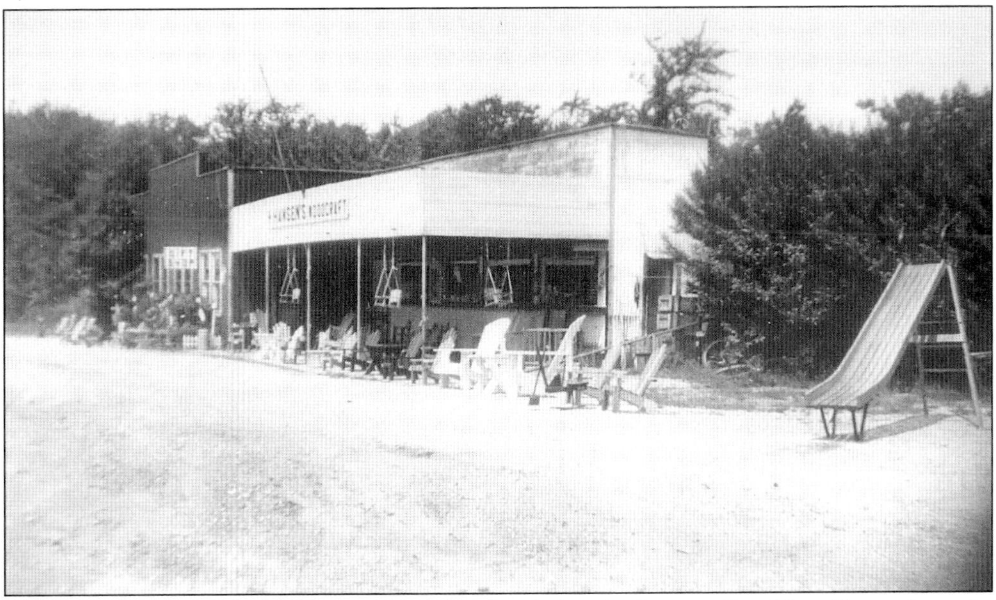

Hjalmar Hansen, a native of Norway, met his Swedish wife, Svea, in Brooklyn. He was brought to Monmouth County to work for Judge Edward Swann, later opening this woodworking shop c. early 1940s in what may have been a former roadside stand. Hansen kept it until 1948, when the Flicka Drive-In opened. The location at 1287 Highway 35 is now occupied by a Steak and Ale restaurant.

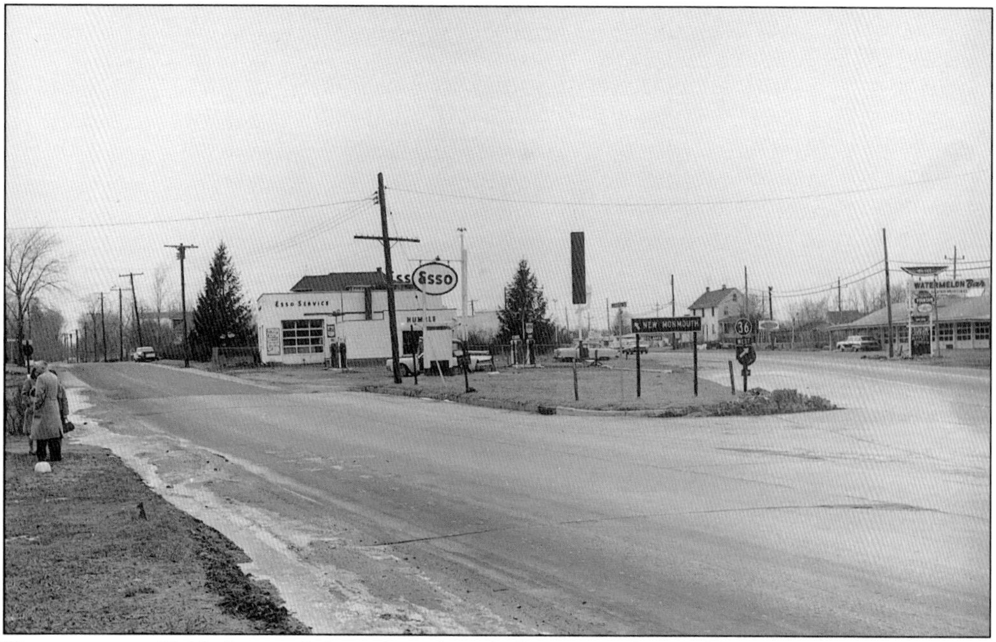

Two views c. 1960 show subtle and profound change at the Middletown border (Leonardo section) with Atlantic Highlands, at this point, Many Mind Creek. The highway was dualized in approximately 1964, and a jug-handle turning lane to enter Leonardville Road was built. The gas station pictured at the top is gone, but the eye-catching watermelon sign remains. A strip shopping center was built in the early 1960s on the Atlantic Highlands side, one that would impact negatively that town's traditional downtown shopping street, First Avenue. Construction did away with the dreadful row of billboards, New Jersey's contribution to the degradation of the American roadside. (The Dorn's Collection.)

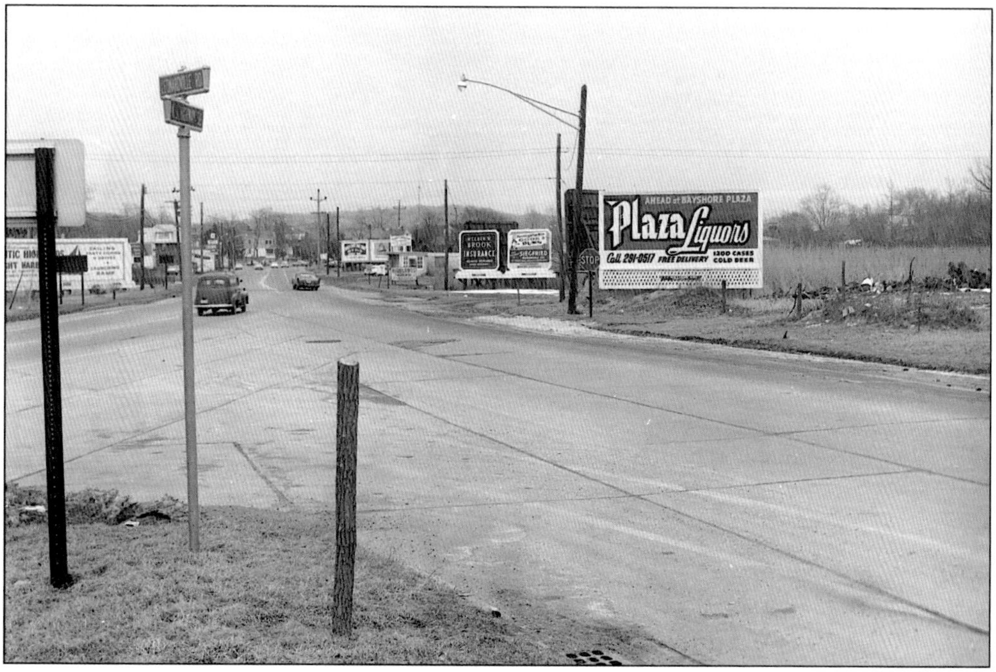

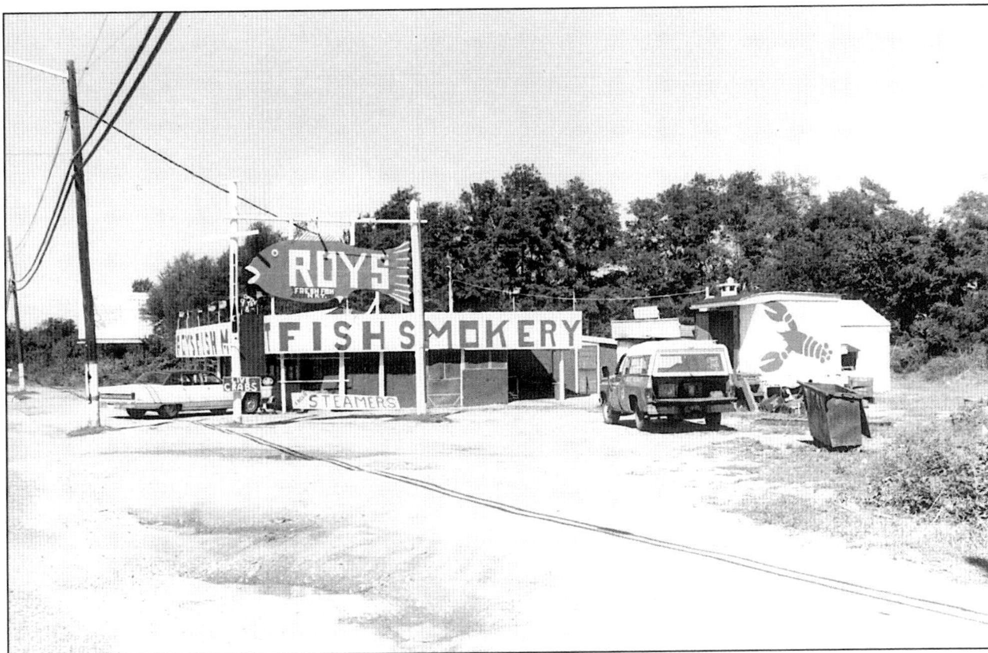

The commercial sign—often large, colorful, and shaped in a popular image—was a classic attention getter and now-nostalgic icon of roadside architecture. Roy's was located on the north side of Highway 36 in Leonardo, east of Avenue D.

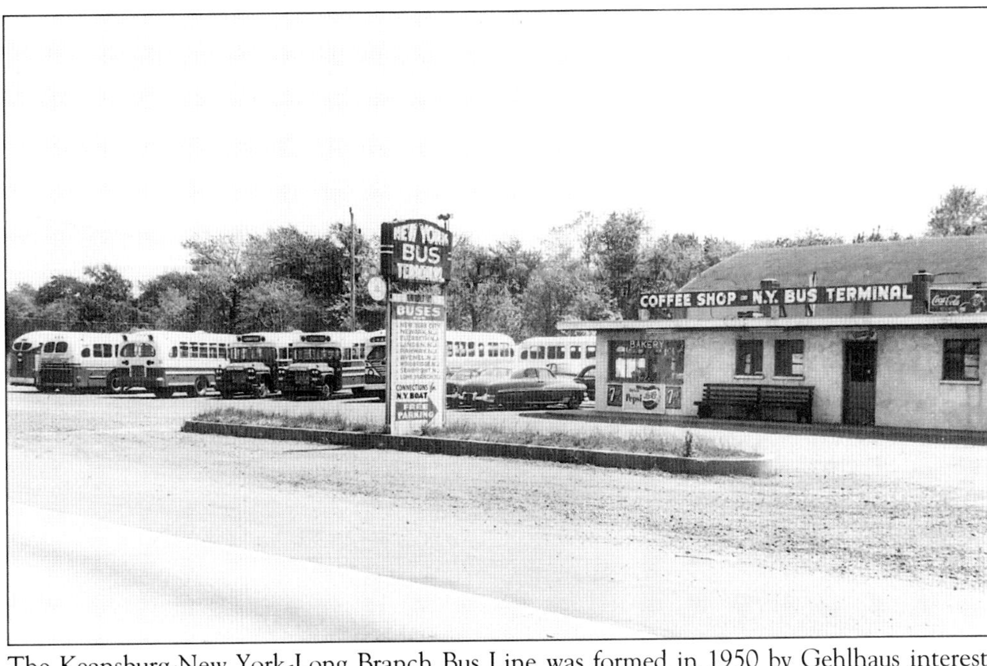

The Keansburg-New York-Long Branch Bus Line was formed in 1950 by Gehlhaus interests in Keansburg, foreseeing the supplanting of steamboats by motor traffic. The Gehlhaus line was sold in 1968. Academy Lines operates this route today, using the terminal on the south side of Highway 36 at Hosford Avenue. Note the sign in this late 1950s photograph indicating connections with New York boats. An expanded terminal remains in use today.

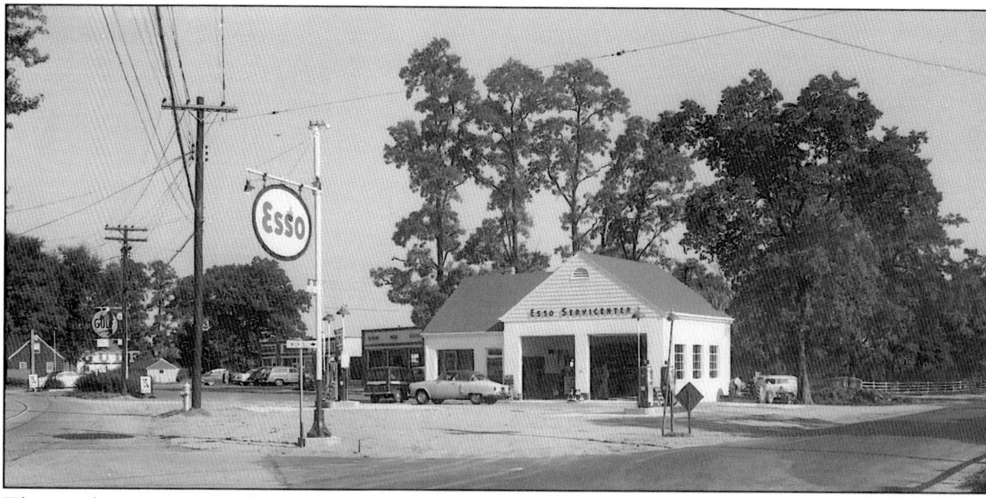

This mid-century view looking east on Newman Springs Road (left) from the Lincroft corners shows that section at the cusp of development. The roads are paved but still narrow, while the tractor at right suggests Lincroft's former rural character. However, the early state of the Village Center, begun by Charles Toop in 1951, is visible in the background. It symbolizes the intensive build up that would follow in the ensuing decades. (The Dorn's Collection.)

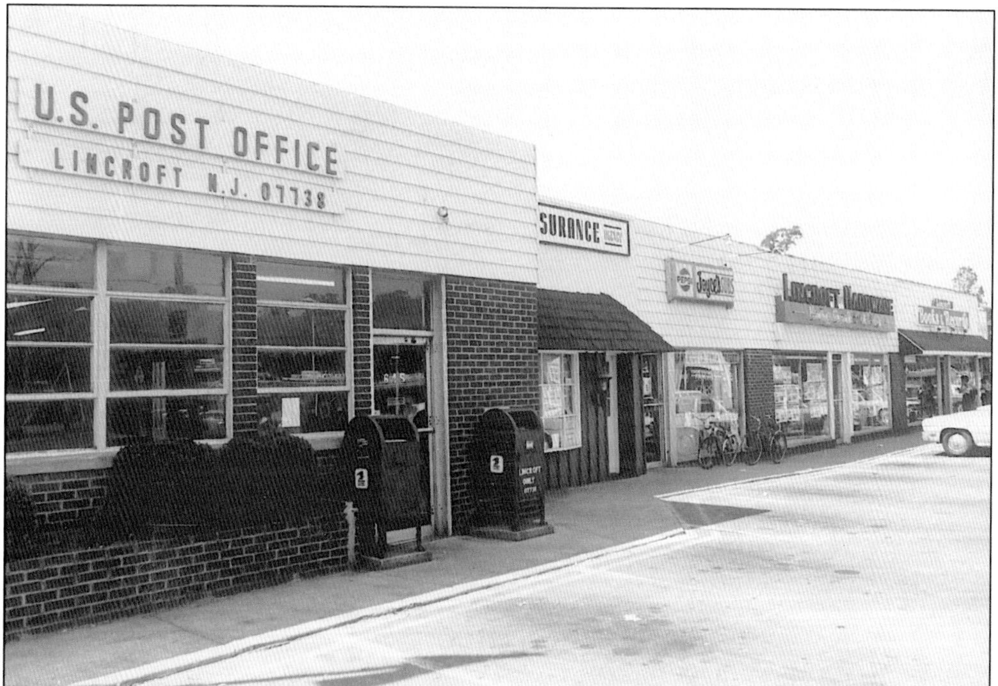

Although this photograph of the Lincroft Village Center on Newman Springs Road dates only from 1982, it shows pointedly how suburban strip shopping centers change. The exterior was given a dignified makeover in the mid-1990s, making the panels over the storefronts appear tacky. Post offices often seek to move from congested village centers to facilitate truck movement, as did Lincroft's. The bookstore is gone, as are so many once-independent small shops. Lincroft Hardware is now Village Hardware and who knows, some may still think an intersection with five traffic lanes is still a village.

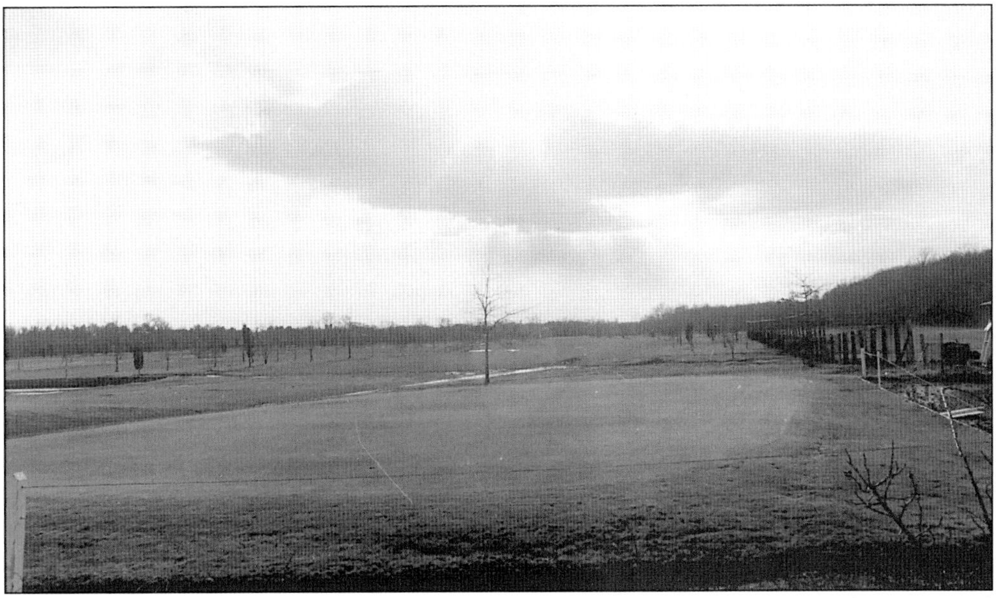

Anthony Piccola opened the Tomahawk Golf Club (visible in an aerial view in Volume II, p. 80) in 1964 on a 56-acre site on the west side of Middletown-Lincroft Road, opposite Turnberry Drive. When it was sold in 1972, the date of this photograph, the golf club was a familiar part of Middletown's recreational landscape. Its new owners changed its name to Fore Lakes.

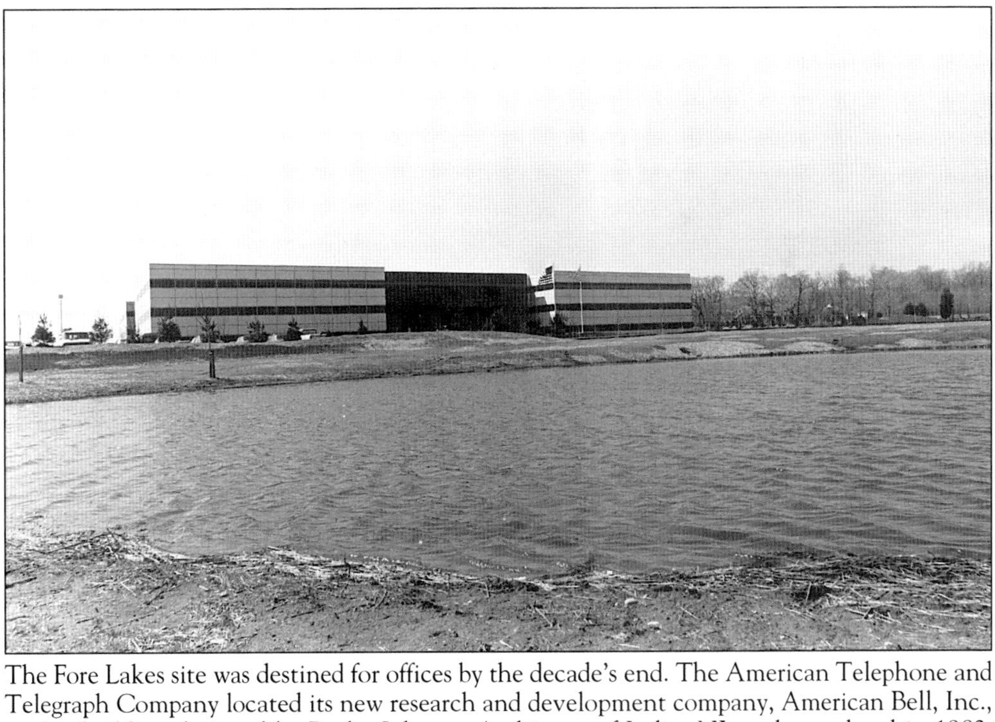

The Fore Lakes site was destined for offices by the decade's end. The American Telephone and Telegraph Company located its new research and development company, American Bell, Inc., in this building designed by Rothe-Johnson Architects of Iselin, NJ, and completed in 1982. A number of organizations in the evolving Bell System have occupied the building, which remains on the site, again housing an AT&T facility.

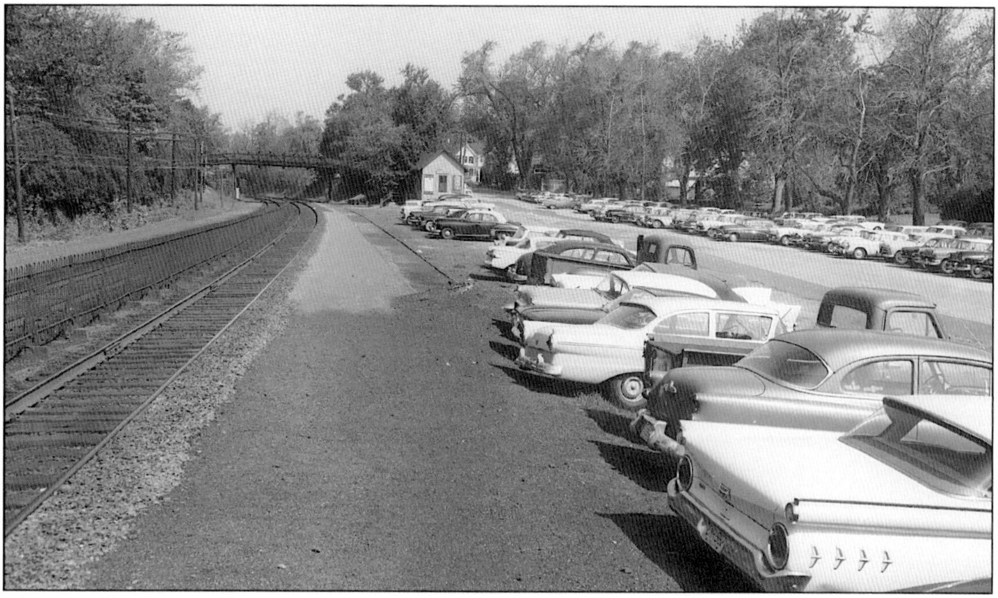

The tiny former Middletown Railroad Station once aptly reflected the town as a minor rural stop, a status it retained with rail schedule makers long after its 1950s population explosion. Many Middletownites commuted from Red Bank in the early days. This parking lot, located west of Church Street and now the metered Lot Number 1, was the only lot when photographed in 1961. Note the former bridge to the Conover estate. (The Dorn's Collection.)

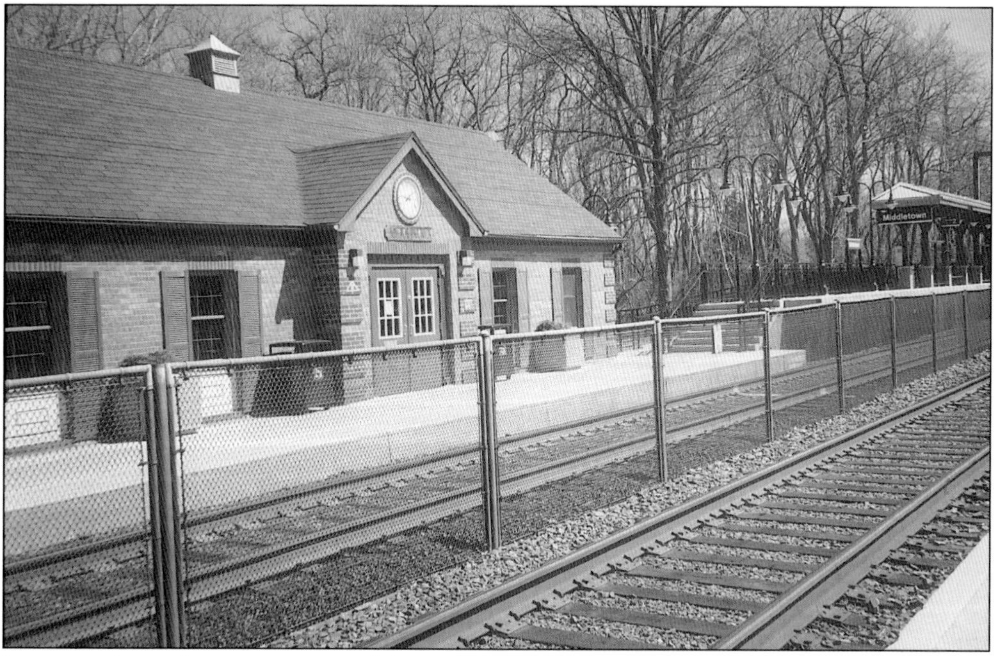

Long-overdue rail improvements of the early 1980s included extension of the New York and Long Branch Line's electric power to Long Branch, the construction of a new Middletown Station, and the replacement of operating equipment. A grade level waiting area was replaced by a raised platform in 1999, visible at right, while new tunnel entrances from permit parking Lot Number 2 make access to the trains easier.

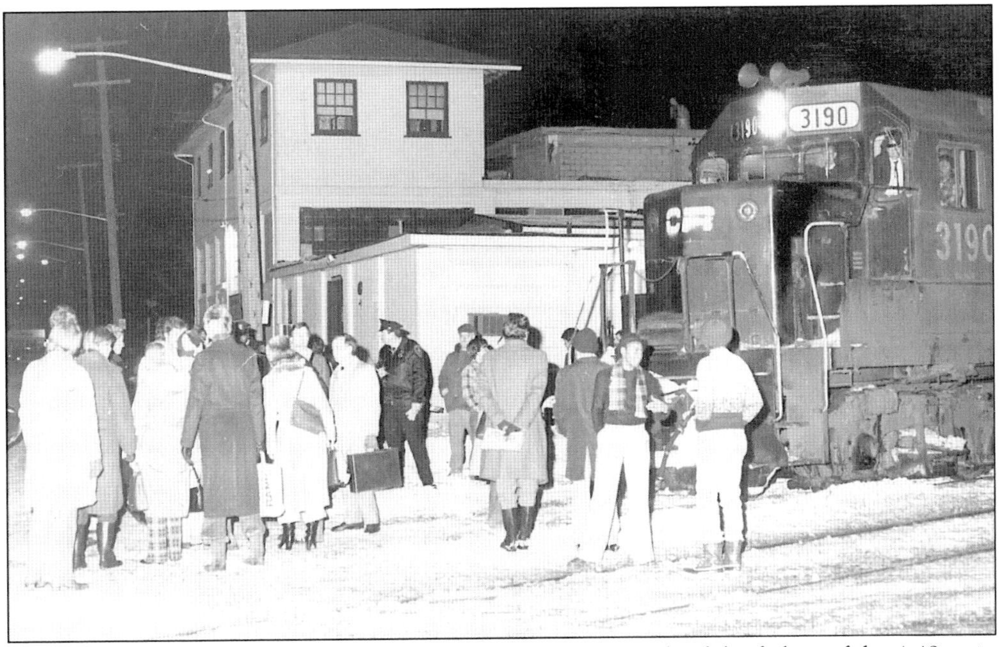

Middletown commuters revolted on February 8, 1978, as a result of the failure of the 4:49 train out of New York to make its scheduled stop at their station. Irate riders blocked the train at Red Bank until given transportation back to Middletown, which was provided by several police cars and a bus. The unprecedented, spontaneous protest had the salutary effect of helping galvanize public support for an ongoing campaign to improve wretched operating conditions and replace obsolete equipment.

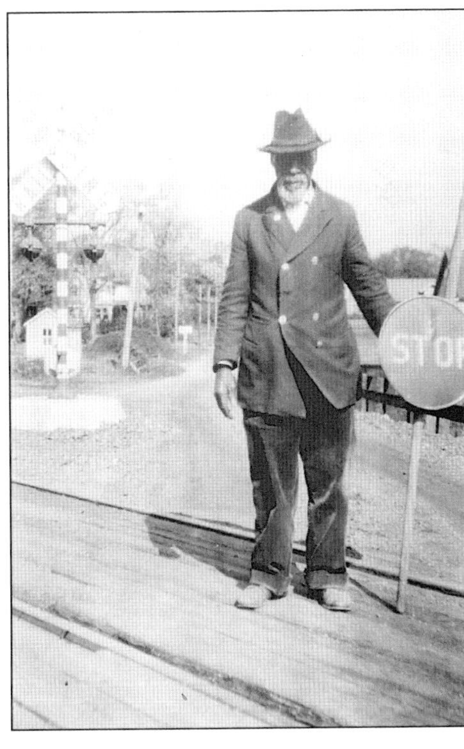

Clinton P. Heath was born a slave in 1856 in New Bern, NC, and came to Middletown in 1885 to work on the Beekman Farm as the first among several of his circle and race to make this migration. He was employed later by the New York and Long Branch Railroad, serving for 16 years as a section hand, and for 27 as a flagman at the Middletown crossing, a function that stopped traffic prior to the use of automatic signals and gates. Heath was awarded a pension on retiring in 1932, a gesture announced as an honor, made well in advance of today's regulation of retirement benefits. He was popular with riders, often receiving small objects as gifts, and was proud of his record of no accidents during his long crossing service. Heath, a co-founder of the Clinton Chapel, AME Zion Church, Red Hill, died in 1936 of injuries sustained in an automobile accident. (Collection of the Monmouth County Historical Association.)

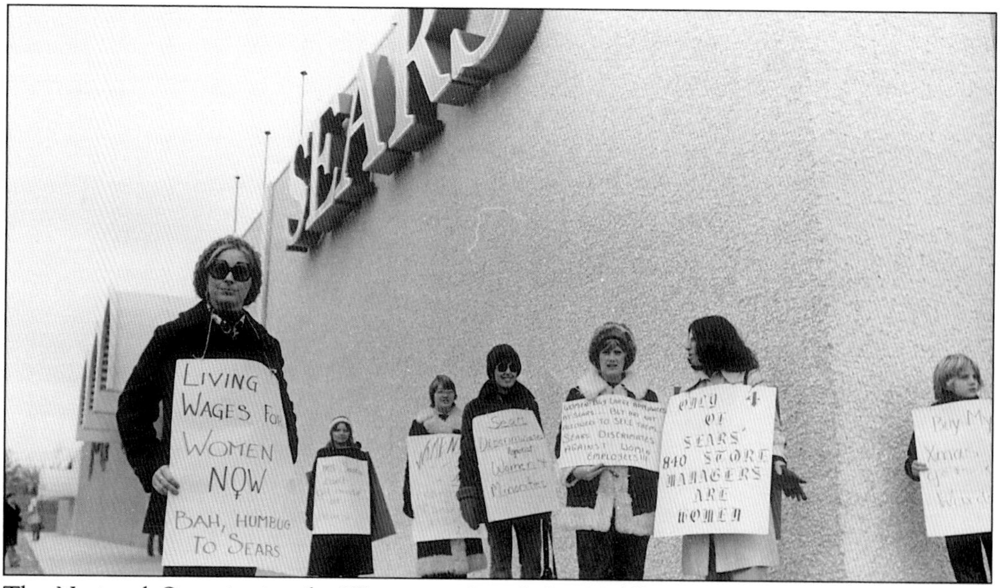

The National Organization for Women picketed the Middletown Sears in December 1974, claiming job discrimination against women. The Equal Employment Opportunity Commission brought suit in 1979, which Sears won, in part because a judge believed women preferred the lesser positions to which they were shunned! Although employment discrimination has lessened considerably in the intervening quarter-century, women in non-traditional roles can elicit a second glance, such as a female garbage collector in the author's neighborhood.

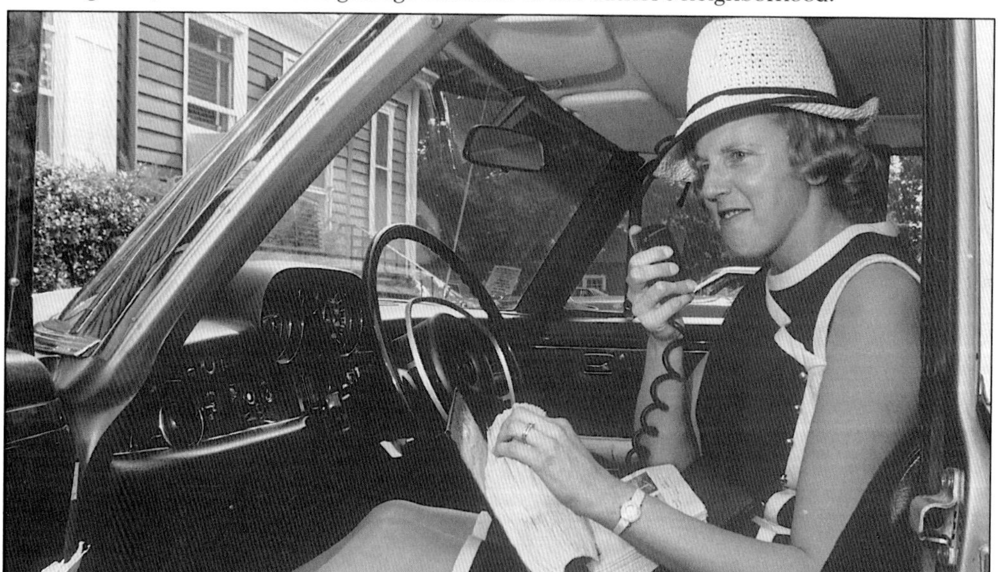

Gloria Nilson, pictured in her trademark hat, of course, was Walker & Walker's star sales representative when she posed here with 1974-style mobile communication. The photograph was taken three years prior to her founding Gloria Nilson Realtors, located in a former restaurant in Shrewsbury. Gloria is now located in another former restaurant, this one in Middletown, where her firm serves "any size house or garden under the sun." This mobile device was tethered as opposed to current cellular phones, which leave one free to telecommunicate anytime and anywhere.

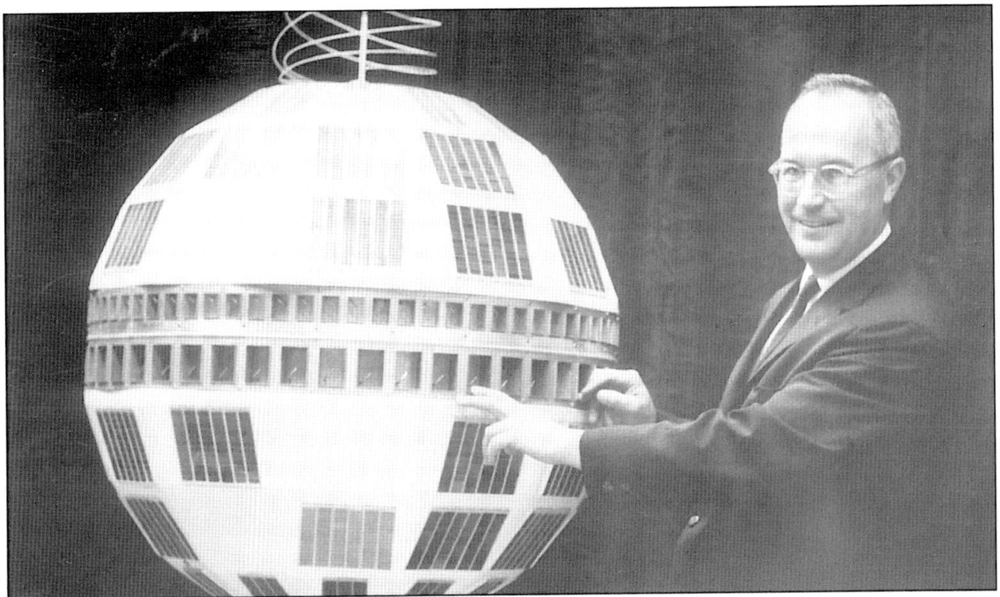

Eugene Francis O'Neill, born in 1918 in Brooklyn, was the engineer directing the American Telephone & Telegraph Company's commercial satellite Telstar project. He is pictured in 1962 with an exact model (the original would never be touched). Telstar's capability of transmitting signals over long distances with minimal ground equipment revolutionized television broadcasting. Although fiber optics provide for more effective transmission now, Telstar's demonstration that electronic equipment could work in space for a prolonged period make it a landmark of the space program. Gene, who worked in several AT&T facilities, has resided in Middletown with his wife, Kathryn, for the past 28 years.

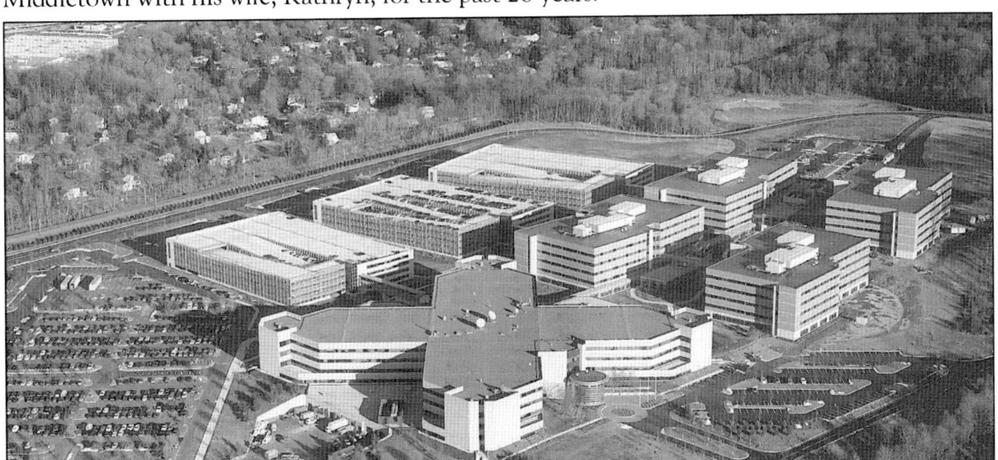

The largest American Telephone & Telegraph Company research and development facility in the world is located on an extensive tract bordered by Laurel Avenue and Holland Road. This aerial view was taken in January 1999. The cross-shaped structure in the foreground is now identified as Building A. It was designed by Jacob Block, who began the project in 1984–85. The four similar buildings to the east, or right, designed by C.U.H.2A. (a firm that identifies itself with the initials of its original partners—Collins, Uhl, Hoisington, Anderson, and Azmy), were completed in 1998. The structures behind them and in front of the railroad tracks are garages. The complex is the township's largest tax ratable.

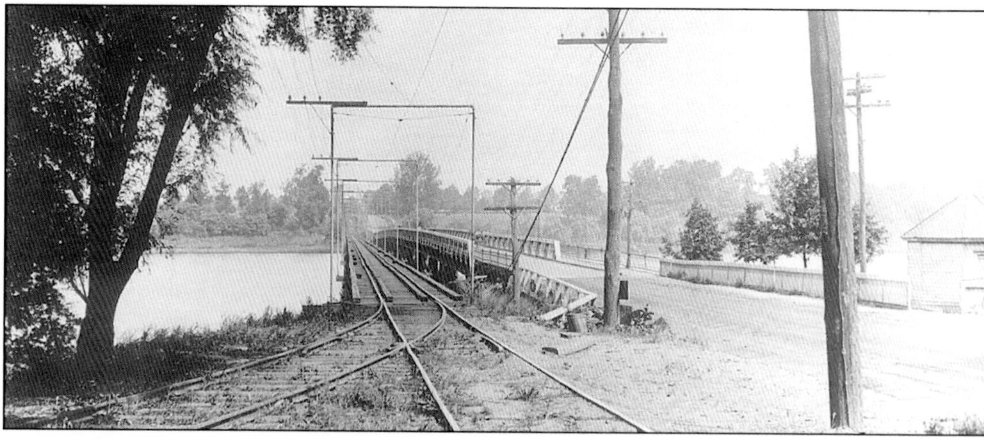

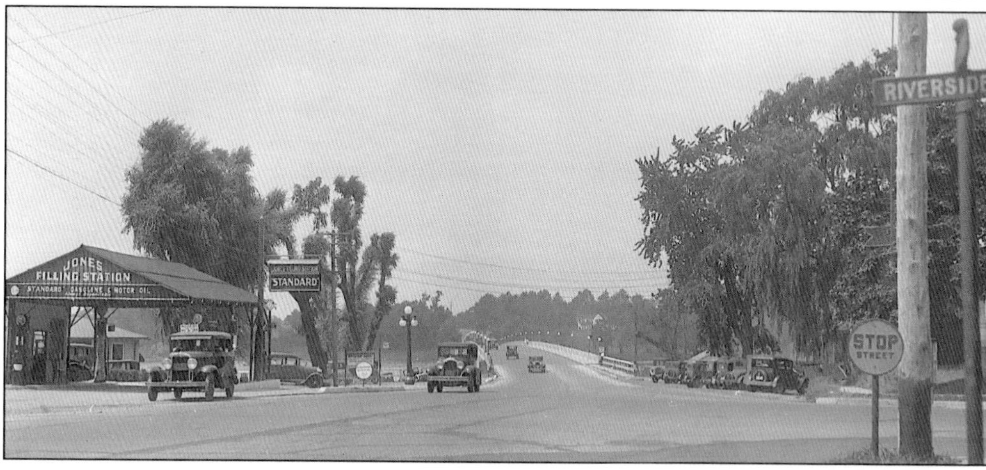

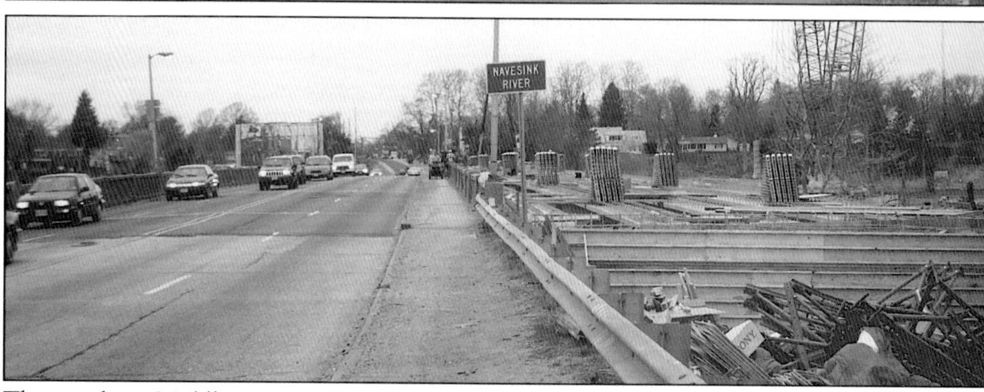

The road to Middletown is paved with impermanent materials, judging by the regular replacement of the Coopers Bridge. The *c.* 1910 photograph at top shows the second bridge, built *c.* 1862 and rebuilt in 1894, along with the trolley bridge then adjacent on the west. The middle photograph from 1929 shows the present bridge three years after construction. Riverside Avenue was later realigned, and although an extensively changed gas station is still on the west side of the road, the recreation facility behind it is long gone. The once impressive concrete bridge of 1926 is now crumbling. Construction of its replacement is well underway at press time, as evidenced by the bottom photograph taken in April 1999. All views are looking west toward Middletown from Red Bank. (Top photo—Collection of Harold Solomon.)

Three

Spiritual Enrichment

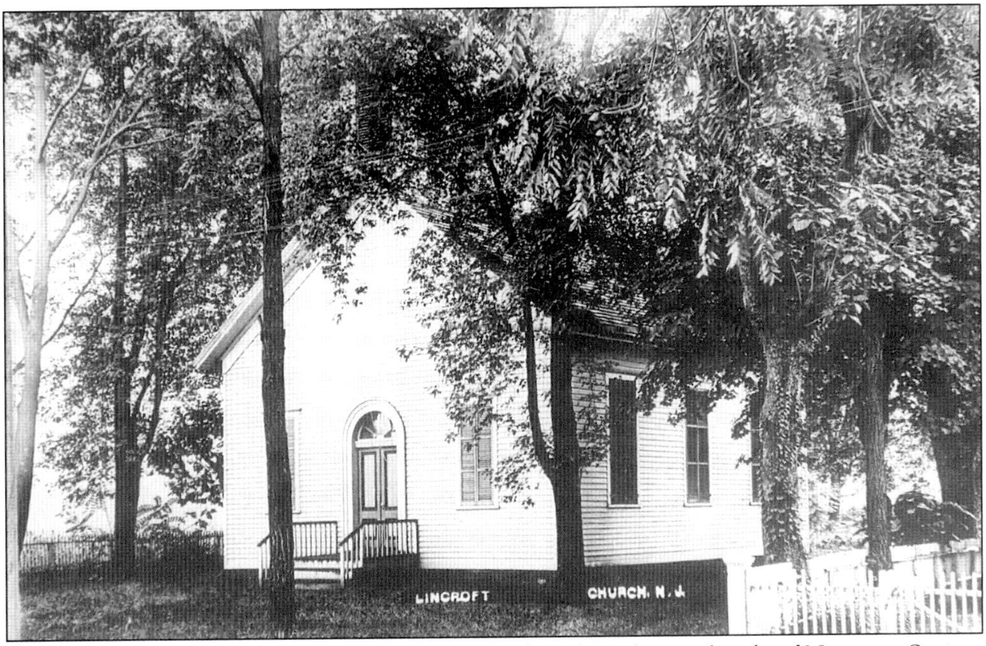

The First Baptist Church of Red Bank built this chapel on the south side of Newman Springs Road in 1868 (dedicated February 17, 1869) following successful revival meetings at the local school conducted during the pastorate of the Reverend Charles W. Clark. Ownership evolved to an independent board of trustees, and the church, in time, became known as the Lincroft Community Chapel. The group changed its affiliation to Presbyterian in 1960, and moved to the northeast corner of West Front Street and Everett Road in 1966. The building, seen on a c. 1910 Merriman postcard, is now a restaurant. (Collection of Harold Solomon.)

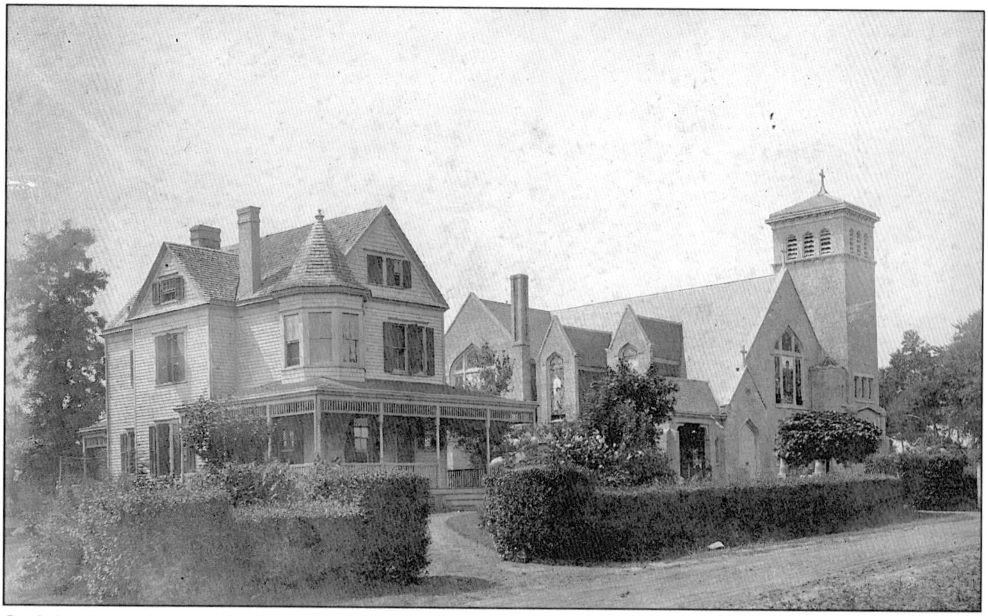

St. Mary's, 26 Leonardville Road, New Monmouth, began the 20th century as the largest Roman Catholic church building in the surrounding area. Its greatly expanded congregation has made the structure small at the century's end, necessitating the use of space in its nearby school for the celebration of Mass. The edifice, designed by New York's Pollard & Steinman, combines Gothic and Romanesque elements and is seen in a c. 1900 photograph. The rectory is shown at left. New construction of an unspecified scope is under consideration at publication.

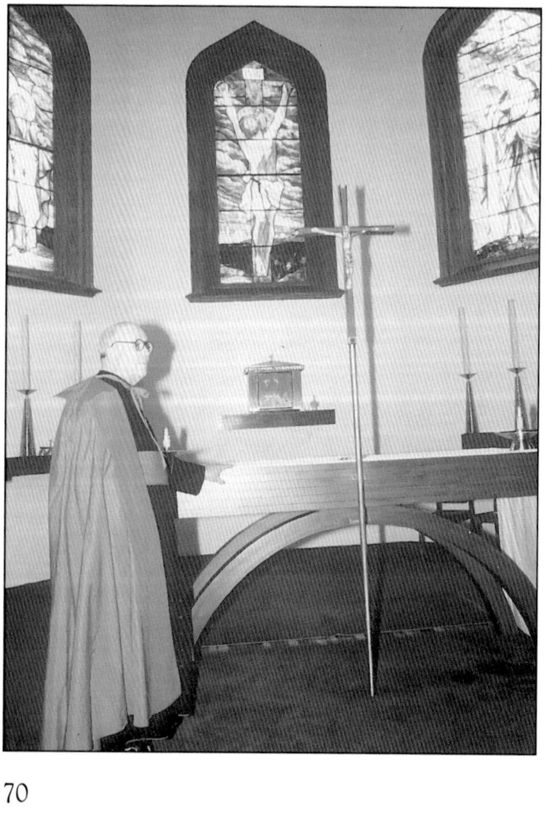

The Reverend Monsignor Robert T. Bulman, born 1913 in South Amboy, NJ, was ordained a priest in 1940, the same year he was assigned as curate to St. Mary's, then a small country church. He was later appointed administrator and, in 1950, pastor. Monsignor Bulman's 52 years at St. Mary's saw the church grow into one of the largest Catholic communities in the Trenton Diocese. His tenure included the opening of St. Mary's Grammar and Mater Dei High Schools in 1953 and 1965 respectively, and the construction of a new convent, later converted into St. Mary's Nursery School. On leaving St. Mary's in 1992, Monsignor Bulman said his dedication to education provided many highlights of his long career there. He now lives in retirement in Manasquan.

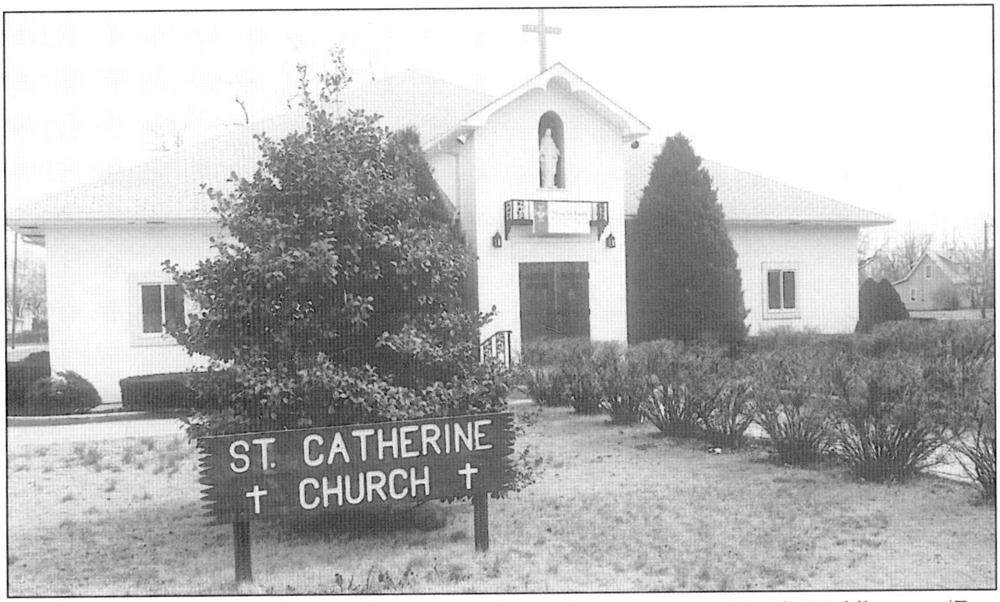

St. Catherine's Roman Catholic Church, 5 Shore Acres Avenue, North Middletown (East Keansburg) was a mission of St. Ann's, Keansburg, from 1927 to 1948, when it was established as a parish. The Reverend Francis P. Gunner was appointed as the first pastor. The original building began as a barn and was remodeled; the church's property expanded as the congregation added a parish hall, school, gymnasium, and convent.

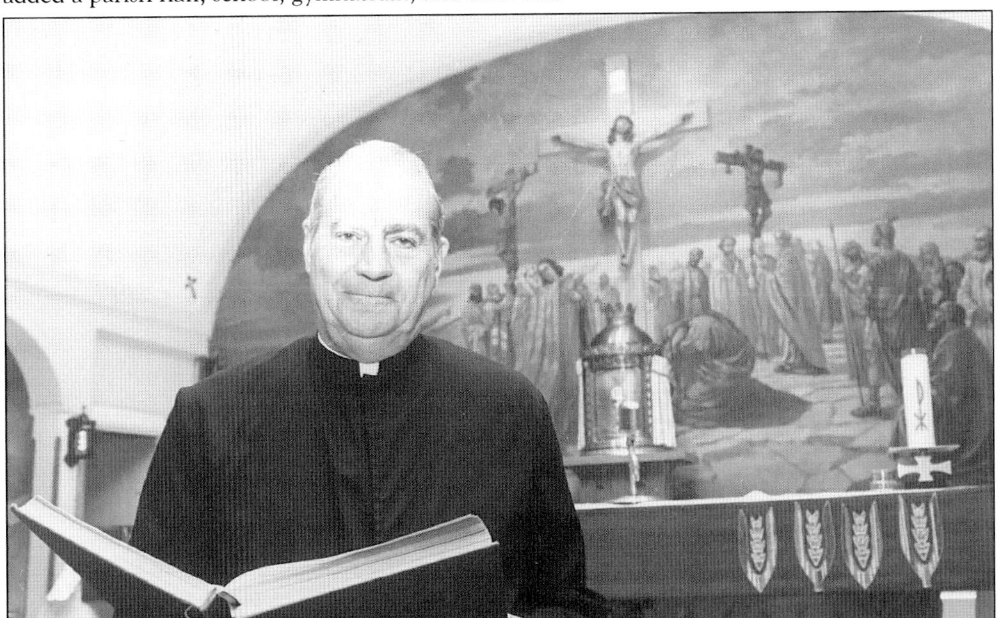

The Reverend John B. Cook, born 1922 in Brooklyn and educated at St. Francis College and Immaculate Conception Seminary, Darlington, NJ, was ordained a priest at St. Mary's Cathedral, Trenton, in 1949. He had served six parishes prior to his 1967 appointment as pastor at St. Catherine's, where he served 20 years. His tenure saw the addition of a gymnasium and kindergarten to the school and the construction of a new rectory. Father Cook, now retired, recently celebrated his golden jubilee as a priest.

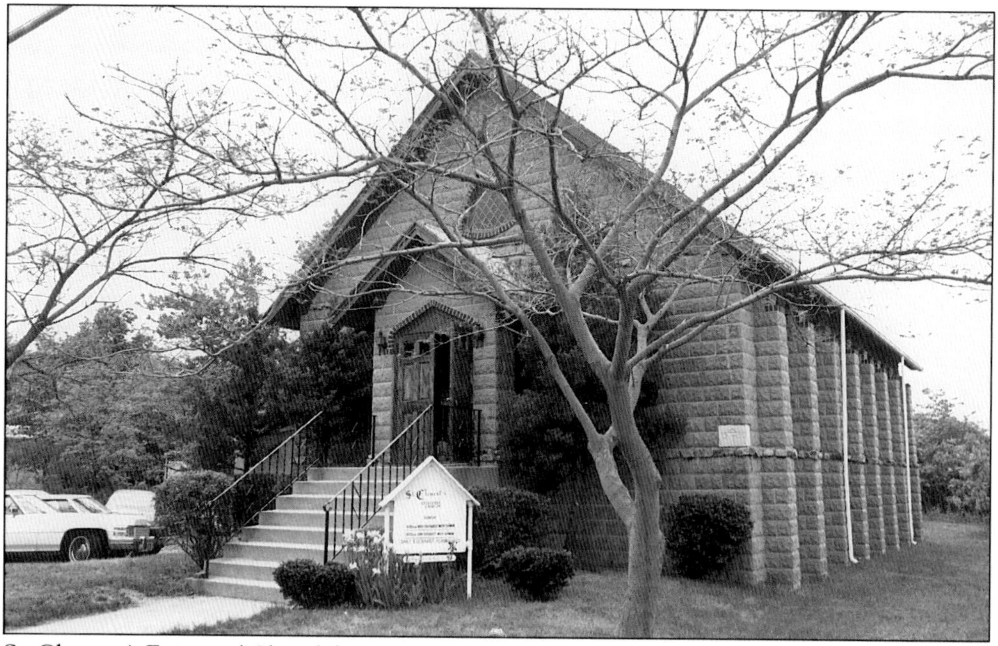

St. Clement's Episcopal Church began as a Sunday school founded by John P. Euler at Campbells Junction on February 14, 1926. A growing following resulted in the establishment of the church on Christmas Day, 1926. The congregation, which later met at a Church Street building near the Belford School, built this 30-by-48-foot church at 300 Church Street, on the south side of Highway 36, in 1930. They received substantial help with donated materials and services. The little-changed rock-face concrete-block edifice is seen here in 1976.

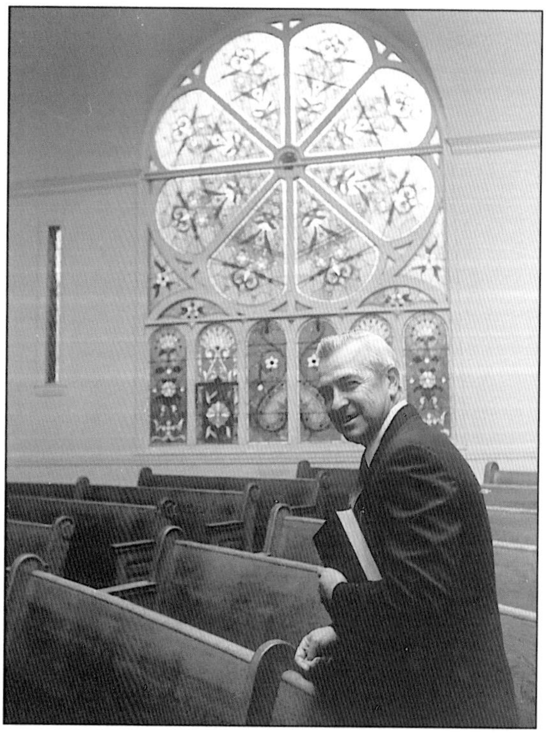

The Reverend Harry W. Kraft, born around 1923 in Irvington, NJ, lived on Monmouth Avenue and was pastor of the Central Baptist Church in nearby Atlantic Highlands. He kept animals on his spacious grounds, using them in his ministry to help children access a spiritual message. Kraft's summer backyard services provided leisurely access to his work in a neighborhood setting. His "Praise Him Band" helped introduce children to music. Kraft is pictured in 1974 when he celebrated his 25th anniversary as pastor.

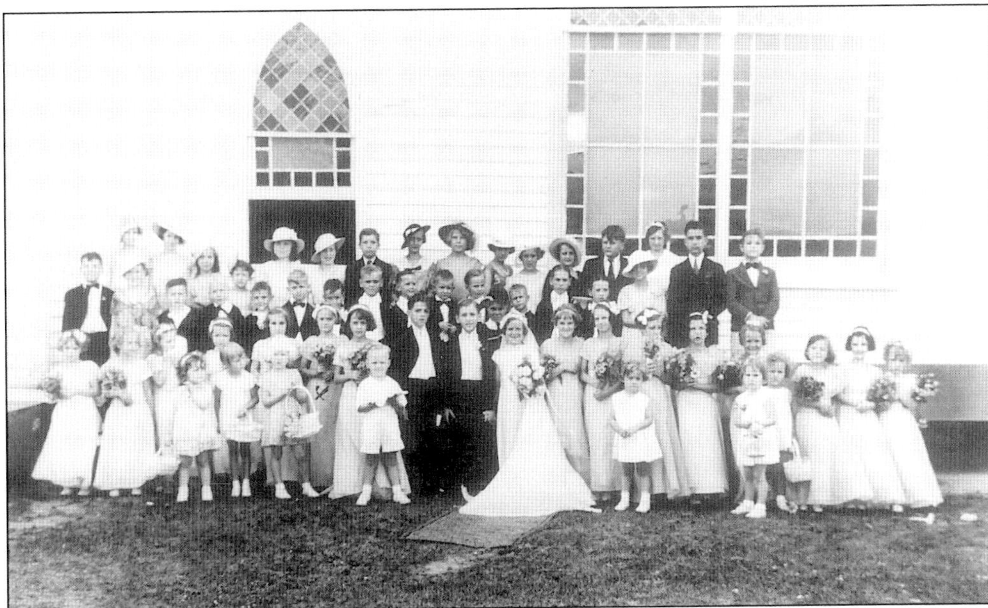

A Tom Thumb wedding was held at the Belford Methodist Episcopal Church at 180 Church Street (Volume II, p. 100) on June 18, 1935. The participants are forgotten, except the one who preserved the picture. Lois Bodtmann, ninth from the left in the first row, is seen as a bridesmaid; the dreaded "x" marks her spot.

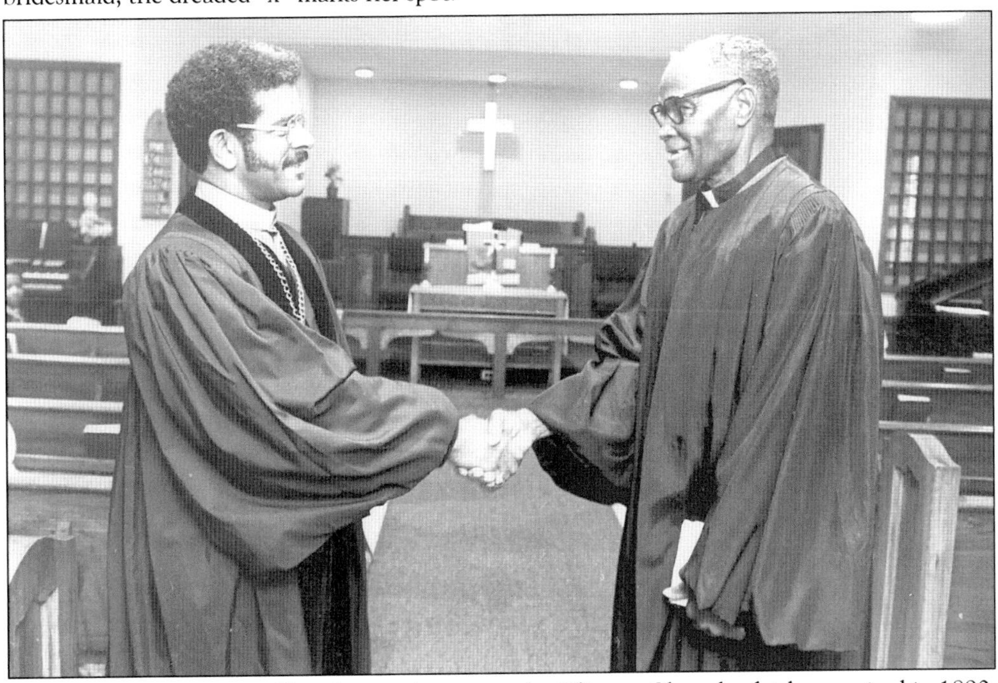

The Red Hill AME Zion Church, now known as the Clinton Chapel, which organized in 1890, was reported to have celebrated their 106th anniversary in September 1976 (perhaps a private prayer practice was regarded as an origin). The Reverend Wallace Stallings (left), pastor, greeted the Reverend Robert L. Kegler, pastor in 1966 when their original church was destroyed by fire (Volume II, p. 68), who conducted the anniversary service.

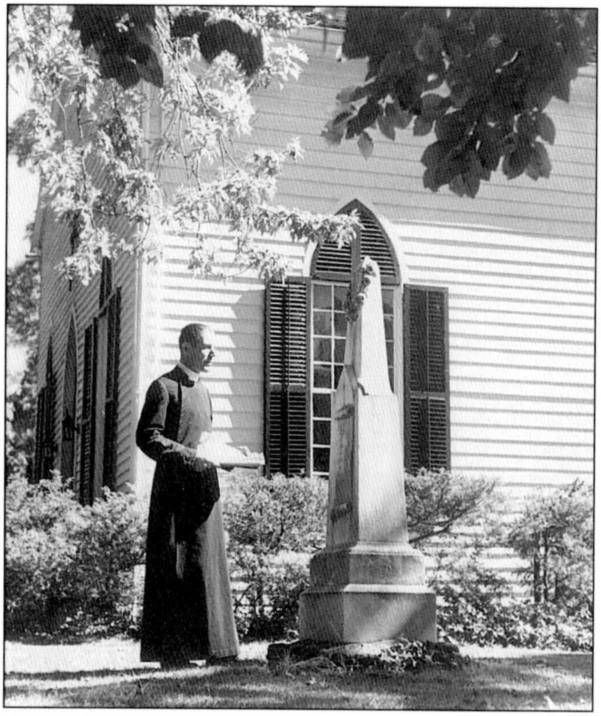

The Reverend Andrew Van Dyke, rector of Christ Church, is seen in 1952 beside a monument erected to the memory of William Leeds. He was a benefactor of Christ Church by his donation of a large farm in Lincroft, when it was a parish combined with the Shrewsbury Christ Church. Van Dyke was born in 1910 in Pennsylvania, and graduated from Hobart College and Virginia Theological Seminary in 1932 and 1935, respectively. He became rector at Christ Church in 1949, leading it to 1960 during a period of growth. The Reverend Van Dyke resigned from the church, having become a teacher at the Lincroft School, where he was later appointed principal. He died in 1974. (Special Collections and Archives, Rutgers University Libraries.)

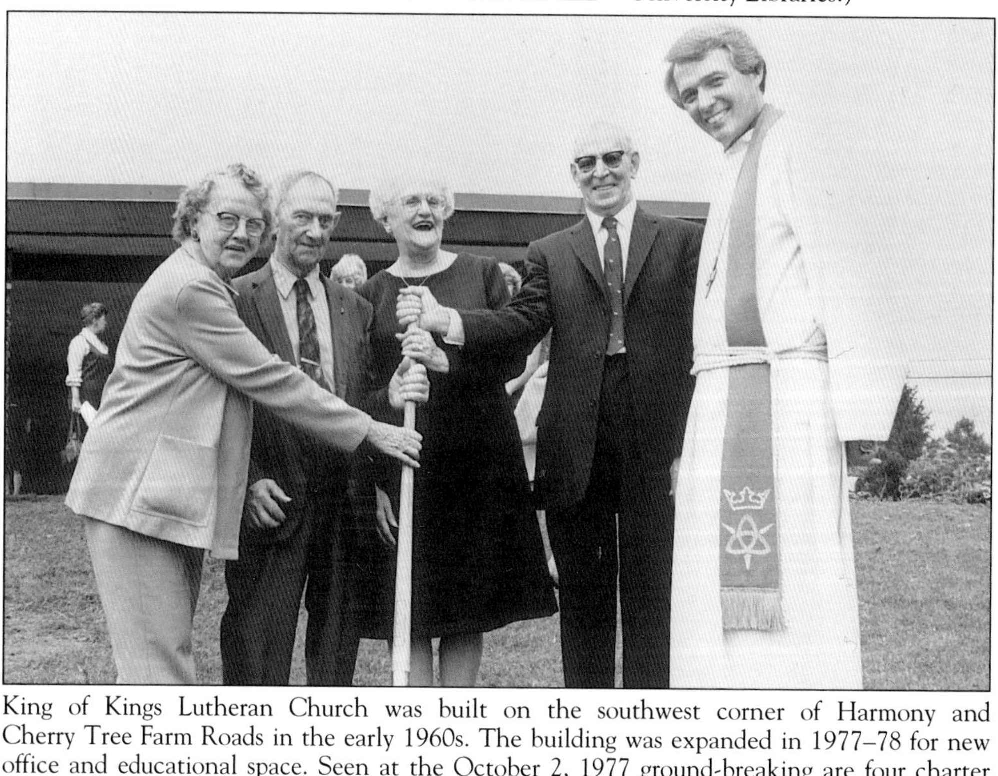

King of Kings Lutheran Church was built on the southwest corner of Harmony and Cherry Tree Farm Roads in the early 1960s. The building was expanded in 1977–78 for new office and educational space. Seen at the October 2, 1977 ground-breaking are four charter members. From left to right are Solveig and Berger Eia, Elsie McCammon, and the Reverend William Hanson.

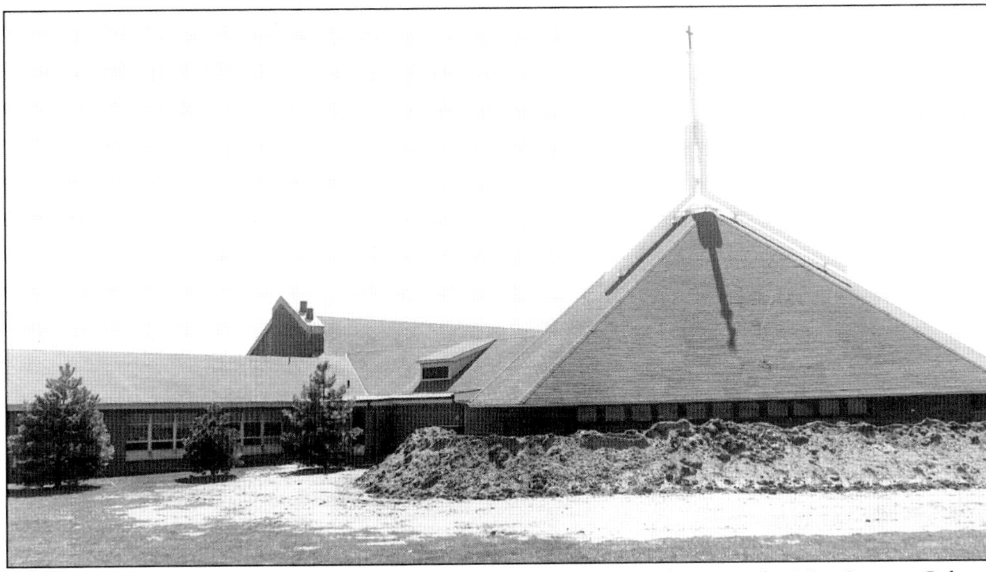

The Middletown United Methodist Church formed in 1965 and met in the Nut Swamp School in their early years. They built an education-meeting space in 1968. After a 1977 building plan had been rejected, the members erected (in 1982) this major addition, which includes a sanctuary, at 924 Middletown-Lincroft Road. The building, designed by Thomas, Kolbe, Thomas and Popori of Cherry Hill, NJ, is seen at the time of its April dedication.

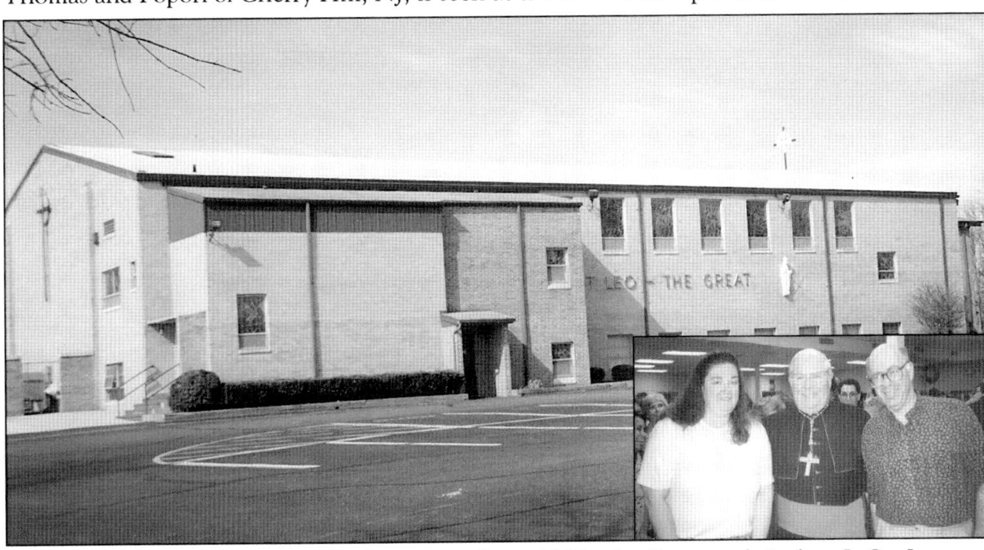

St. Leo the Great was established as a parish in 1958, the Reverend Arthur J. St. Laurent, pastor, with its early masses celebrated at the Lincroft School. The present church at the northeast corner of Newman Springs Road and Hurleys Lane was completed in 1960, and was designed by Carl W. Karlberg, architect, Trenton, with T. Harry Moran, consultant. The structure was intended to serve as both church and school, notably as a gymnasium. It was built with the expectation that it would be given to educational use alone at some point, which has not happened. Alterations were later made on the east entrance. This view is the south elevation. Bishop John M. Smith, who visited St.Leo's for evening prayer on September 16, 1997, soon after appointment as the ninth Bishop of Trenton, is seen there with the author and his wife, Barbara.

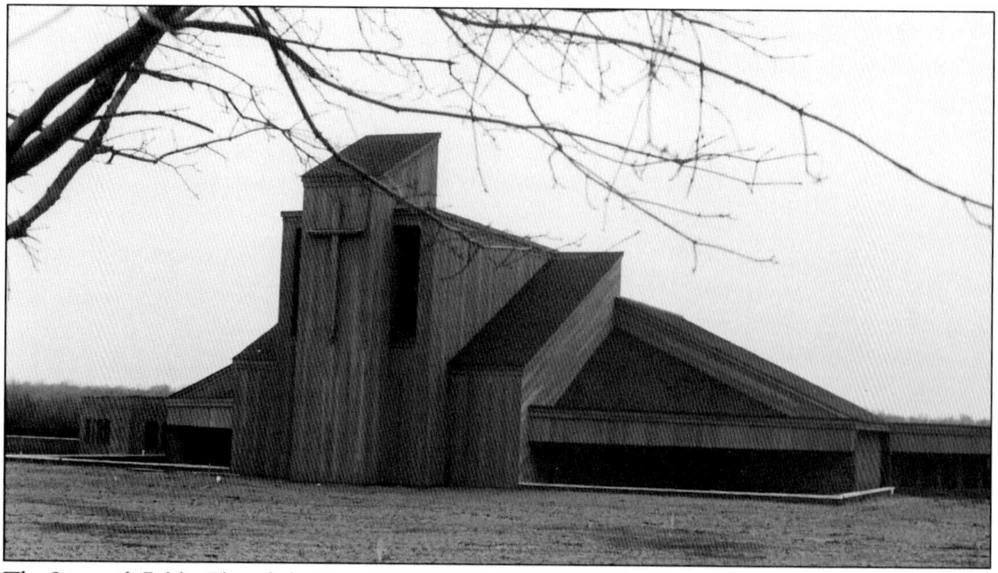

The Lincroft Bible Church began in the 1960s as a small Bible study group, later in that decade renting meeting space in the Fairview School. They built a small church on West Front Street around 1970, and this edifice at 790 Newman Springs Road, which was completed in 1983, the time of the photograph. Its architect was Edmund H. Gaunt Jr. of Kaplan Gaunt De Santis, Red Bank, who recalled working closely on its modern design with the Reverend James Persons. The building was designed to meet the congregation's religious philosophy, accounting for the high central element, a radial plan that brought the worshippers closer, the pulpit as the center of the church, and made extensive use of interior wood finishing to reflect a warm, welcoming ambiance.

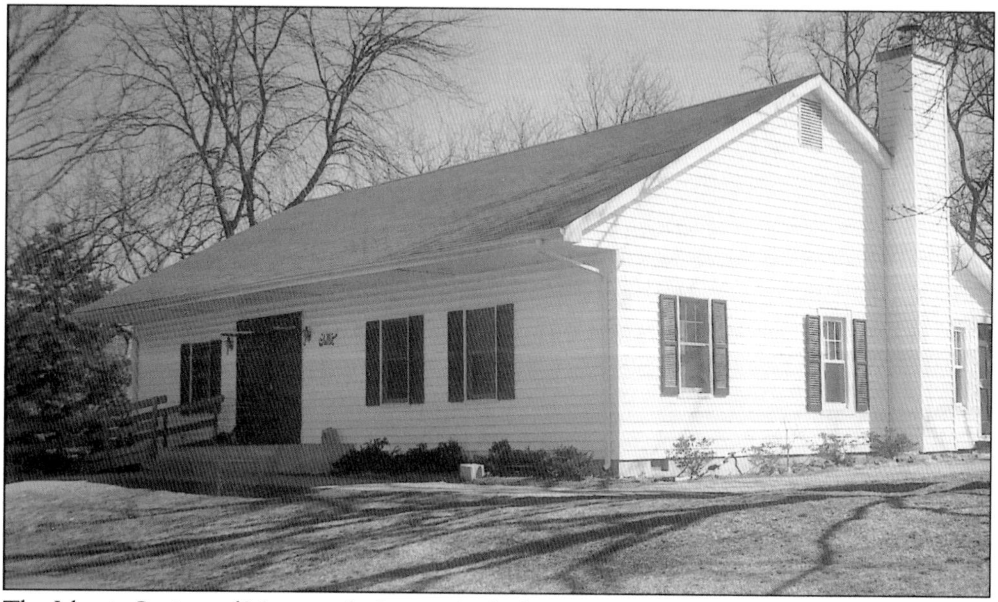

The Islamic Society of Monmouth County built the newest house of worship in the township. This mosque is on about 6 acres at 496 Red Hill Road, and opened in 1995. The rapid growth in the number of worshippers has already strained the capacity of the building's approximately 1,300 square feet of prayer space, notably at Friday afternoon services.

Four

Education and Culture

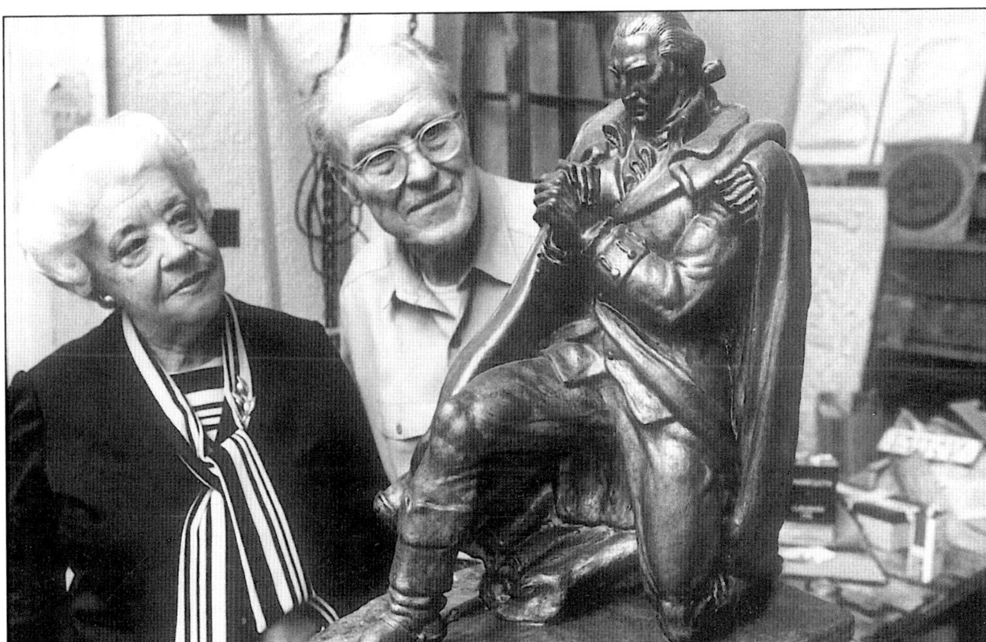

Figurative sculpture was in the artistic mainstream in the early decades of the 20th century, but was in critical decline by the time the career of Donald DeLue, born 1897 in Boston, reached its peak. However, he was a major figure in that field for the second half of the 20th century. His work ranges from medallic art, with some subjects local to his adopted home, to large, cast monumental public sculptures. *Washington at Prayer*, installed at Valley Forge, PA, is one of his better-known works. He is seen here in 1976 with its maquette in his Leonardo studio. DeLue died in 1988.

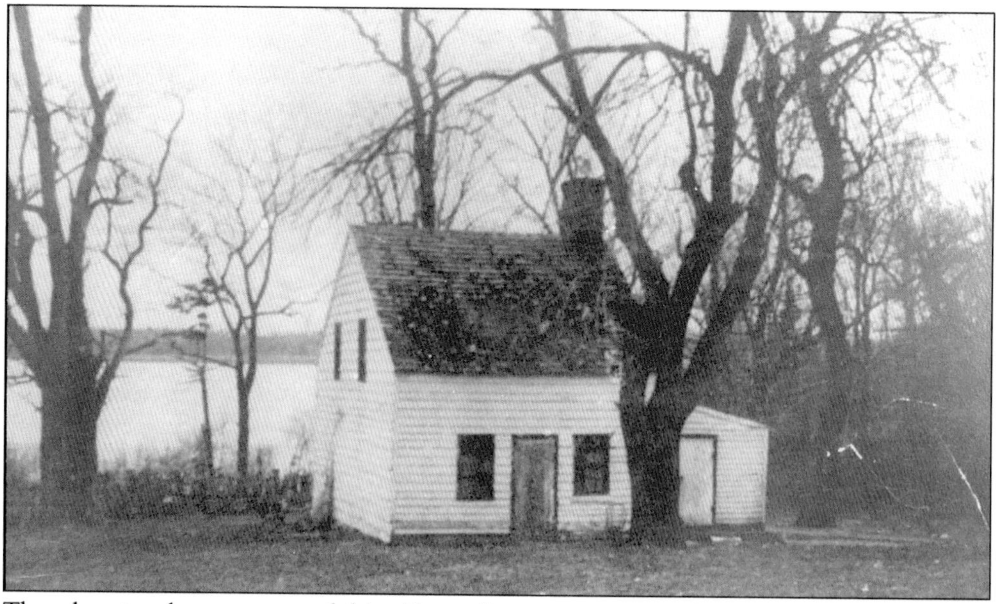

The educational provenance of this old, small structure seen in the picture is unknown. The picture dates perhaps *c.* 1900, and is believed to be reliably labeled "private school-Hartshorne estate." However, it symbolizes early instruction in the township as the irregular, often private undertaking that characterized schooling prior to the mid-19th-century construction of one-room schoolhouses. The building was a residence prior to its destruction, perhaps at the time of the federal government's *c.* 1941 purchase of Rocky Point acreage (in today's Hartshorne Woods) for the Highlands Army Defense base (see p. 106).

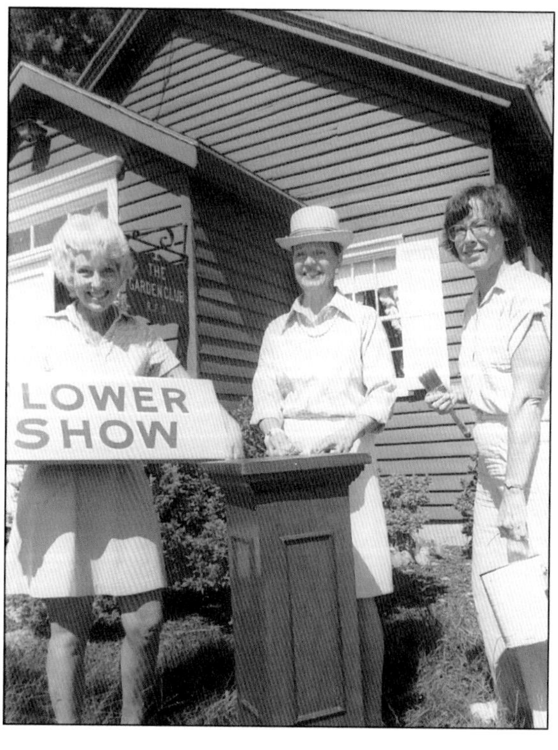

The township's one-room schoolhouses were replaced in the first quarter of this century, typically by two- or four-room brick schools that were later expanded. Most of the buildings no longer stand, but the Headdens Corner and Everett Schools were converted to dwellings, while Nut Swamp, at the southwest corner of Middletown-Lincroft and Dwight Roads, was adapted for use by the Garden Club RFD. Seen in 1978 planning for their "September Harmonies" flower show are, from left to right, Mrs. Malcolm H. Markendorf, Mrs. Walter Zimmerer, and Mrs. John Chappell. The building still stands, its changes in over 150 years relatively minor.

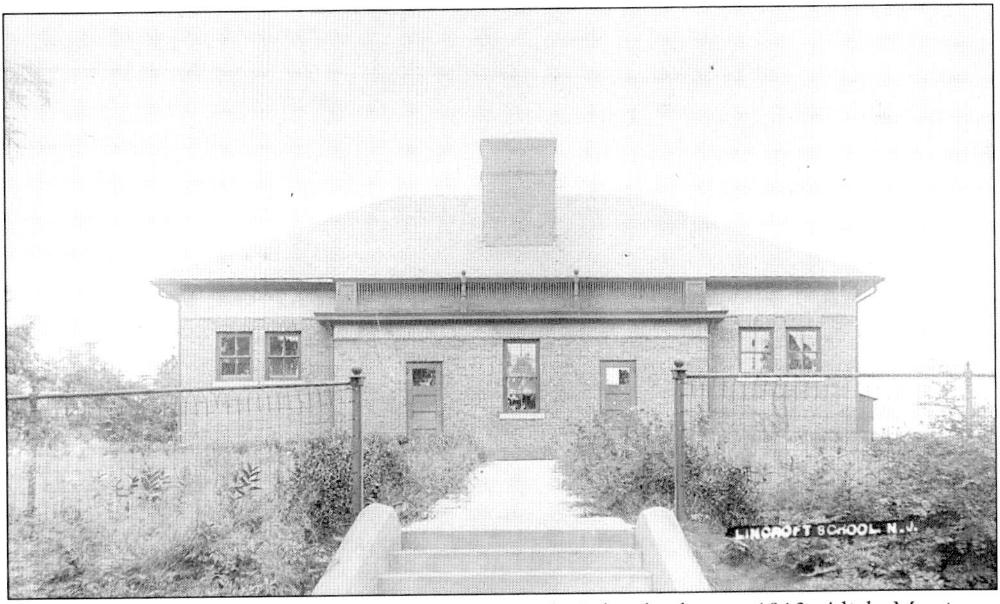

The earliest known picture of the 1907 Lincroft School, this c. 1910 Alick Merriman photographic postcard, reveals an attractive balustrade over the entrance (a feature not found in later images) and wild vegetation. An extension was built on the west, or left, of this building at 722 Newman Springs Road. This facility was replaced in 1957 by the present Lincroft School, but served as an annex into the 1960s. The 1907 school is now the Lincroft branch of the Middletown Public Library. (Collection of Harold Solomon.)

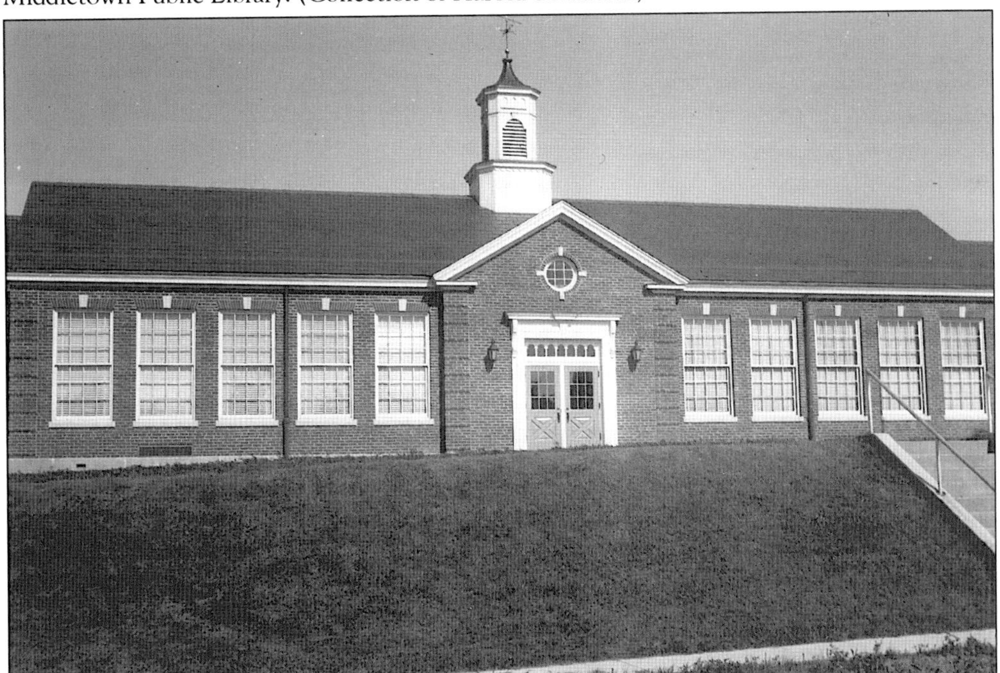

The Middletown Village School was completed in 1941, replacing the school near today's Township Hall that was gutted by fire in 1939. The school is pictured here when new, prior to several additions.

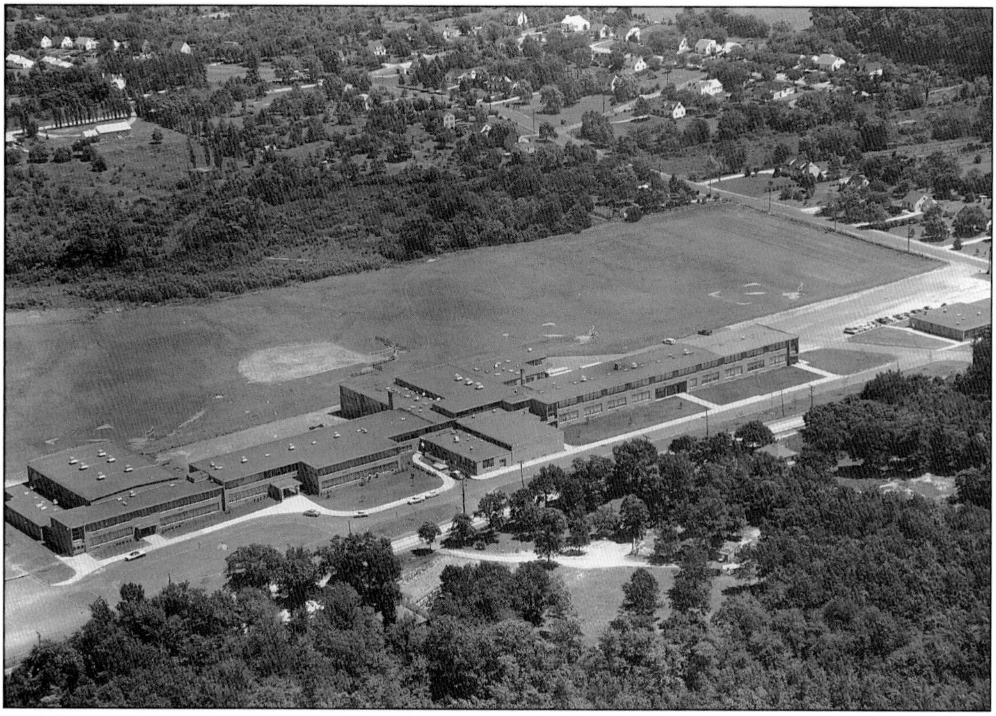

Middletown High School North, Tindall Road, originated as a central elementary school in 1953, a time when the township's high school was in Leonardo. It was expanded in 1955 and again in 1964, when it was converted to a high school.

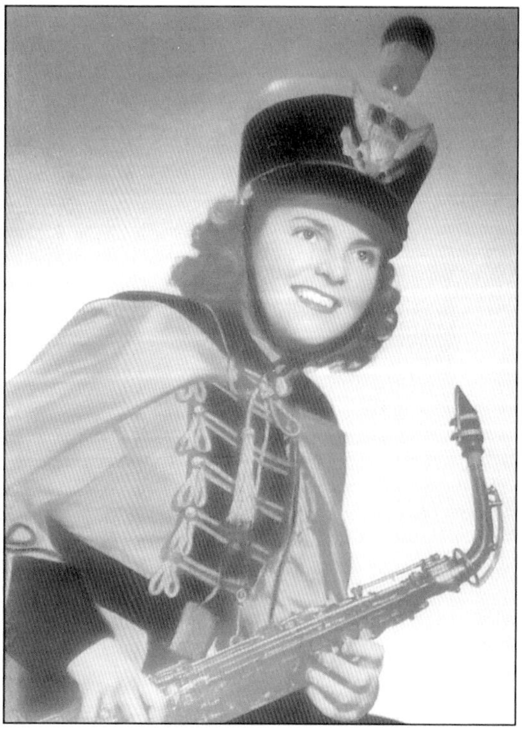

Rose Marie Hansen Boyle was born in 1928, and began playing in the seventh grade in the Middletown school system. She is seen here *c.* 1944 in her Leonardo High School band uniform, and recalled that music led her to a lot of fun, including "all the games" and an annual competition in Asbury Park for the better performers. She sang with a message, too, as Rose Marie's four children learned that her breaking into "God Bless America" meant "I'm angry—be quiet!"

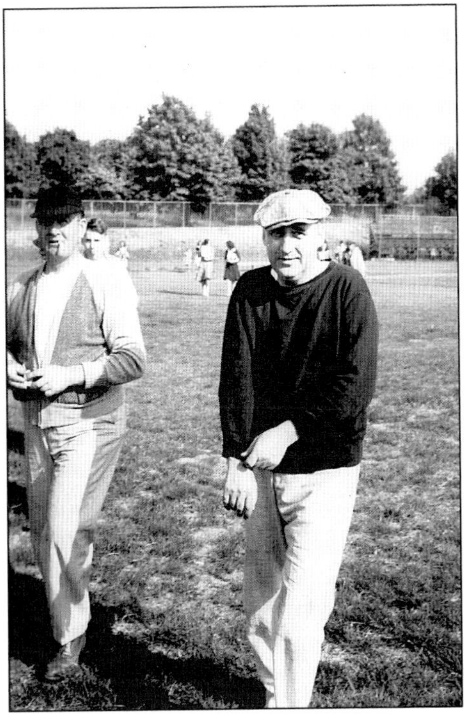

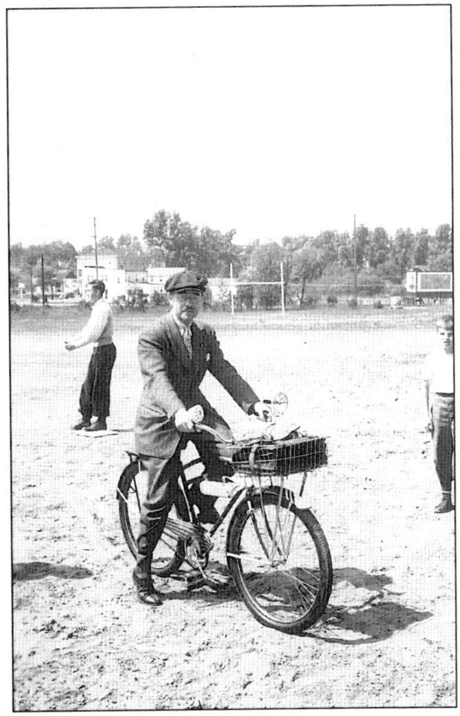

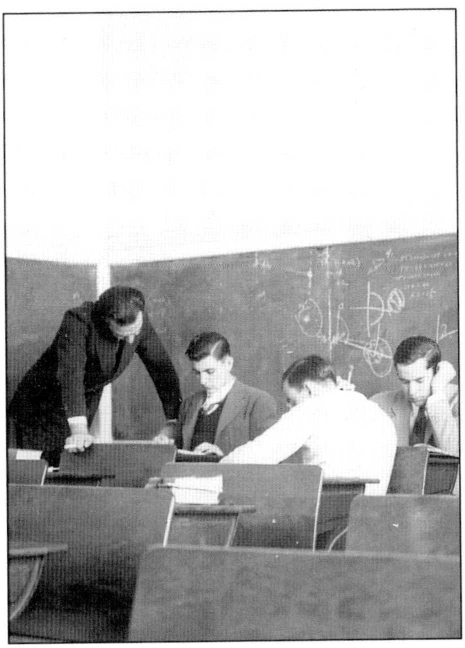

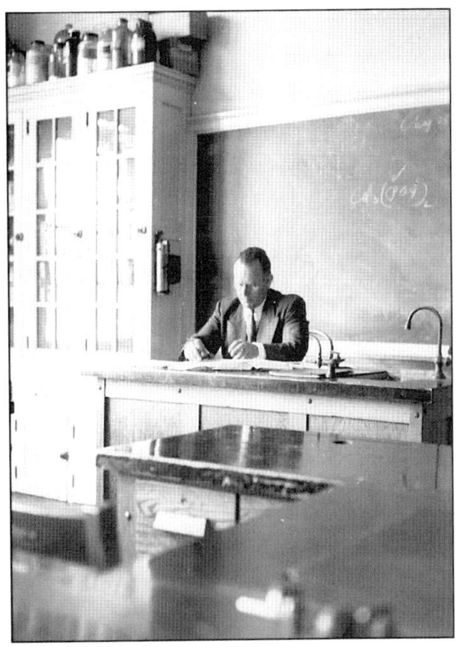

Four c. 1942 snapshots give a glimpse of key Middletown educational figures of the period. Clockwise from the upper left are Lawrence Scott Jr., president of the board of education, and to his left, Wylie Pate, supervising principal; Kenneth H. Meinert, history teacher, on the bicycle; a contemplative Lewis H. Blood, a gym teacher and athletic coach, perhaps drawing a new play; and Lloyd T. Tingley in his math class.

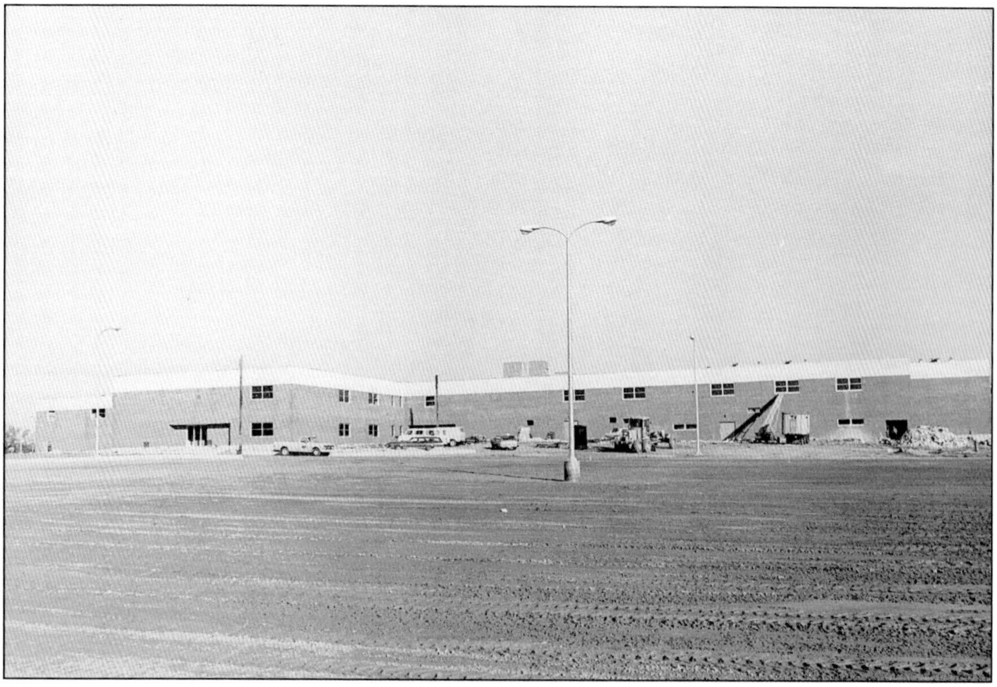

Despite overcrowding and double sessions for years at the township's only high school, a long, public struggle was required to secure approval to build what became Middletown High School South, seen here nearing completion in October 1975. The school, designed by Elsasser & Miller, with educational consultants Engelhardt & Engelhardt, was built with open class space, reflecting a then-fashionable educational idea. The concept proved unsatisfactory, requiring reconstruction in addition to major repairs in the 1990s.

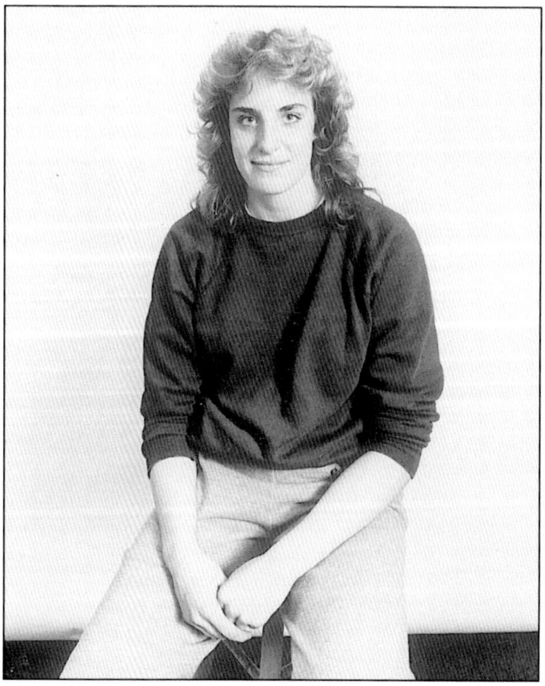

Middletown High School South's girls' basketball program enjoyed its greatest success during the four-year career of Andrea Ashuck, the school's all-time leading scorer. The team won the Shore Conference tournament during her 1984–85 senior year. Andrea was a scholarship winner to Boston University and was elected to that school's athletic hall of fame.

Pat Houston, born 1945 in Elizabeth, NJ, starred at guard on Elizabeth's Sacred Heart basketball team, playing later for the College of Santa Fe, a Christian Brothers school. He is seen here in December 1974, when he became coach at the then-only Middletown High School, where he served for two seasons before organizing the program at the new High School South, coaching there through the 1983–84 season. Houston had one great team, his 1979 squad, which had an unequaled 27-1 record. However, all of his teams were instilled with qualities of discipline, teamwork, intelligent play, and a strong work ethic. Pat's coaching was usually worth an extra 2 or 3 wins per year in this observer's opinion. As principal of Thompson Middle School, call him Mr. Houston now, or those remembering the old days, "coach," an honorific fitting for life.

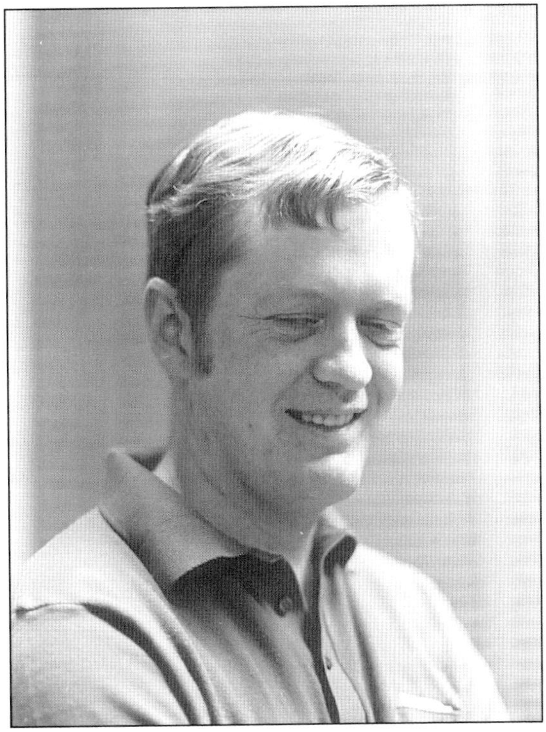

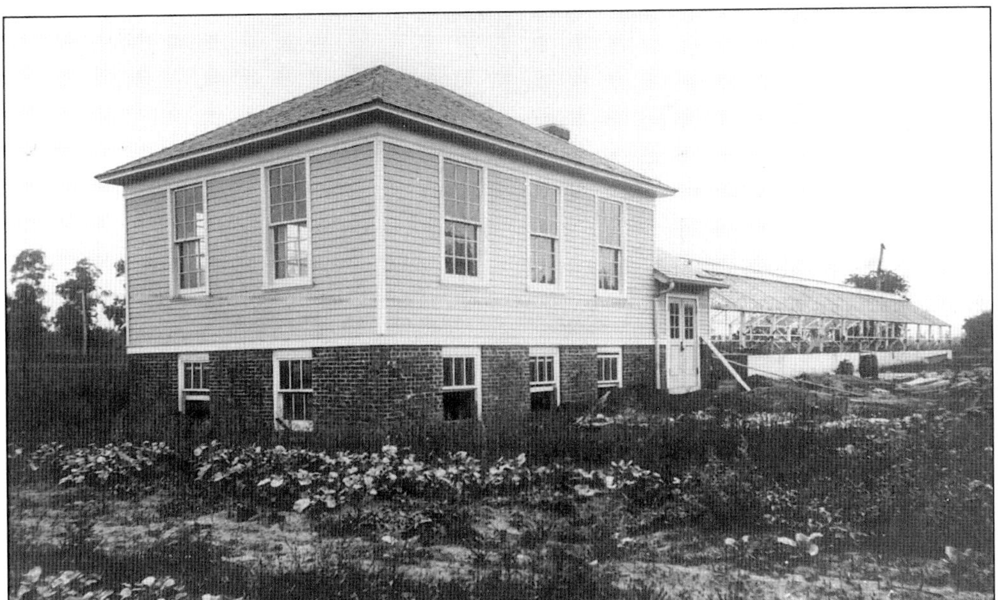

The township was rural and agrarian when the new Leonardo High School was built in 1913. It maintained an agricultural program for years, with many activities centered in its greenhouse. This is probably their second one, built in 1930, which was described when new as one of the most advanced in the country. Sales of flowers and plants raised significant funds to support the program. The greenhouse was demolished in the late 1950s, the dawn of the space era, when technology was replacing agriculture there, recalled four-year program veteran Joseph Dineen. (Collection of the Shrewsbury Historical Society)

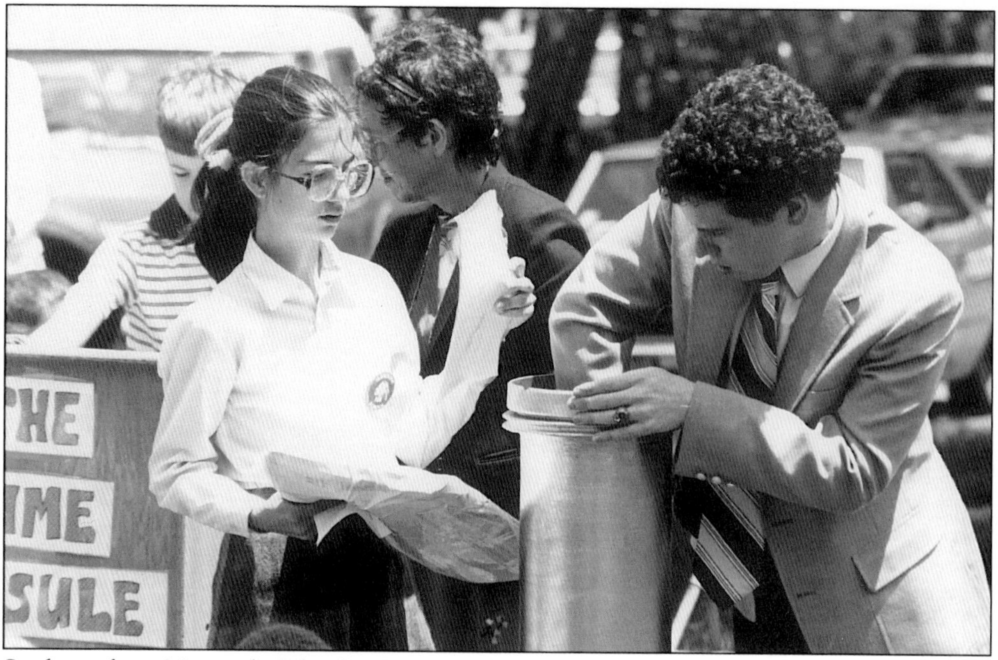

Students from Navesink School's "Project Challenge" buried a time capsule in two 5-foot cylinders donated by Earle Naval Weapons Station, on June 8, 1982. William Presutti, a learning specialist (a title only an educator can appreciate), is seen assisting a student insert an artifact. The capsule is scheduled to be retrieved after only 30 years. A variety of reports were buried, along with objects including a Rubic's cube, a backgammon game, and a postage stamp. They will be nostalgic at the old postal rate in 2012! A reproduction of Pac-Man (remember him?) was included, recalling fears once expressed that video arcades would corrupt the youth of America! Surveyor Tom Finnegan donated a marker to denote the spot.

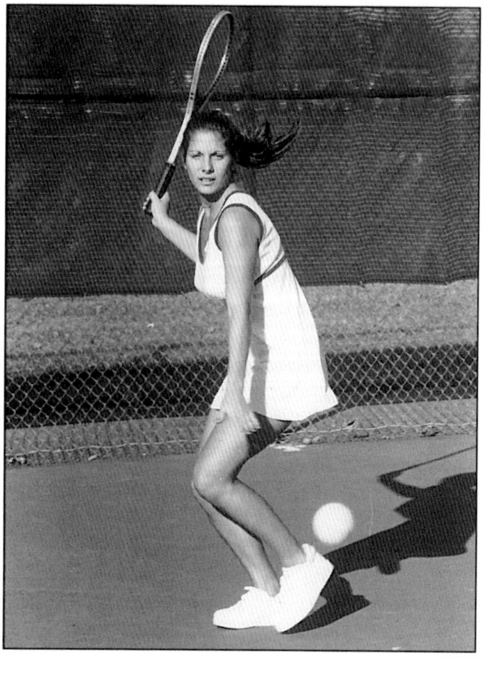

Brookdale Community College enjoyed early success in a number of its athletic programs, notably baseball and women's tennis. Doris Bello is seen here in October 1978, as the team, coached by Kevin Haytor, completed an undefeated season.

Brookdale Community College opened in the fall of 1969 on the former Brookdale Farm. Many farm buildings were remodeled for educational use. Much of the conversion work was designed by Kellenyi Associates, Red Bank, a firm that also designed most of the new construction there for many years. This aerial view shows the Natural and Applied Sciences Building and the gymnasium, with the Swimming River Reservoir in the background. (Historian, Fort Monmouth)

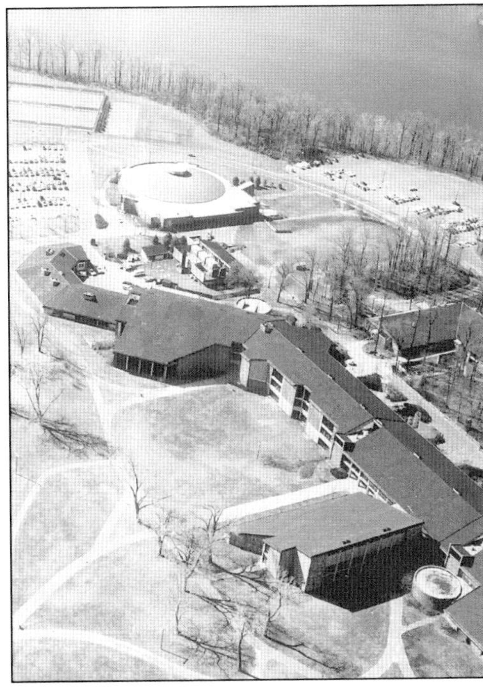

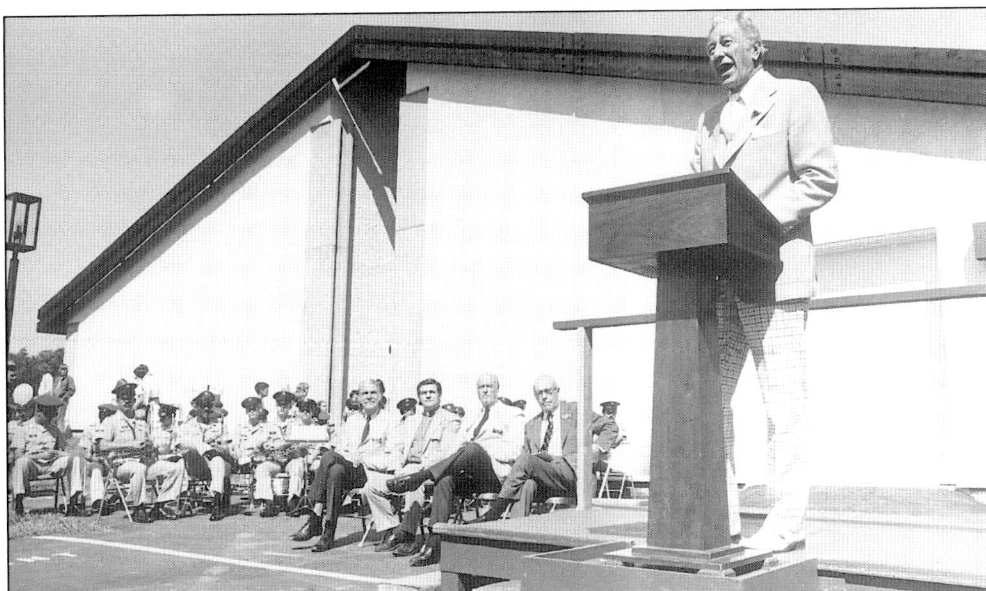

The Monmouth Museum, founded in 1962 as a "museum of ideas," one that would not collect, was housed in its early years in inadequate rented space. Their own $536,000 structure, designed by Bernard Kellenyi, was built in 1974 on the Brookdale Community College campus, financed by public subscription. Freeholder Director Joseph C. Irwin gave the keynote address at the September 15, 1974 dedication. Members of the 389th Army Band, Fort Monmouth, are in the rear. Seated in front, from left to right, are as follows: Dr. Mason W. Gross, trustee and chairman of the fund drive; the Reverend Paul McCarty; William B. Leonard, museum president; and Charles B. Harding, chairman of the board and a major force in the building of the museum. The museum exhibits embrace a variety of cultural and scientific subjects.

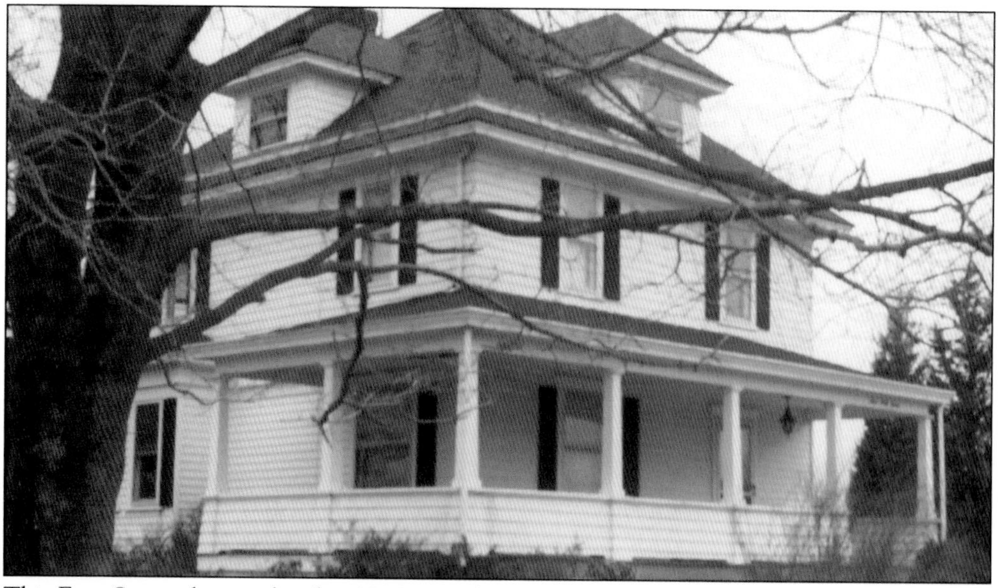

This Four Square house, dated c. 1910, was the seat of the once 60-acre former Gould poultry farm. It was for sale in 1983 by Joseph Panetti, a physical education teacher who retired from the Eatontown system, and learned of its interest by the Oak Hill Academy, a new private school in nearby rented quarters. His enthusiastic backing occasioned him to withdraw from the market while the school secured financing to purchase the property and public approval for its educational use. The school opened it in 1984, soon expanding the facilities. Most of the porch was enclosed and educational space has been affixed to the former house.

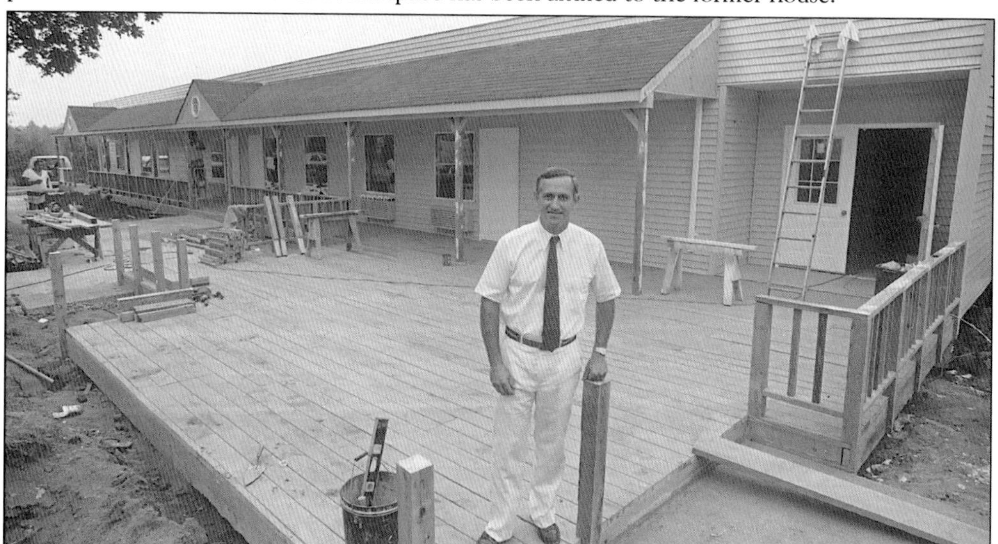

Joseph A. Pacelli, a Middletown native and graduate of Washington and Jefferson College, earned a masters degree from Seton Hall and taught at the Christian Brothers Academy. Seen in the summer of 1984 preparing for the school year, he is the long-serving headmaster at Oak Hill Academy and has shaped an educational philosophy believing in each child's individuality and ability to learn, while providing a homey atmosphere with small class sizes. Excellence in reading and writing is not merely expected, it is routine here, including documented research papers in the eighth grade.

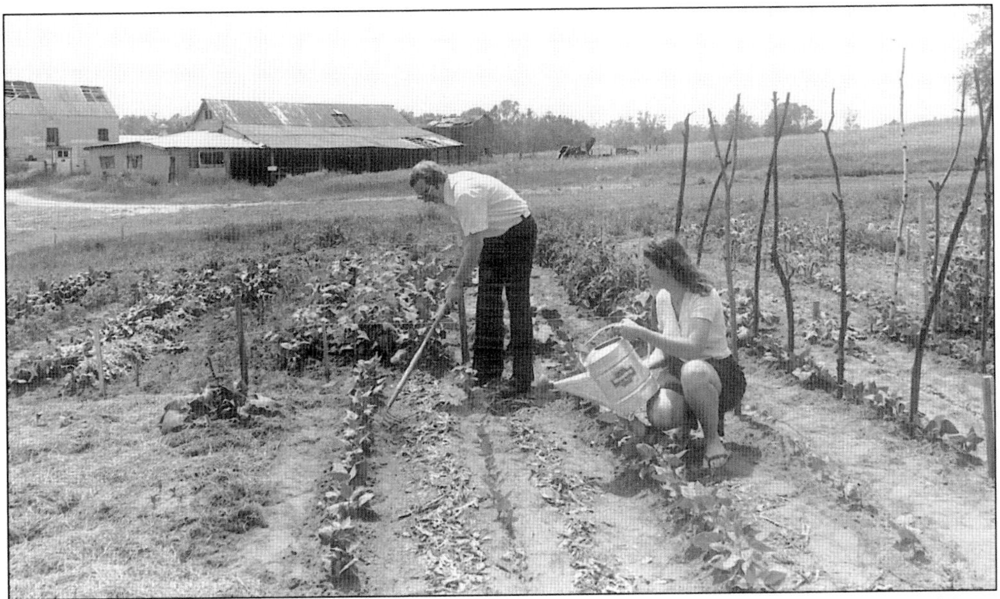

To appreciate the restored state of Poricy Park's Murray Farmhouse (Volume I, p. 17) and barn (Volume II, p. 59), one should realize the extent of the effort made by the founders, including Marcia and Louis Rissland and Pete Brady (see p. 94), to reveal the place from what had been the shabby Gebhardt Farm. Later additions to the old barn were demolished, the original house was uncovered from unsympathetic additions and remodelings, and the place's significance was discovered through Marcia's primary research. Seen "farming" in 1974 are Michael L. Trotta, assistant director of parks and recreation, and Denise King, an intern from Penn State.

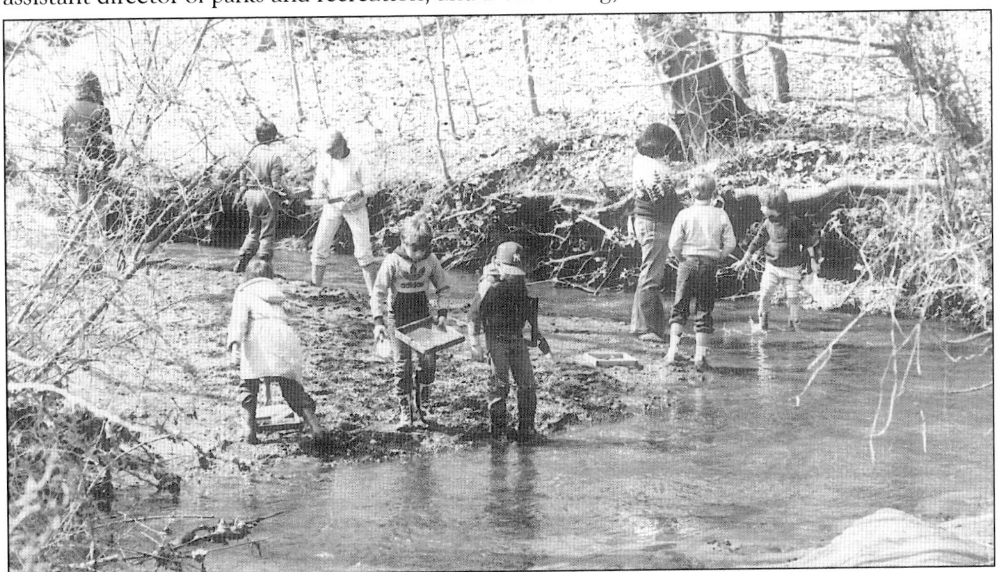

Poricy Park originated from an environmental campaign to reroute a sewer trunk line away from the Poricy Brook stream bank, an effort that resulted in the preservation of 250 acres of open space. The brook, which became a very popular educational-recreational site, was discovered to have fossil beds, containing shells, shark teeth, and other fossils 100 million years old. Seen in a 1983 photograph, the fossil beds can be accessed from a parking lot on Middletown-Lincroft Road, opposite Crawford Road.

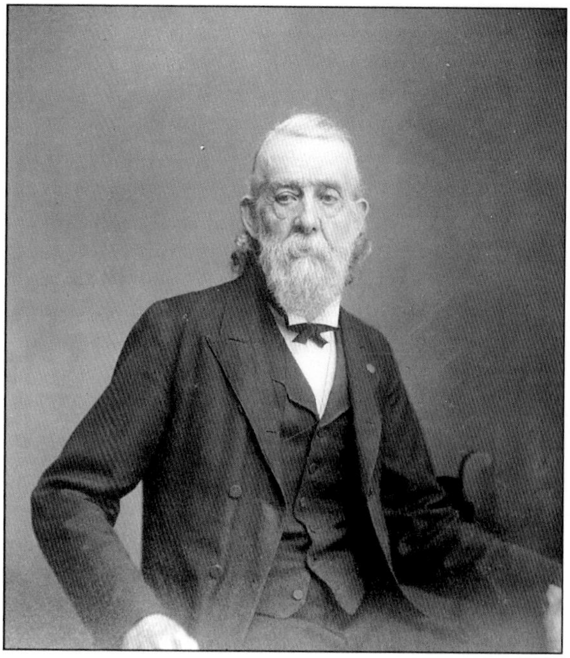

Harvey Jenkins, a New Jersey native who lived most of his life in New Monmouth, labored for years in poverty as a portrait painter and music teacher, prior to dying there in 1908. The Civil War veteran was a member of the Red Bank Arrowsmith Post Number 64 of the Grand Army of the Republic, and painted at least one picture for them. Jenkins was "discovered" nearly three quarters of a century after his death, largely through a compilation of his oeuvre, made through holdings of descendants of his subjects. Jenkins never married, was a member of the New Monmouth Baptist Church, and a longtime superintendent of its Sunday school; he is buried in Fair View Cemetery. (Collection of the Monmouth County Historical Association.)

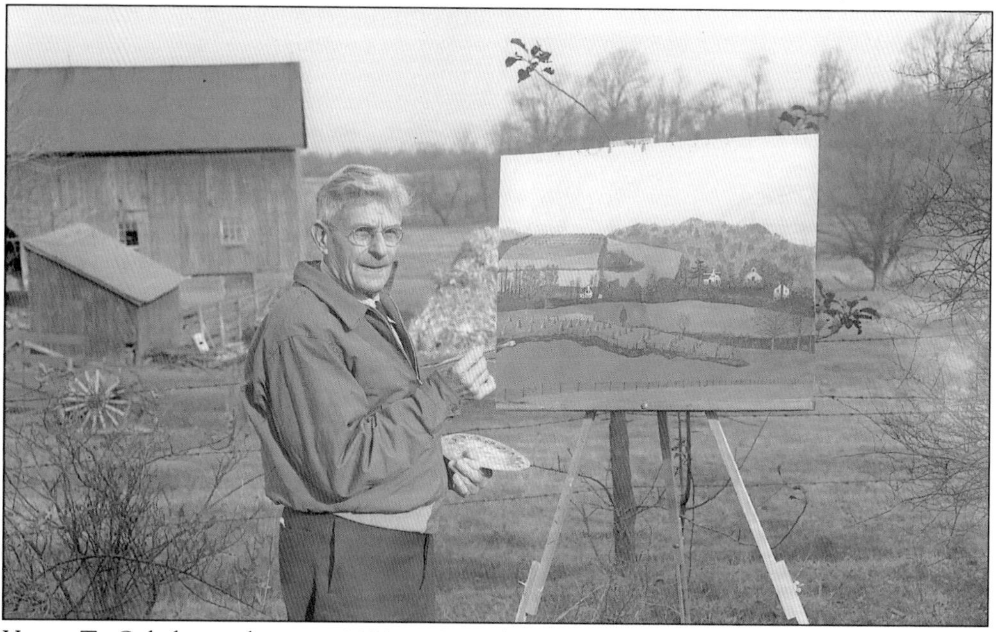

Henry T. Gulick was born in 1872 in Manalapan, graduated from Chattle High School, Long Branch, in 1891, and moved with his family to a Holland Road farm in the 1920s. He began painting in 1946, in part to ward off the effects of arthritis, soon achieving success and recognition through a self-taught style embracing a simple, realistic vision that captured the public's imagination. He is seen in 1948, when several paintings were exhibited at the Newark Museum. His subjects were typically rural, and often farm scenes near his Middletown home. Gulick had a one-man exhibition at the art gallery at Seton Hall in 1964, shortly before his death, and a major retrospective at the Montclair Art Museum in 1974. (The Dorn's Collection)

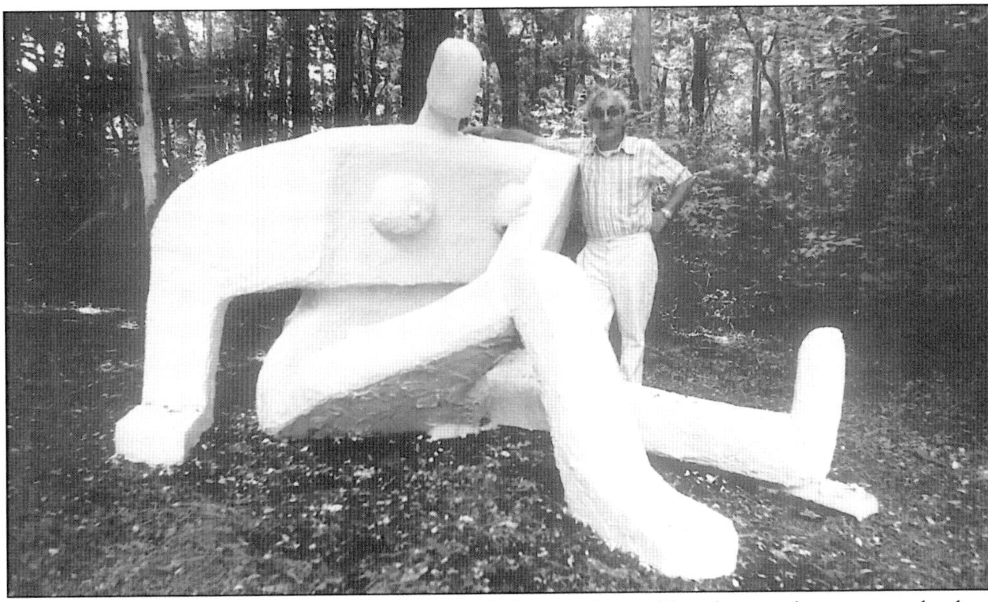

The proportions of Sid Martin's (1920–1996) large, blown fiberglass sculptures can be best appreciated compared with objects of recognizable size—in this 1979 photograph, the artist himself. He was often inspired by subjects in action, or contemplative poses, and made a maquette in clay, which was later fabricated to his specifications by a foundry. The early work of this style was concrete on a wire armature, but he eventually used blown fiberglass. A businessman by day and an artist in his leisure hours, Sid had a long and varied output in a number of styles and media.

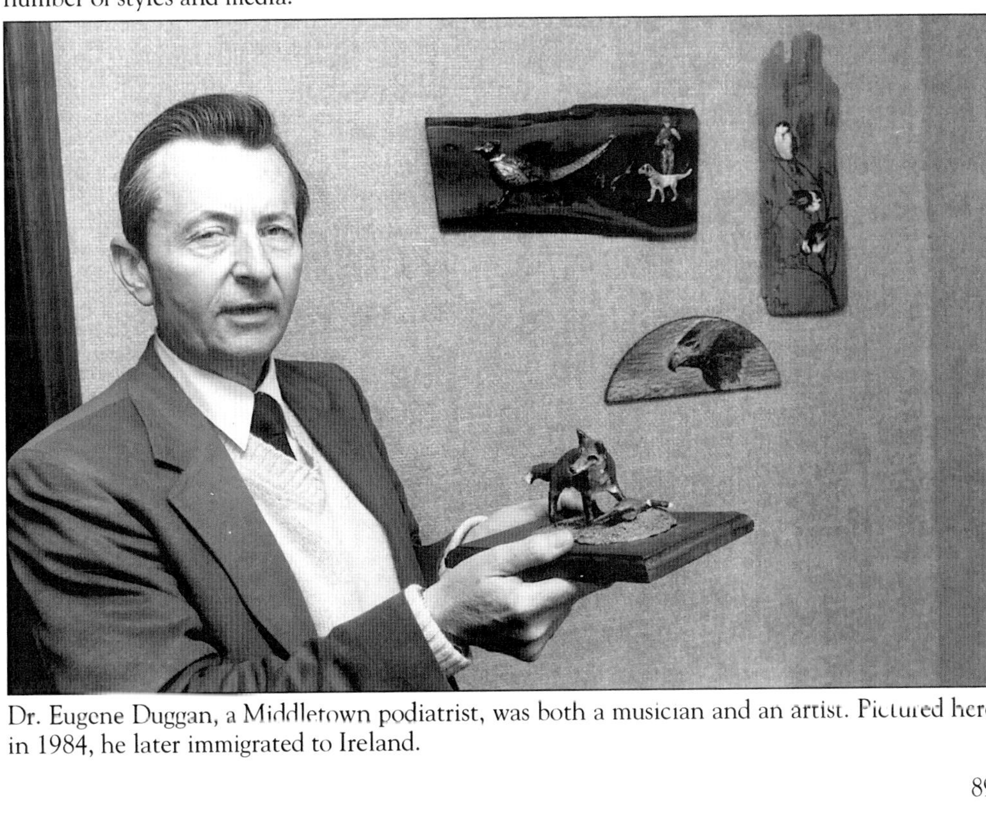

Dr. Eugene Duggan, a Middletown podiatrist, was both a musician and an artist. Pictured here in 1984, he later immigrated to Ireland.

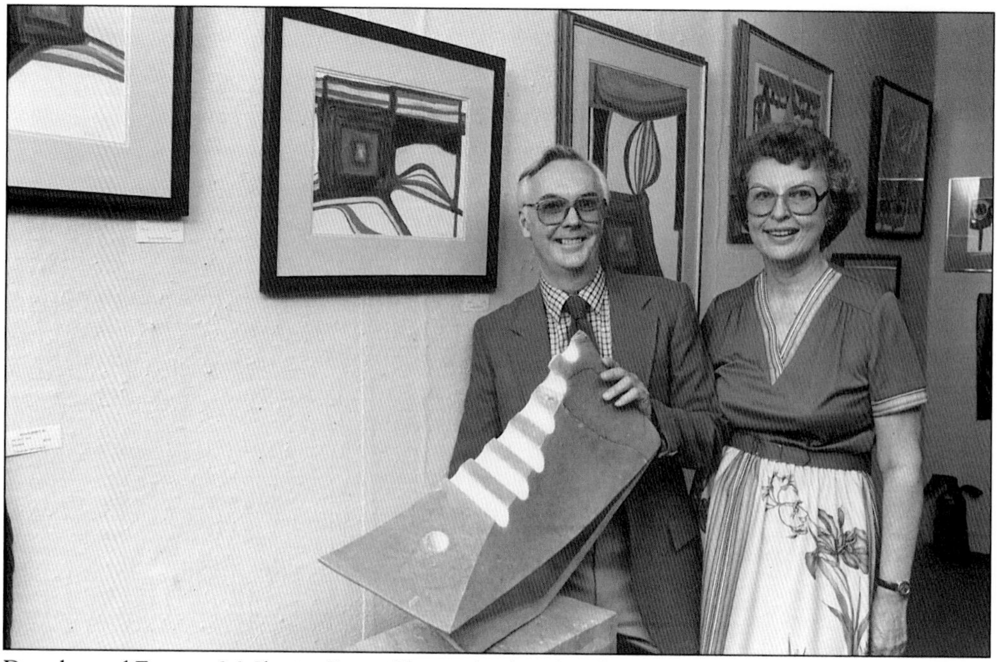

Douglas and Frances McIlvain, River Plaza, a husband-wife artist pair, are both retired teachers, he from Red Bank and she from Tinton Falls. Doug sculpts and Fran is a watercolorist. Although some of his most notable work is semi-abstract subjects in wood, Doug works in a number of media, and his output includes non-representational pieces. Much of Fran's work is landscapes, frequently painted on location, often in bright colors. They are pictured with their art in 1982.

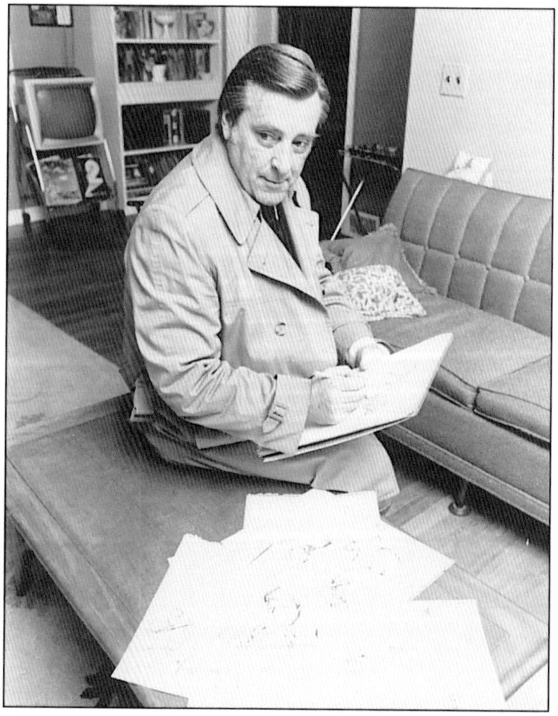

Thomas C. Dunn, who studied at Villanova and the Pratt Institute, enlisted in the Marines in 1942, taking his brush to war as a combat artist. He saw extensive action in the Pacific, including Guadalcanal and Iwo Jima. He was a leading book-cover artist for Doubleday in the 1950s and 1960s. Tom's war-honed ability to capture a subject quickly led to a ten-year career beginning in 1972, the year of this photograph, as a courtroom artist for the ABC television network. He also does portraits, draws the maritime activity near his Belford home, and is pleased about this year's election to *Who's Who in American Art.*

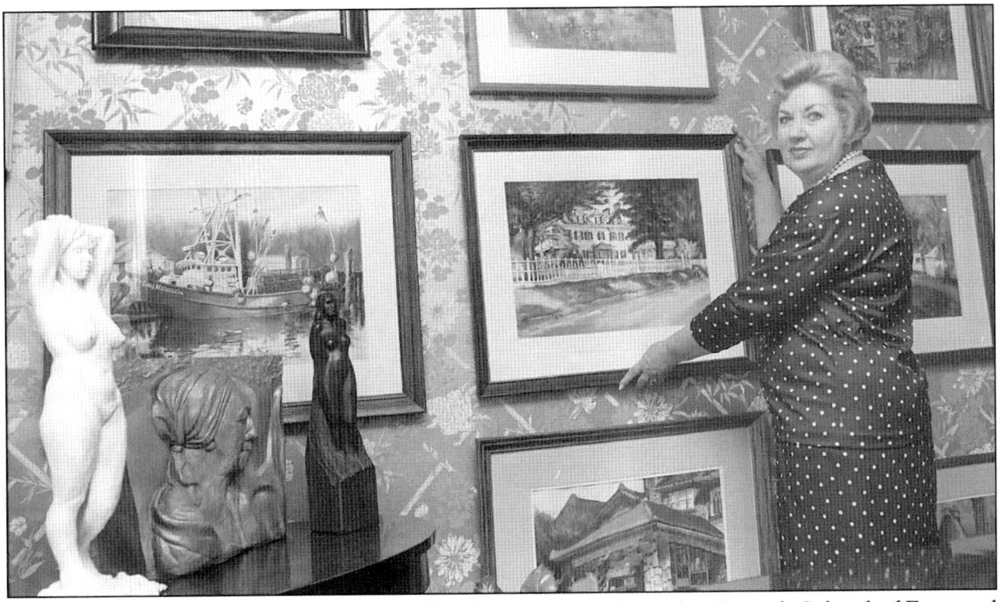

Dorothy McComb Senk, born in Far Hills, NJ, graduated from the Newark School of Fine and Industrial Art in 1942, the year of her first exhibition and commercial work. She has exhibited a variety of media and subjects since, including marine topics, animals, landscapes, and a highly refined specialty, houses in watercolor. Dot, a resident of Lincroft, also sculpts and is a skilled miniaturist. She is pictured in 1984 with her work.

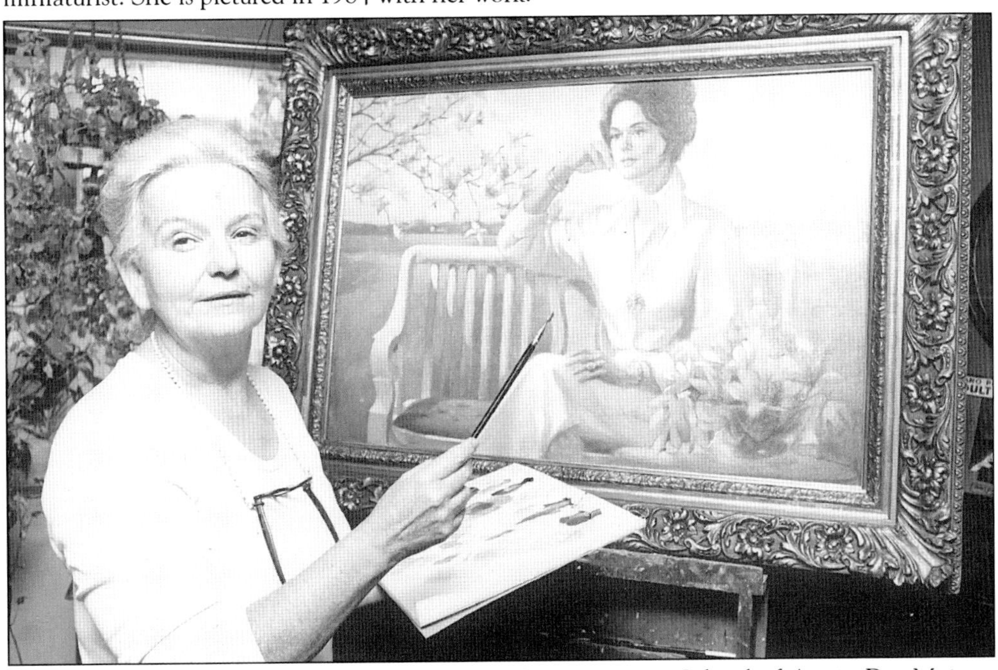

Mary Sheean, born in the Midwest, studied at the Cummings School of Art in Des Moines, IA, and had early commercial art experience in Omaha, NE, prior to working in a New York advertising agency in the mid-1940s. She taught herself portraiture, using a number of media, working from many sittings to capture an insightful image of the subject. Mary is pictured in 1975 working on a portrait of Mary Weir.

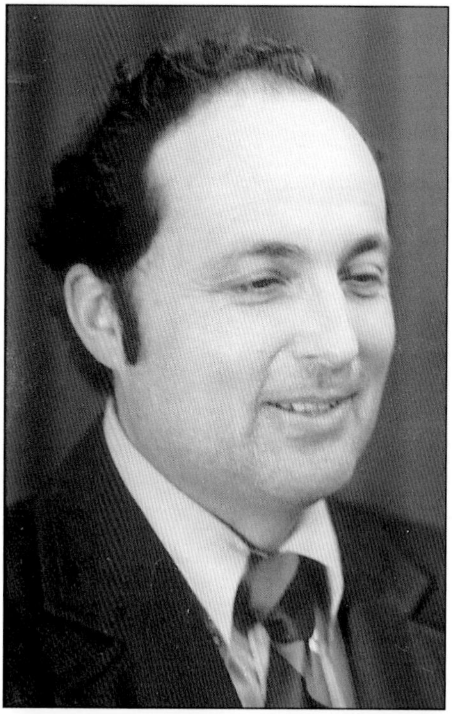

James Truncer was born in 1936 at Parvin State Park (his father, Joseph, was a careerist with the New Jersey system), spending his adolescence in Allentown, where he met his wife, Ramona Rue Truncer, of the early Monmouth family. Jim earned bachelors and masters degrees in resource management at Michigan State University and began his career with a brief stint in the National Park Service. After a position within the state park system, he became the new Monmouth County Park System's first professional employee. Jim and Ramona have two grown children, live in Holmdel, and plan to return to Allentown. He holds memberships in numerous professional and service organizations, having held the presidency of several, and is now the system's secretary-director. He has led the establishment of a nationally recognized park and recreation system headquartered in the former Thompson grounds at Thompson Park, Lindcroft. However, he is quick to share the credit with a supportive public and governing body and the vision of the county's first planning director, Charles Pike.

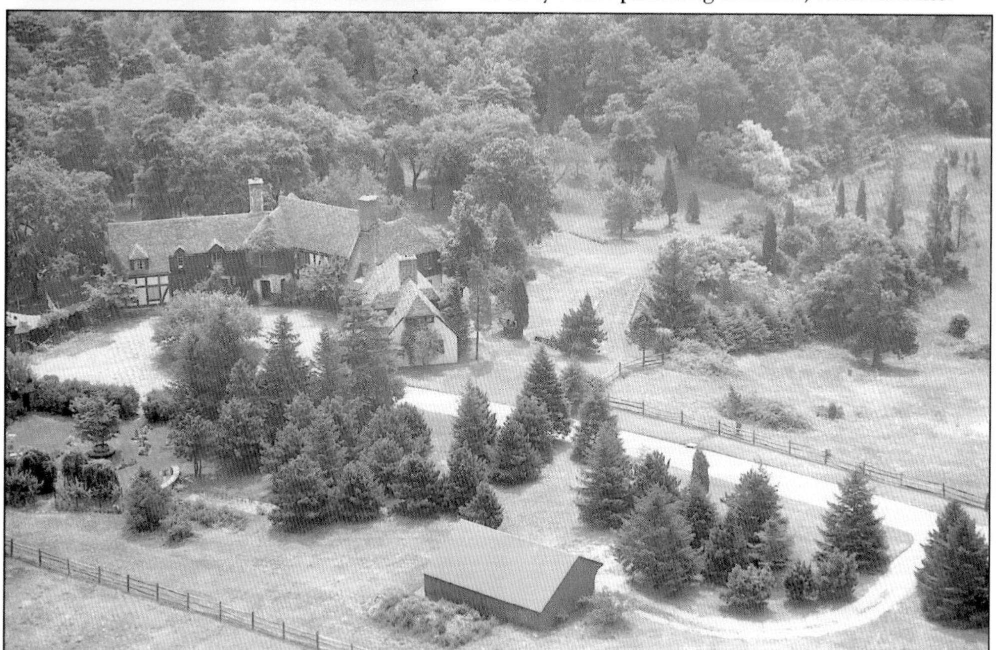

The Hans Huber house, seen from the air in 1963, was designed by Edwin Howard in the style of a German-Swiss manor and built in 1927. It is on an extensive tract along Browns Dock Road, facing Navesink River Road, with much of it now the Huber Woods of the Monmouth County Park System. The house, containing an environmental center and historic displays, is also used for public programs. (The Dorn's Collection)

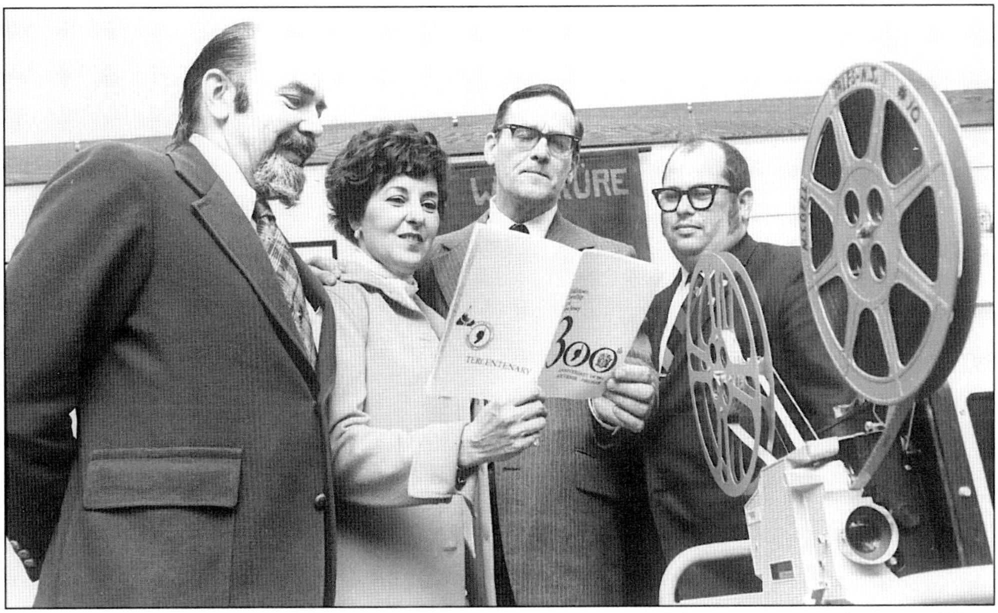

Middletown's Bicentennial Commission met at the township's library on December 8, 1975, to view *Tales of New Jersey*, a historical documentary film made by the New Jersey Bell Telephone Company. Seen here looking at a copy of the 1964 Middletown Tercentenary Souvenir Program are, from left to right, William Le Kernec, director of the Middletown Library, Catherine Lentz and Charles Walker, commission chair and vice chair respectively, and William "Tex" Zober.

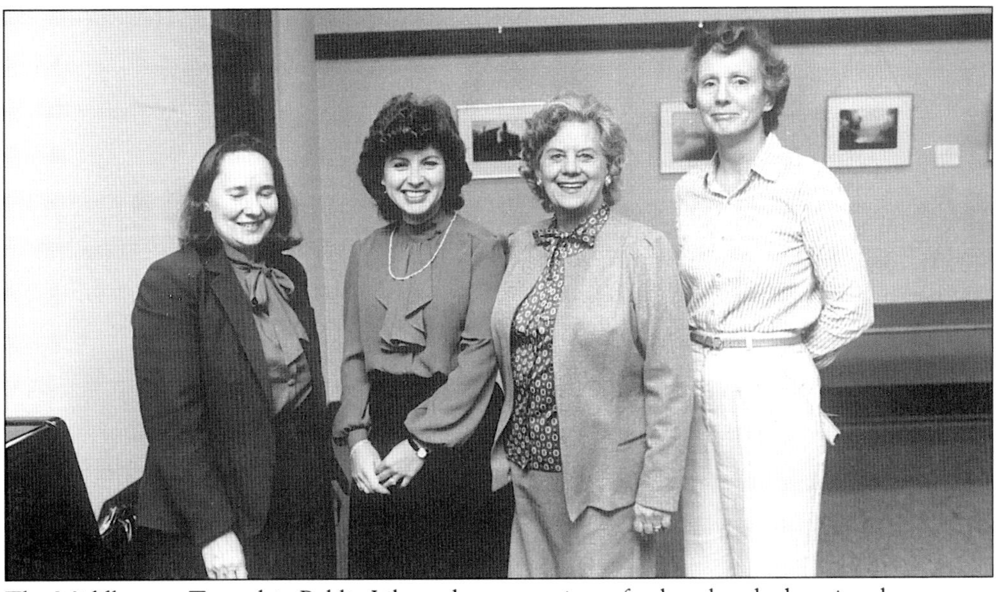

The Middletown Township Public Library hosts a variety of cultural and educational programs, exhibitions, and lectures. Its musical capabilities were enhanced by the donation of a piano by their Friends of the Library organization. Seen at its October 1984 unveiling are, from left to right, Dorothy Rice, Friends president, Joann Strano, a reference librarian whose long-term reference assistance to the author deserves public recognition, Olga Boeckel, library trustee, and Elaine Anderson, Friends secretary-treasurer (probably a lifetime position).

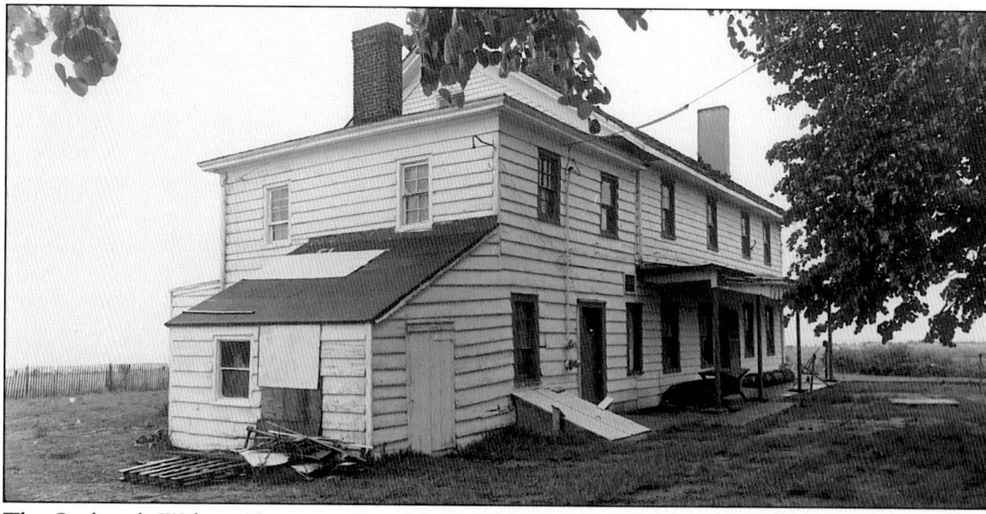

The Seabrook-Wilson House on Port Monmouth Road at the foot of Wilson Avenue is seen in May 1971, as Middletown Township was acquiring the building that would have a long run as the "Spy House." It was a misnamed label for what was interpreted as a "folk museum of the bayshore people." Gertrude Neidlinger, its longtime, dedicated but dictatorial curator, was forced aside in the early 1990s, and died in 1998. Without a viable plan for its future, the township transferred, for a valuable consideration, an emptied building to Monmouth County in 1999. The county, through its park system, is evaluating the site's history and planning a different future usage as this book goes to press in 1999.

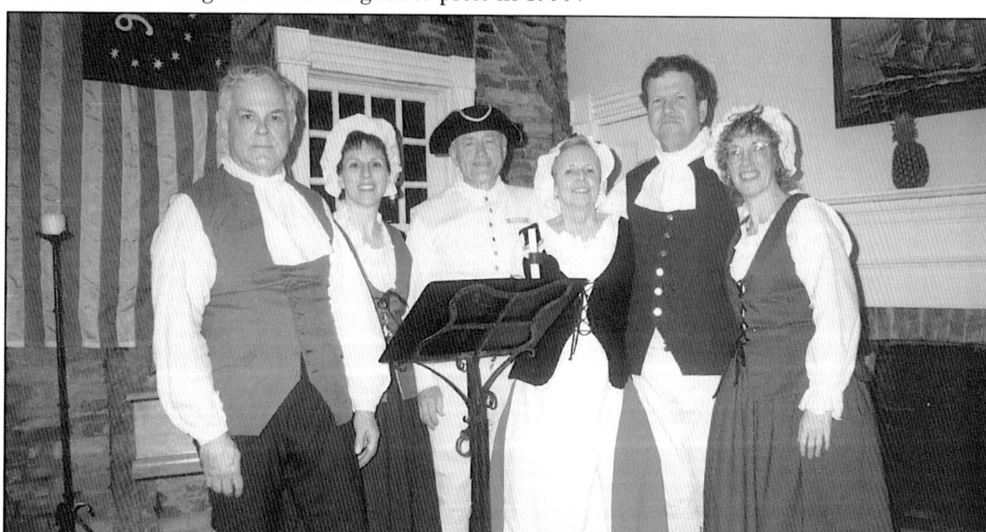

Interests in the past are interpreted in many ways. The D-Major Singers bring to life Colonial-era ballads and "songs of the people," most with themes as popular now as in the 18th century, including drinking, lust, murder, love, humor, and a dated one, farming. The ballads are carefully researched and typically performed in historic properties. From left to right are Paul "Pete" Brady, their founder and international song sleuth, Irene Hauge, two longtime supporters, Louis and Marcia Rissland, and singers Jim Cusick and Lois Lyons. The scene is the newly emptied Seabrook-Wilson House, site of the February 1998 *Ballads on the Bay* presentation, in a property undergoing a new incarnation as part of the Monmouth County Park System's Bayshore Waterfront Park.

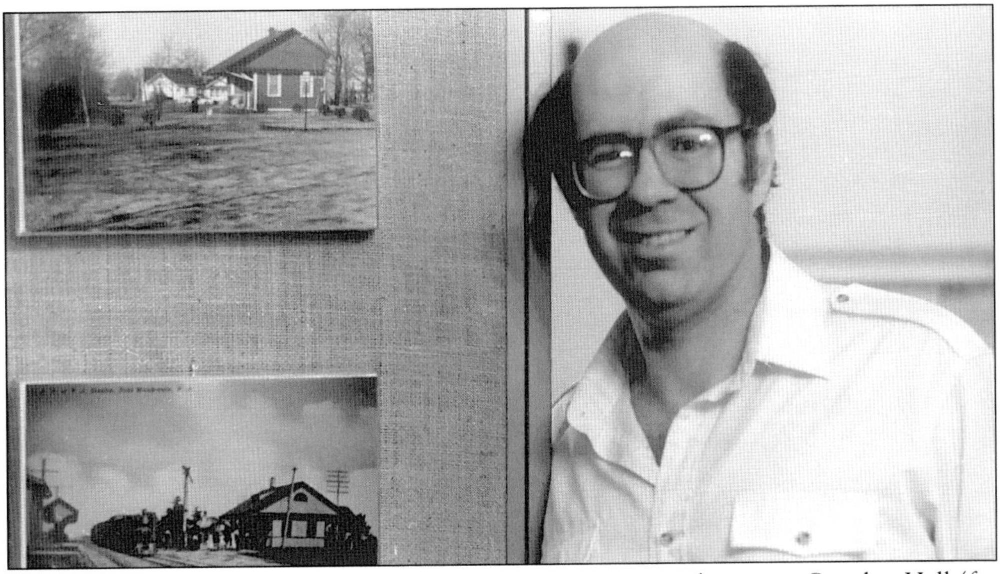

The grade floor of the Donald MacLeod-Melvin A. Rice House, known as Croydon Hall (for the private school that later occupied it), was leased to the Middletown Township Historical Society in 1984. Society President Randall Gabrielan is seen in 1985 at their first exhibition, which he organized, "Middletown: Then and Now." He later observed that many of the "now" scenes were becoming "then" scenes, often sadly, such as this example, the Port Monmouth Railroad Station (Volume I, p. 84). The building, later the home of local charity Middletown Helps Its Own, was destroyed by an incendiary fire in 1997. A replacement is planned.

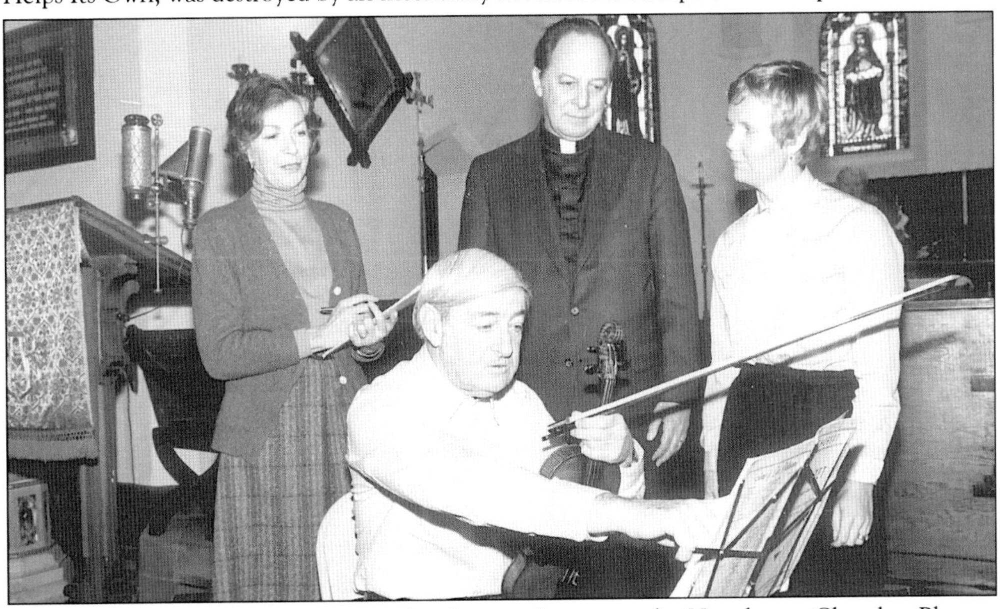

John Karlin founded a string quartet that became known as the Hartshorne Chamber Players. He is seen in January 1985 at the music stand at one of their favorite venues, All Saints Memorial Church. John has retired from playing, but the group holds an annual Candlelight Concert there each October to help raise funds for the National Historic Landmark property. It is a splendid setting for delightful classical music programs, one worthy of readers' support. Their former pastor, the Reverend Harry Sorenson, is behind him.

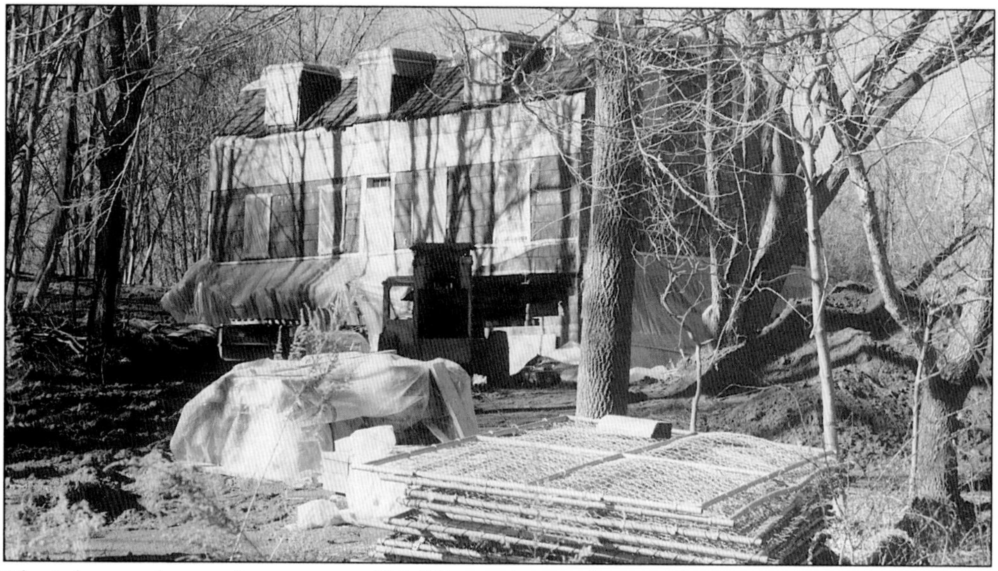

The Johannes Luyster house, one of Middletown's most historic houses, was part of an ancient farm complex at the northeast corner of Holland Road and Laurel Avenue, until it was moved in December 1998 to the west side of Red Hill Road, north of Holland. The original site in the historic Holland neighborhood now appears ripped apart. The conservation of historic properties will be lacking a vital element until builders are compelled to make provision for on-site preservation as part of their development plans, with sound, workable protection for the old property required before approval to build is granted.

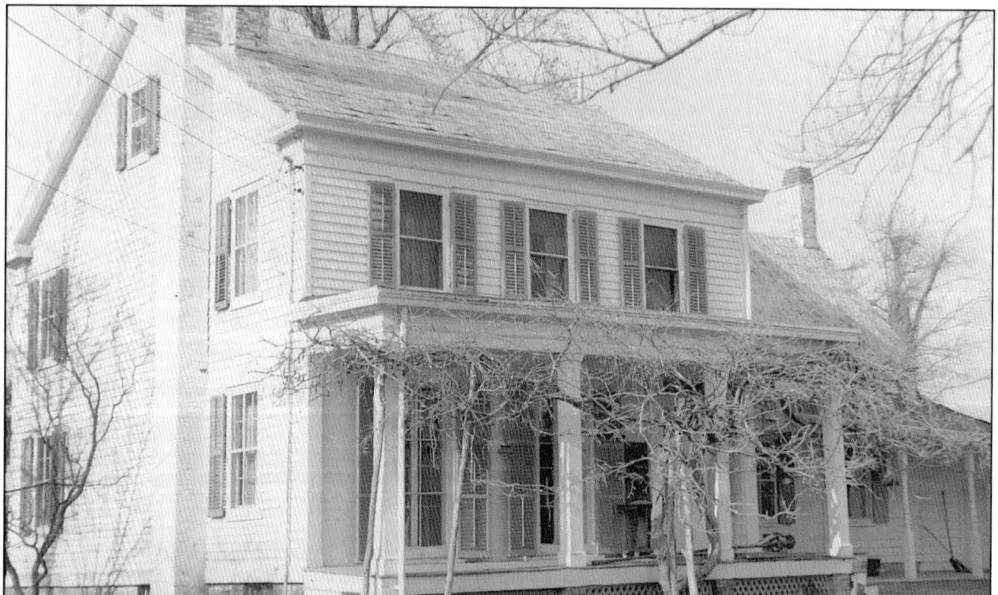

The Thomas Henry Grant house was the seat of a large farm at 940 West Front Street. A 131-acre tract of it was partially sold and partially donated to the township in 1978 by longtime mid-20th-century owner Dr. George S. Stevenson. The house consists of a mid-19th-century main block, seen at left in this 1964 photograph, attached to its 18th-century origins, now the side ell (at right in a partial view). The house is in the midst of the township's Stevenson Park.

Five

THE MILITARY PRESENCE

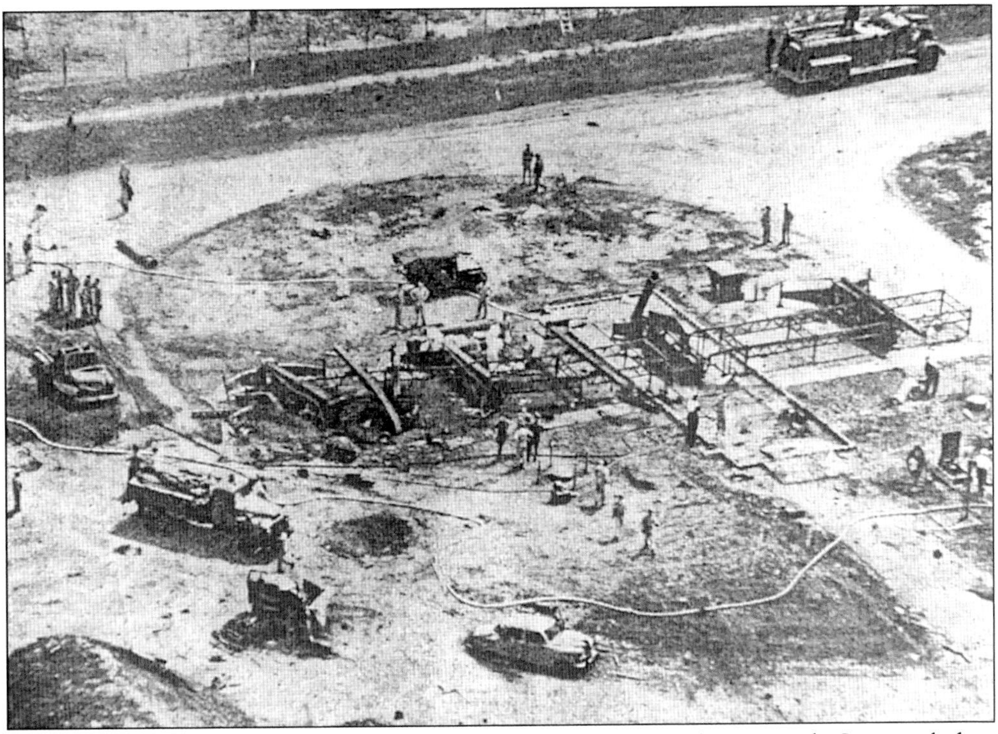

Numerous Nike anti-aircraft missile bases formed a ring around New York City, including batteries at Sandy Hook, Holmdel, and Chapel Hill. Eight missiles exploded at the latter on May 22, 1958, killing six soldiers and four civilian workers. Three others were injured in an accident "that could not happen," which scattered debris around a 3-mile radius. Fire was controlled, as the area became jammed with rescue and other vehicles. Houses were built in the 1980s on the site, a short distance west of the Navy railroad and south of Kings Highway East.

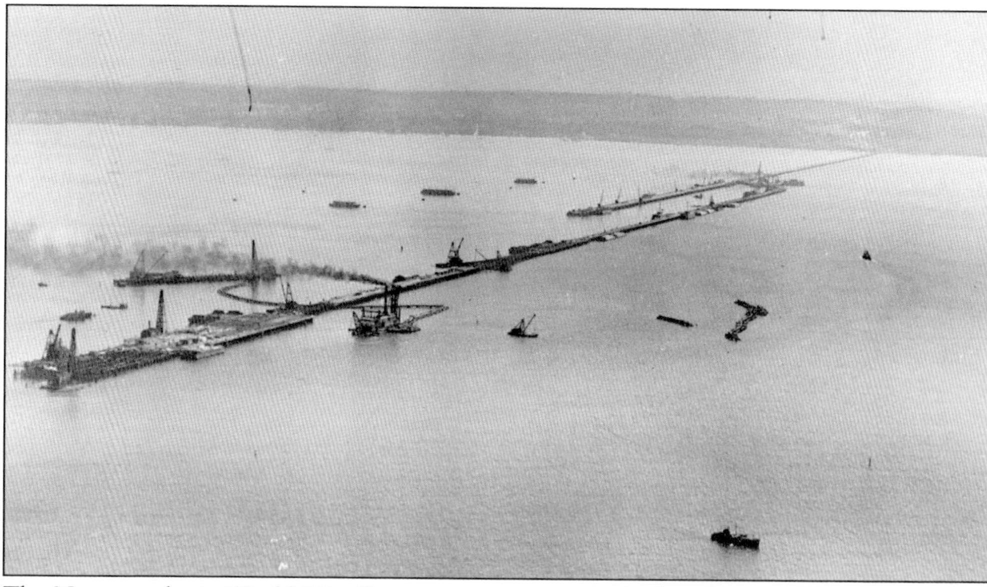

The Navy sought in World War II an eastern munitions facility that would combine inland storage and shore shipping capabilities, located away from a major population center. Central Monmouth County provided a site for the former, a extensive, largely wooded tract in three rural townships, while the latter was located on the Leonardo bayshore. A major land acquisition was begun in 1943 and the base was completed in 1944. This May 3, 1944 aerial photograph shows Piers One and Three, along with the beginnings of Pier Two. (Official United States Navy photograph.)

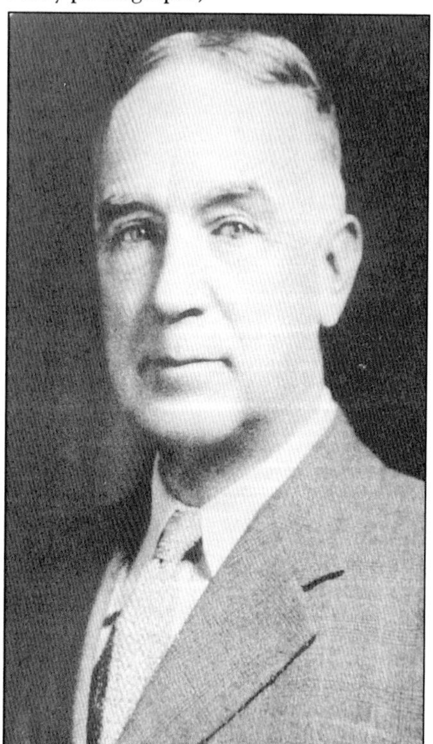

The first commanding officer of this base, Captain Burton H. Green, placed his personal imprint on the facility, guiding work with his motto, "Our primary purpose is to furnish ammunition to the fleet; all else is secondary." The base, however, was named for Rear Admiral Ralph Earle, born 1874 in Worcester, MA. Earle was an 1896 graduate of the U.S. Naval Academy. He was decorated for valor in the Spanish-American War, specialized in ordnance and rose to be chief of the Bureau of Ordnance of the Navy and commander of the Naval Proving Ground at Indianhead. Earle went to sea after World War I, commanded the battleship *Connecticut*, and resigned in 1925 to become president of Worcester Polytechnic Institute, a position he held at his death in 1939.

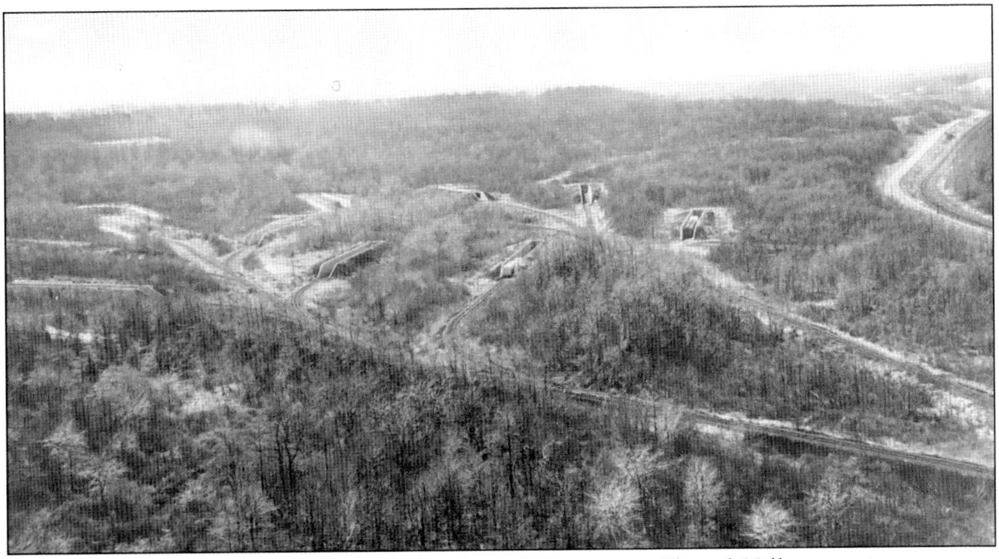

The Middletown Earle unit also includes about 720 acres in Chapel Hill, appearing on maps as a roughly octagonal-shaped break in the street plan south of Leonardville Road and north of Kings Highway East. The area, which once contained a number of summerhouses, had been bisected by Chapel Hill Road, formerly a through street. Numerous sidetracks, their ends surrounded by concrete barricades, were once used for overnight storage of munitions-laden railroad cars. However, current practice is to unload ordnance the day it is delivered to the pier area. Normandy Road is visible at right in this 1968 aerial photograph. (Official United States Navy photograph.)

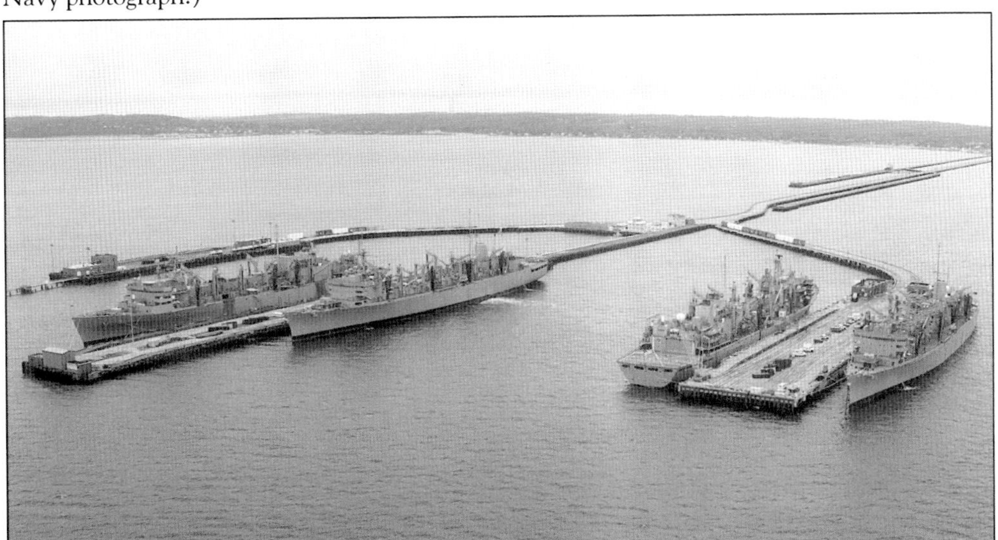

The Leonardo pier complex, one of the longest "finger piers" in the world, consists of Piers Two, Three, and Four, connected to land by a 2-mile trestle. The latter, at right, was completed in 1990. Pier One branches off one mile from shore. Earle is home port to four supply ships—floating warehouses for the remainder of the fleet. This May 1998 aerial records the first (and unlikely) occasion that the four ships were in port together. They are, from left, the USS *Arctic*, USS *Seattle*, the appropriately named USS *Supply*, and the USS *Detroit*. (Official United States Navy photograph.)

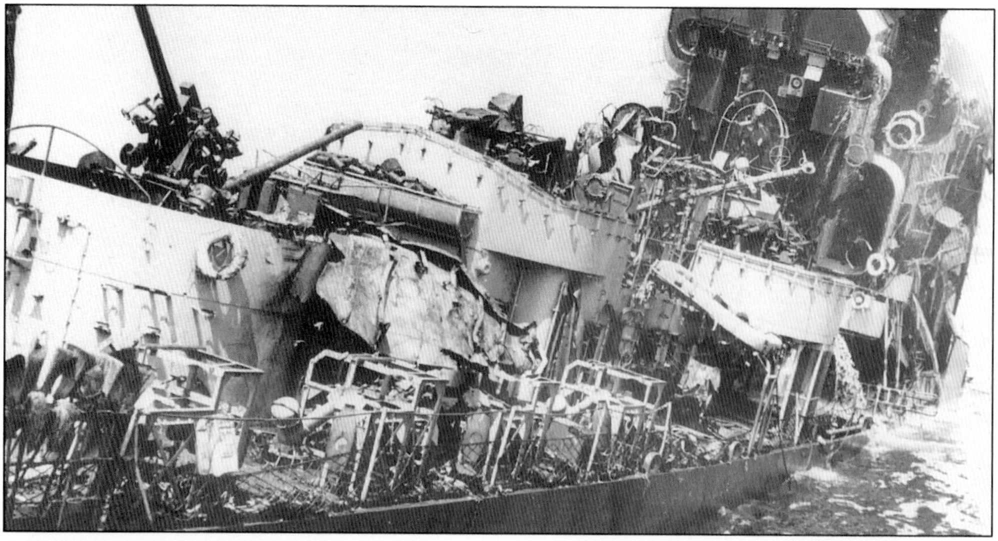

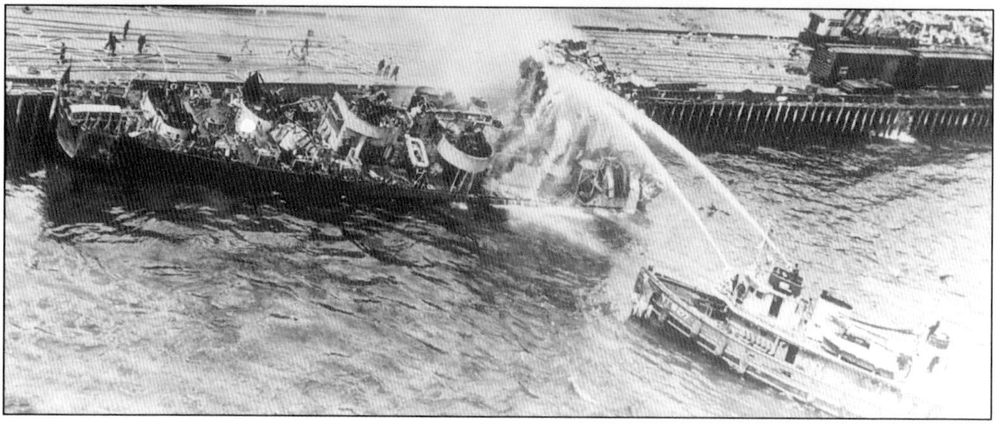

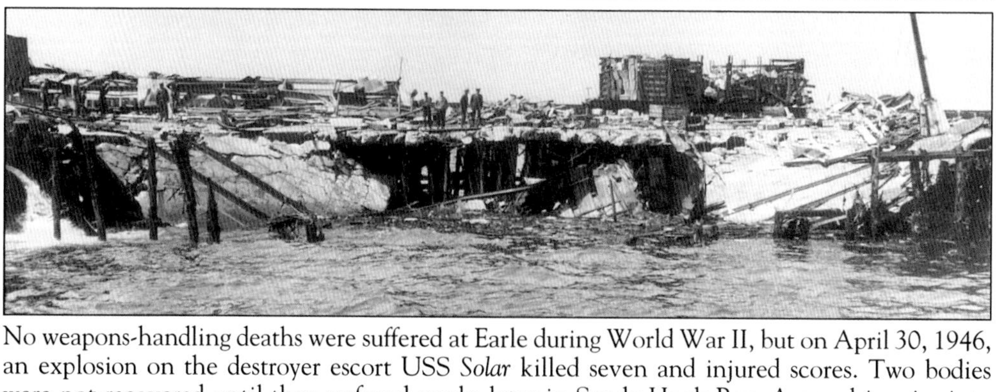

No weapons-handling deaths were suffered at Earle during World War II, but on April 30, 1946, an explosion on the destroyer escort USS *Solar* killed seven and injured scores. Two bodies were not recovered until they surfaced weeks later in Sandy Hook Bay. A naval inquiry into the origin was not positively conclusive, but it appears the cause was the dropping on board of a "hedgehog," a small anti-submarine weapon that contained 35 pounds of torpex, a volatile explosive. The death toll would have been higher if it were not for a command to abandon the ship, made soon after the initial explosion. The loudness of the explosion caused some residents to believe it was much closer to them, even to those located miles away. (Official United States Navy photographs.)

This memorial is inside the Leonardo gate on Highway 36: "DEDICATED TO OUR UNITED STATES NAVY AND COAST GUARD SHIPMATES WHO WERE LOST WHILE SERVING ABOARD DESTROYER ESCORTS IN PEACE AND WAR." It was erected by the Garden State Chapter of the Destroyer Escort Sailors Association on June 11, 1994. It lists 15 casualties, beginning with the USS *Leopold* on March 9, 1944, and ending with the *Solar*. The jagged piece of metal is debris from the *Solar* explosion.

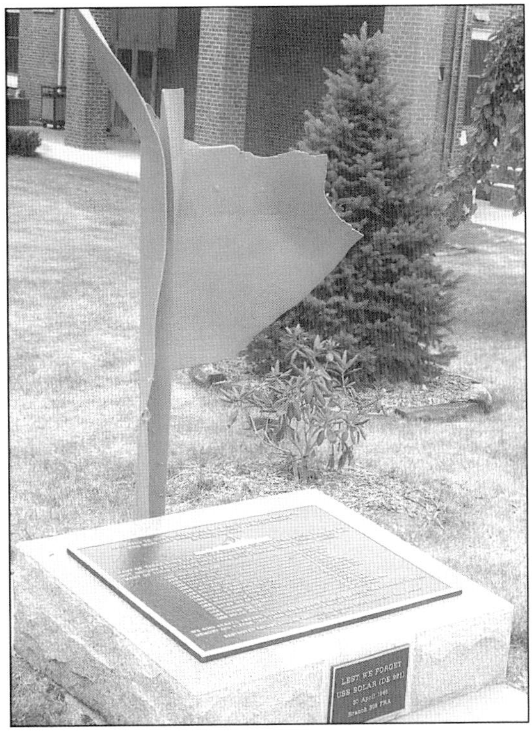

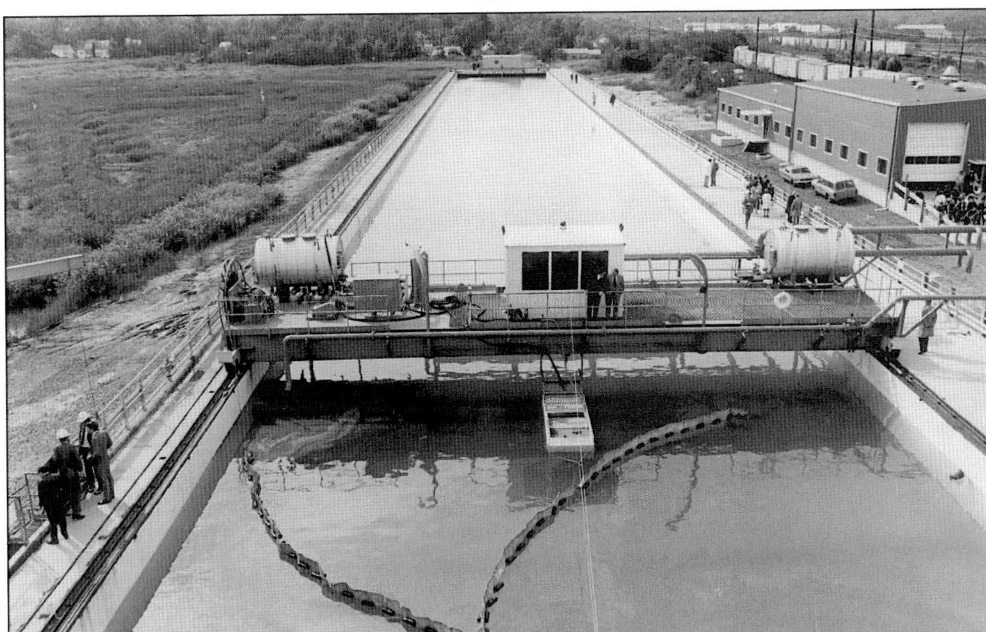

An Environmental Protection Agency Oil and Hazardous Material Simulated Test Tank, known by an inevitable governmental acronym, OHMSETT, is located at Earle. The concrete tank, seen here when new in 1974, has water surfaces of 667 feet by 65 feet, with an 8-foot depth. It provides a safe place for the testing and development of devices and techniques for the control and clean-up of oil and hazardous material spills. A generating device can make waves to simulate varied water conditions.

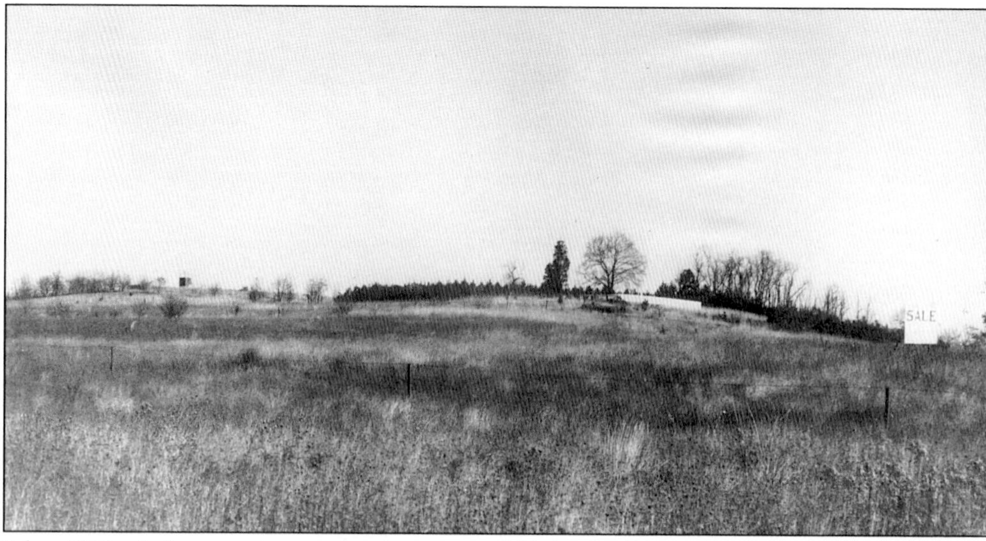

John Giblon's farm at the northeast corner of Newman Springs and Half Mile Roads was surveyed c. 1940, in preparation for the purchase of 46 acres by the federal government for Fort Monmouth's Field Laboratory Number One. It was dedicated October 1, 1942, as Camp Coles. (Historian, Fort Monmouth.)

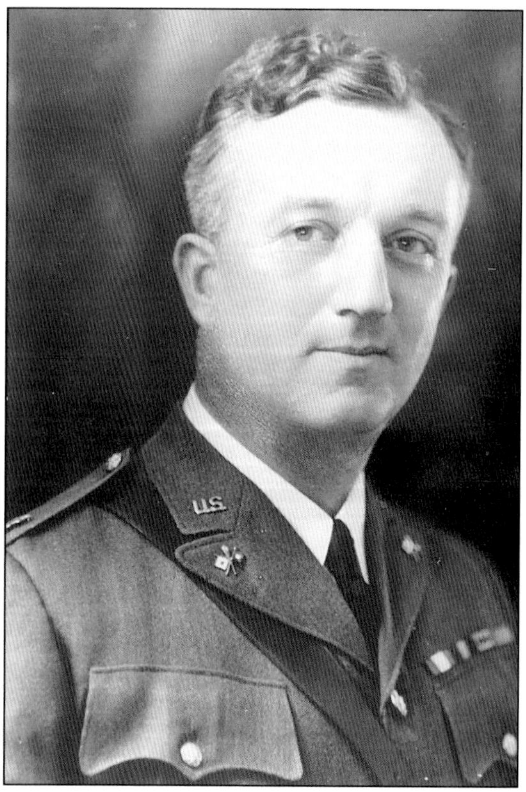

Roy H. Coles, born 1887 at Warren, IN, was commissioned an infantry second lieutenant after his 1909 graduation from the United States Military Academy. He studied at the Signal School, Fort Leavenworth, in 1916, and held a number of positions in the office of the chief signal officer in the World War I era, including a period as chief in Europe, attaining the temporary rank of colonel. Coles was executive officer at Fort Monmouth in 1936–37, transferring in 1937 to the General Staff in Washington. He died there in January 1938, had his rank of colonel posthumously restored, and is buried in Arlington National Cemetery. (U.S. Army Electronics and Communications Museum, Fort Monmouth.)

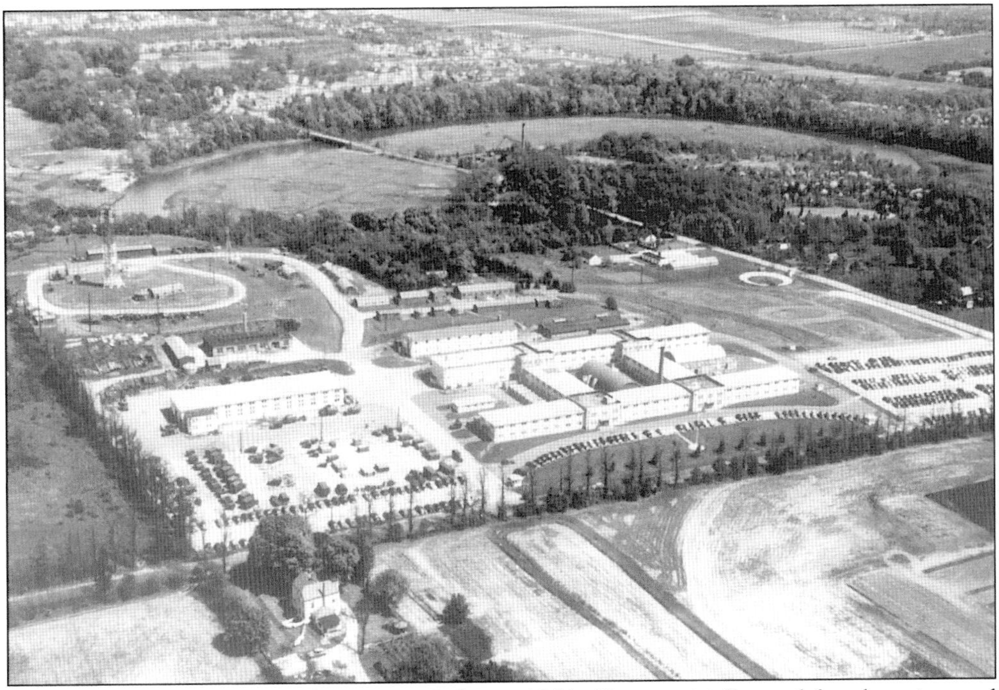

The costly laboratory erected at Camp Coles in 1941–42 was initially used for observing and measuring pilot balloon ascensions. This c. 1965 aerial shows Half Mile Road at bottom, forming a "V" with Newman Springs Road (at right). Visible on the latter street adjacent to Coles is the series of greenhouses built for the raising of orchids by George J. Ciejka, formerly of Hubert K. Dalton's Rumson Willowbrook estate. (Historian, Fort Monmouth.)

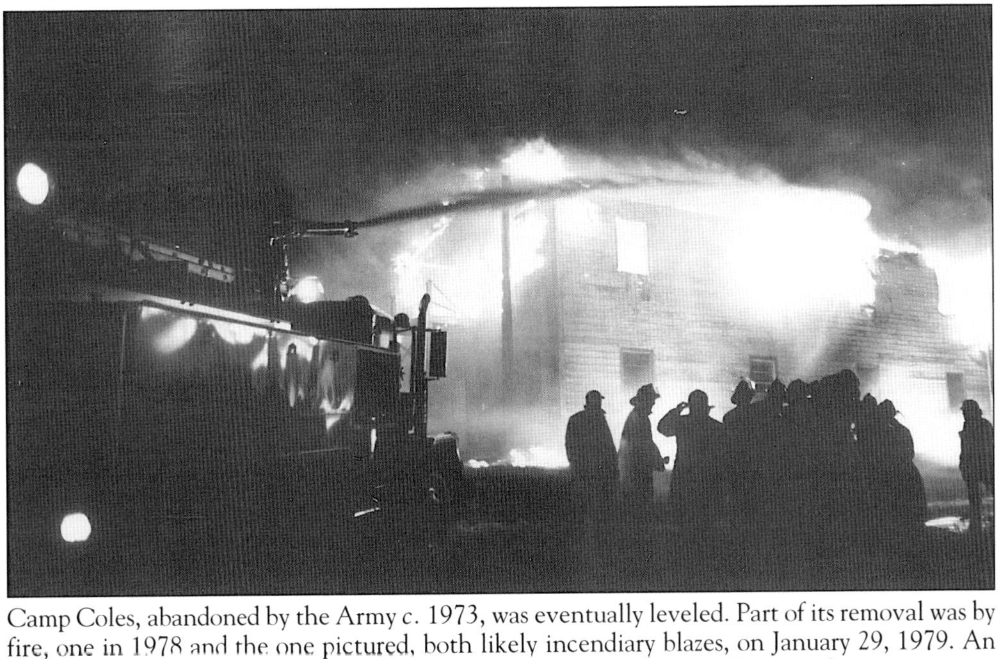

Camp Coles, abandoned by the Army c. 1973, was eventually leveled. Part of its removal was by fire, one in 1978 and the one pictured, both likely incendiary blazes, on January 29, 1979. An office-type building, completed c. 1983, housing the Armed Forces Reserve Center, occupies the site now.

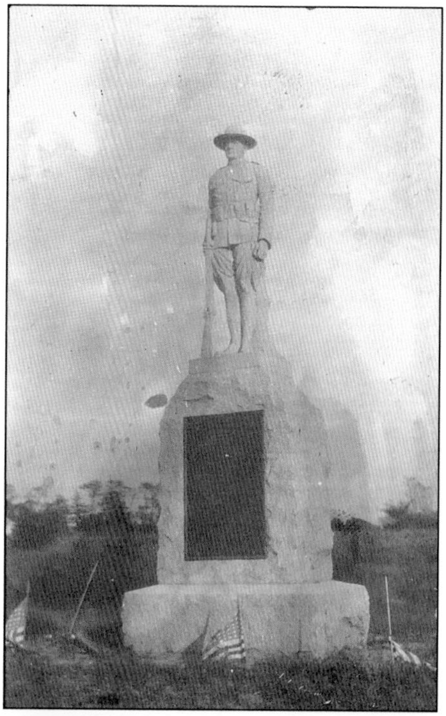

The memorial park on Church Street, Belford, was laid out in 1919 on a 100-by-150-foot lot donated by Elmer Compton, brother of Harold, one of three Belford men killed in World War I. The others were Clarence Walling and Fred Crane. Work was begun in early May, while exercises at the park were held that Memorial Day when funds were raised for the doughboy monument, seen in a c. 1920s photograph. It is presumed its dedication was conducted as announced for New Years 1920, as no post-event account was found. Shrubs are now close to the statue, while a field artillery piece was placed in front of it.

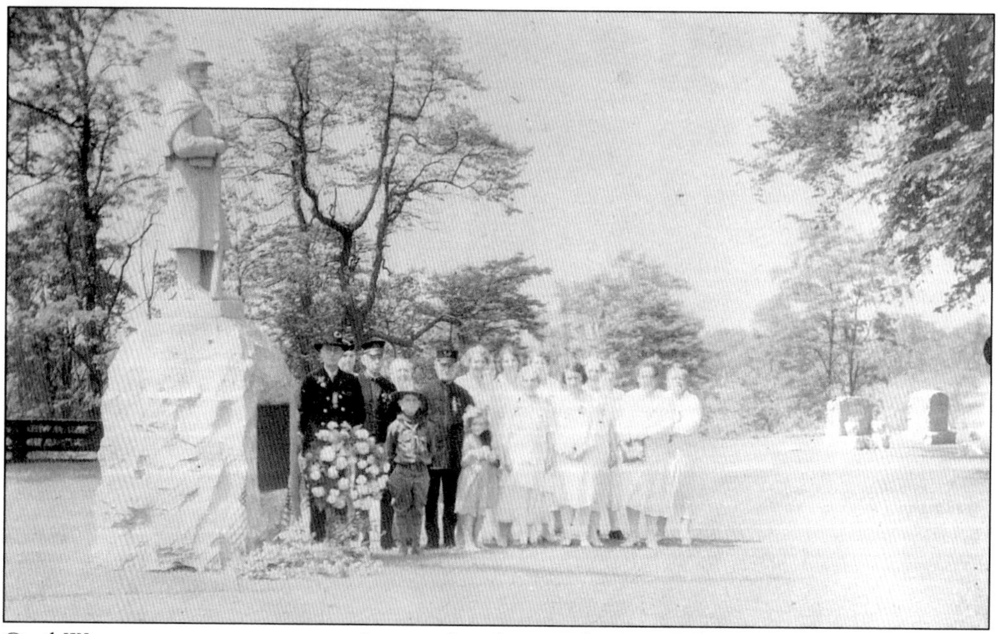

Civil War veterans were venerated soon after that conflict's end, leading to the remembrance now widely commemorated as Decoration, or Memorial, Day, on the last Monday in May. This monument was unveiled in 1925 on May 30, the former fixed date of the holiday, in honor of the 29th Regiment of the New Jersey Volunteer Infantry, a group organized at Camp Vredenburgh, near Freehold. Civil War veterans were a fixture at annual ceremonies. The small girl who attended this one in the early 1930s, Elizabeth "Betsy" Hall Albert, also preserved the picture.

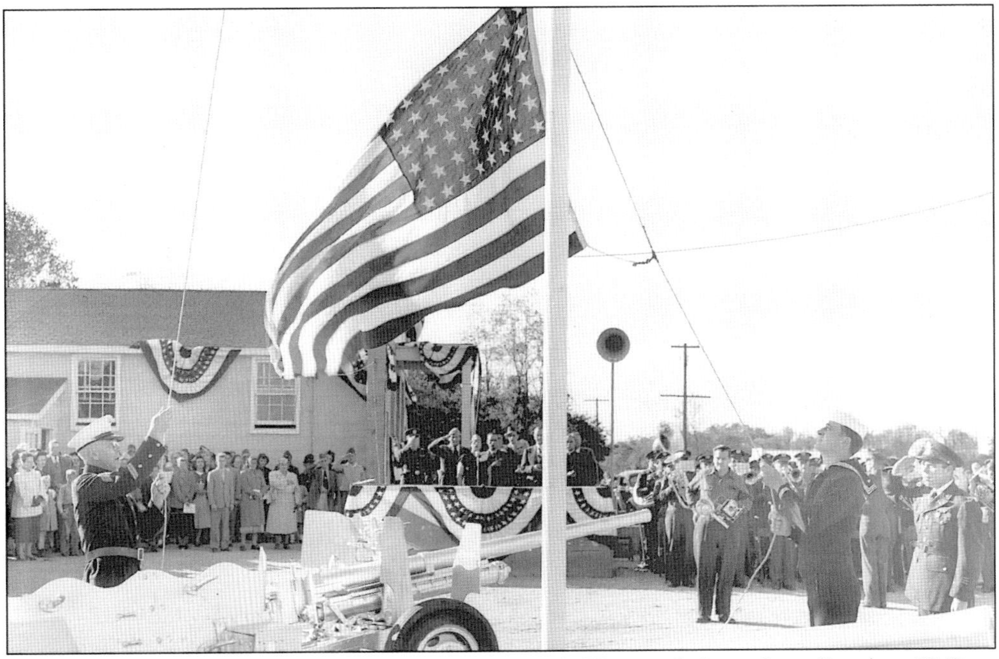

A new house for Veterans of Foreign Wars Post 2179 was dedicated in October 1949 at 1000 Highway 35, just west of the Middletown Township Hall. The principal speaker was General George L. Van Deusen, retired commander of Fort Monmouth. The post's present house is on Highway 36, Port Monmouth; this building presently serves as a real estate office. (The Dorn's Collection.)

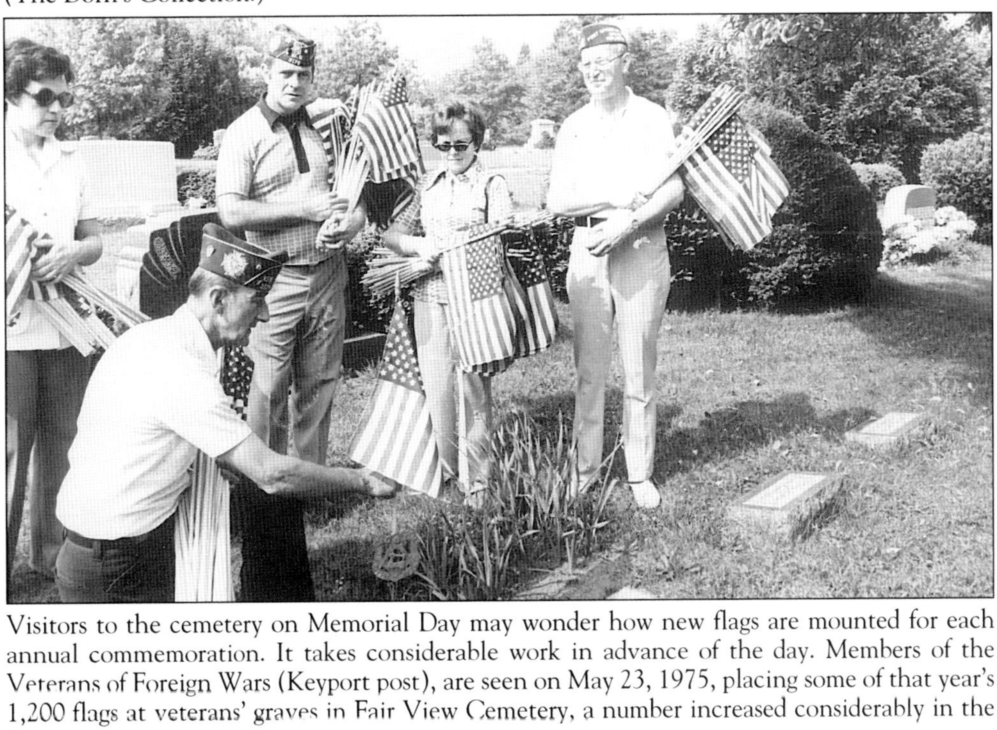

Visitors to the cemetery on Memorial Day may wonder how new flags are mounted for each annual commemoration. It takes considerable work in advance of the day. Members of the Veterans of Foreign Wars (Keyport post), are seen on May 23, 1975, placing some of that year's 1,200 flags at veterans' graves in Fair View Cemetery, a number increased considerably in the intervening years.

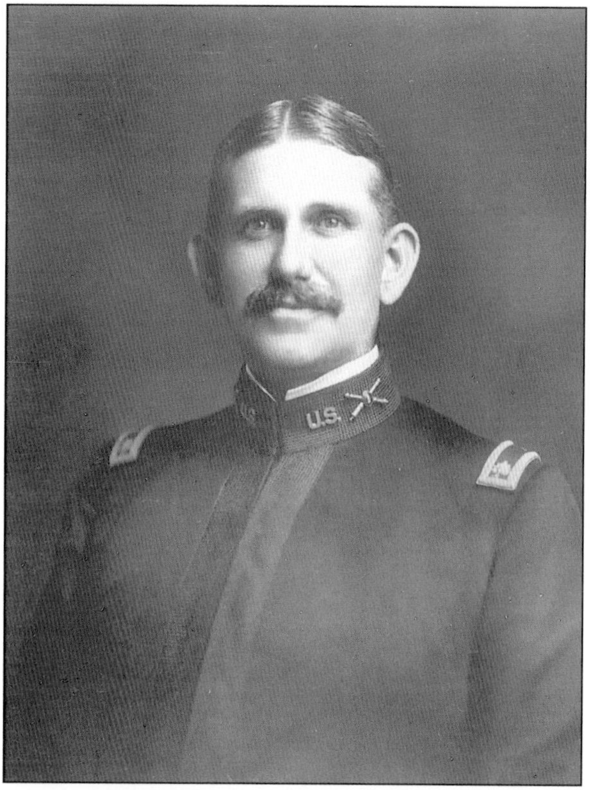

Isaac Newton Lewis (1858–1931), was commissioned second lieutenant in the 2nd Artillery upon his 1884 graduation from the United States Military Academy. He was technically skilled and invented, or perfected, a number of devices. Lewis's work also embraced coastal defense and he began the modern corps organization of artillery. His most famous invention, the Lewis machine gun, was initially rejected by the American government, but was later accepted, with over 100,000 supplied to the Allied forces during World War I. The 16-inch gun battery at the new Highlands Army Defense Base in the Middletown hills was named for him in 1942. The base is now part of Hartshorne Woods Park. (United States Military Academy Library, Special Collections.)

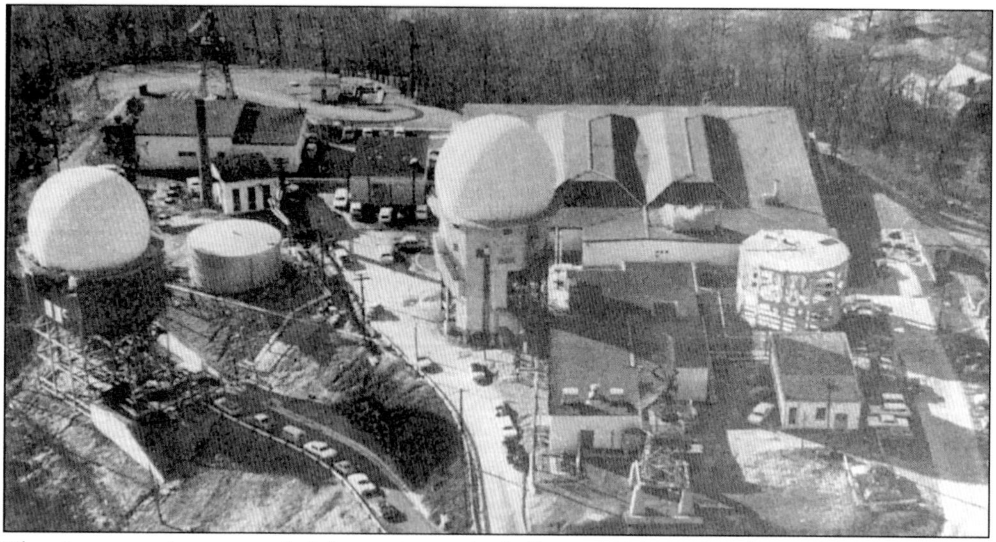

The Army sought a coastal defense site in the hills, c. 1941, as the elevated location would provide better protection against airborne attack, and a longer gun range. Its 16-inch gun, installed in 1943, was obsolete by the end of World War II, and scrapped c. 1949. The base was chosen as the site for the metropolitan New York area Missile Master command, and control center for NIKE anti-aircraft missiles in 1959. It is seen here in a 1960s photograph. The NIKE base was closed in 1974. Although the site was transferred to the Monmouth County Park System c. 1984, the heavy equipment was not dismantled by the Army until c. 1995.

The USS *New Jersey*, the second battleship of the Iowa class, was built in the Philadelphia Naval Shipyard and was commissioned May 23, 1943. Her distinguished career included World War II service as Third Fleet Commander Admiral William "Bull" Halsey's flagship, participation in the Korean and Vietnam wars, and 1980s fire support for Marines in Beirut, Lebanon. Armament includes nine 16-inch guns that fired shells with a 23-mile range. The deactivated ship is sailing from Bremerton, Washington, and is expected to arrive in New Jersey waters in the fall of 1999, for eventual public display. The *New Jersey* is 887 feet long; its beam of 108 feet will make a tight squeeze through the Panama Canal. The foundation that has raised the funds to bring the USS *New Jersey* to our state is headquartered in Middletown. On-going support for the costly project is needed. The Battleship New Jersey Foundation may be reached at One Arin Park Building, 1715 Highway 35, Middletown, New Jersey 07748.

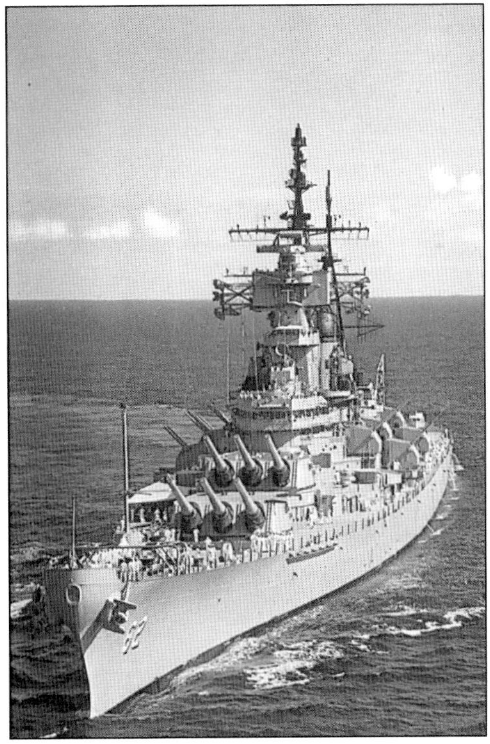

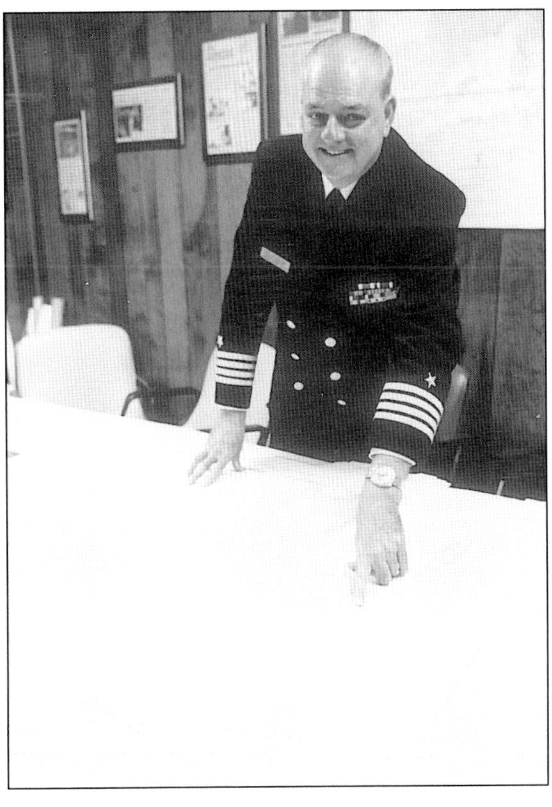

Joseph Azzolina, born in 1926 and raised in Highlands, joined the Navy in 1944, beginning an active and reserve career of 42 years. He graduated from Holy Cross College, joined his father in the grocery business, and built the Food Circus chain of supermarkets into one of the region's major food retailers. Joe has served in the New Jersey State Senate and is now a representative in the Assembly. His honors for public service include a humanitarian award for aid to the Deborah Hospital Foundation, and the Monmouth County Council, Boy Scouts of America, Joshua Huddy Distinguished Citizen Award. He is seen in an October 1983 photograph following three months active service on the battleship USS *New Jersey*, a ship headed for display in New Jersey waters following his leadership of a successful campaign to bring her here.

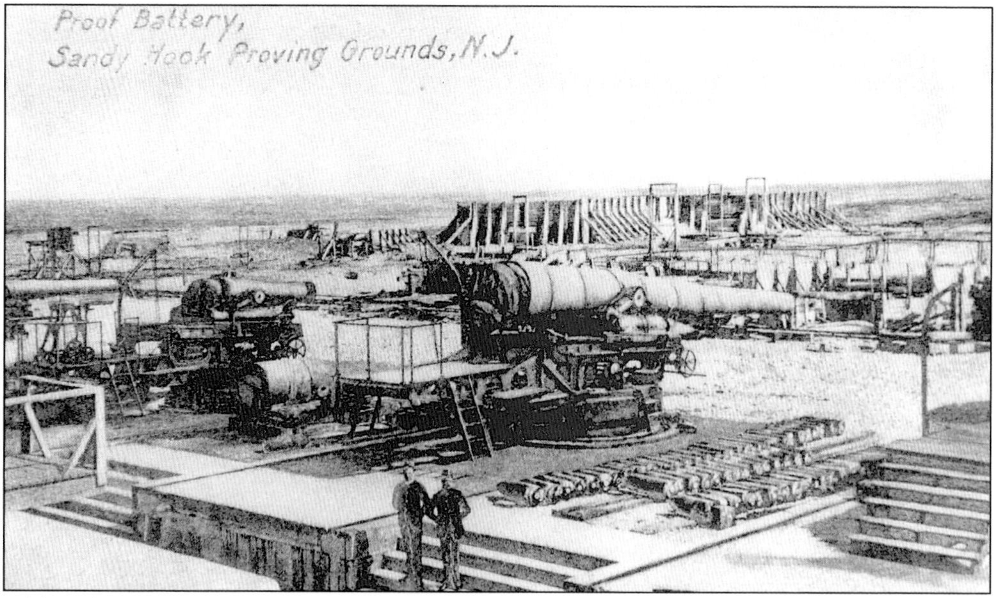

Although it is not widely known, Sandy Hook is part of Middletown Township. The Army built a gun and ordnance proving ground there in 1874 that tested experimental guns and all large guns manufactured for field deployment. A second proof battery, pictured on this c. 1910 postcard, was later built nearby, serving until the proofing operation was moved to Aberdeen, MD, in 1917. The remains of this concrete platform are still present, but all other traces of its military use disappeared long-ago(assuming all ordnance has been removed from under the beach). For a full account, see the author's *Sandy Hook* (Arcadia Publishers, 1999). (Collection of John Rhody.)

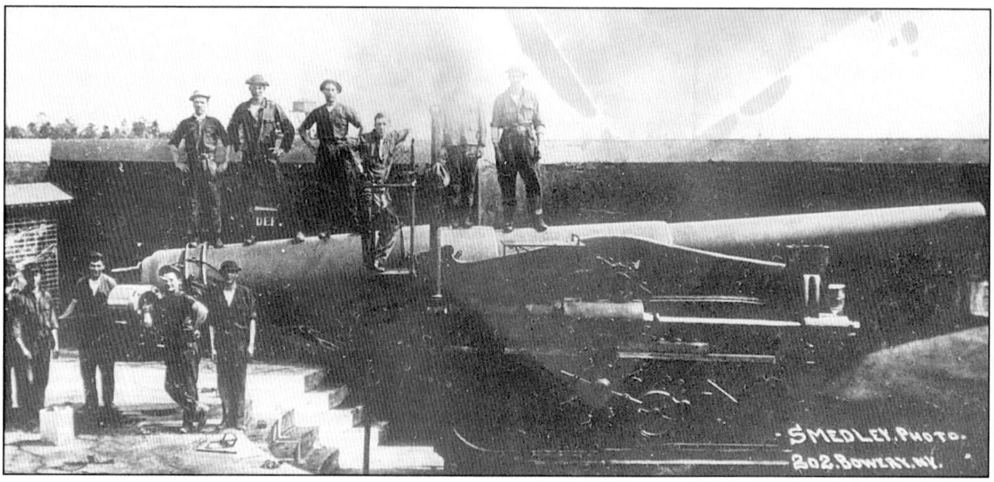

A coastal defense fort, begun at Sandy Hook before the Civil War but obsolete before the war's end, was left unfinished. A new fort was begun in 1891, was named Fort Hancock in 1895, and became operational in 1897. The facility was one of the most heavily armed fortifications in America for nearly half a century. Its weaponry and their deployment were adjusted regularly to combat evolving offensive weapons, but the fort was made obsolete by aerial bombardment tactics developed by the end of World War II. This 10-inch gun, believed to be located at Battery Granger, is seen c. 1915, probably during target practice. (Collection of Harold Solomon.)

Six

THOSE WHO SERVE

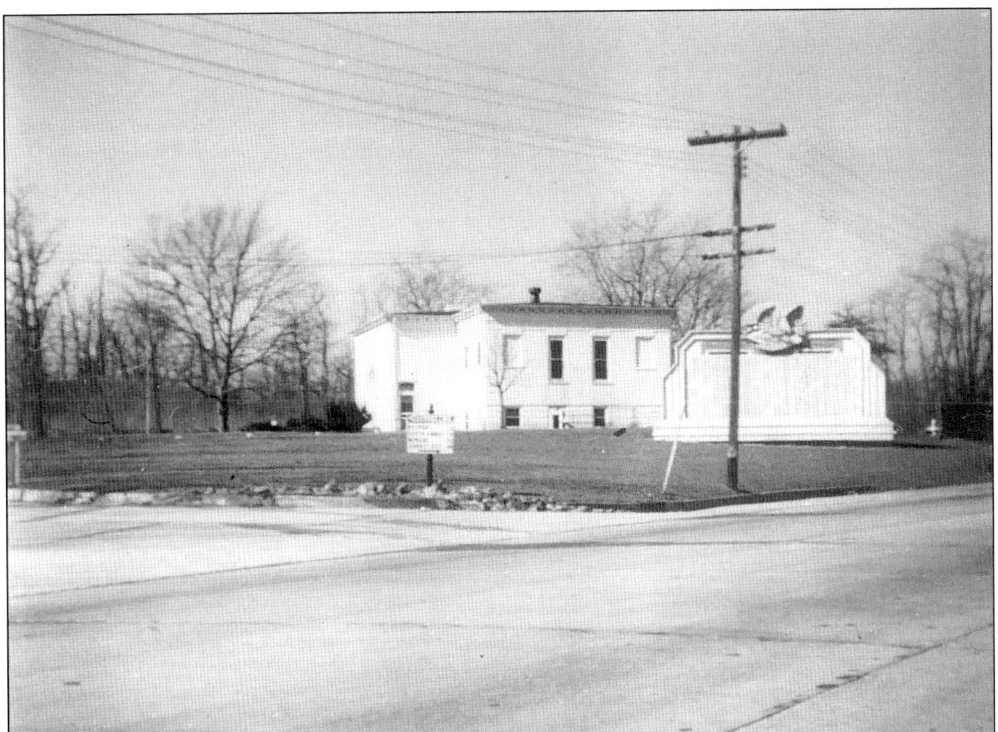

The Middletown World War II service memorial was erected on Highway 35, outside the Middletown Township Hall, which was formerly located in the remodeled Middletown Village School. The building is now a recreational annex, while a permanent memorial is near the site of the temporary wood-frame structure. Today, this intersection, where Tindall Road and Kings Highway merge into Highway 35, is one of the township's most dangerous. The picture is dated c. 1949.

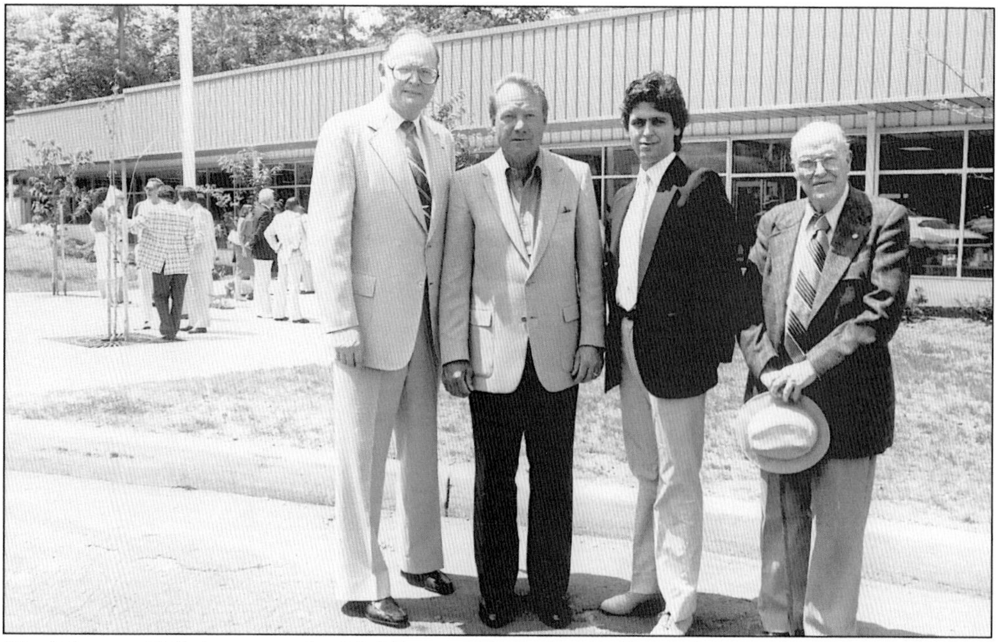

The Johnson-Gill Annex to the Middletown Township Hall was designed by Robert De Santis of Kaplan Gaunt De Santis, Red Bank architects. It was begun in 1982, finished in 1983, and dedicated that June 12. Attending, from left to right, were Mayor Paul A. Linder, William Johnson Jr., Matthew Gill, sons of the honorees, and Donald De Lue, sculptor. De Lue sculpted busts of Johnson and Gill, which are mounted on pedestals inside the front door.

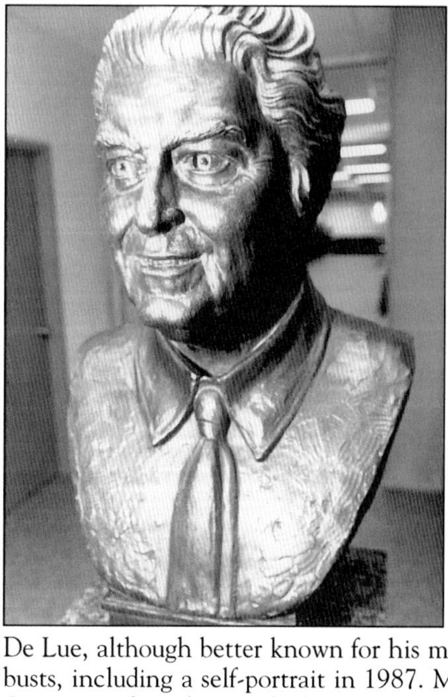

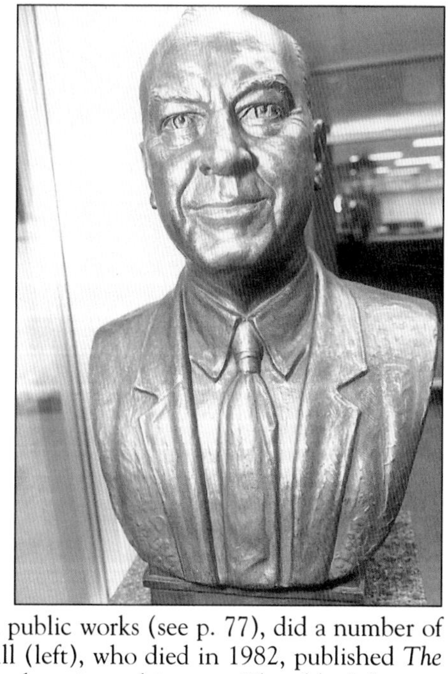

De Lue, although better known for his monumental public works (see p. 77), did a number of busts, including a self-portrait in 1987. Matthew Gill (left), who died in 1982, published *The Courier*, and was known for his uncommon love for and service to his town. The elder Johnson, who died in 1981, was president of the Keansburg-Middletown National Bank and was known as "the banker with a heart."

A memorial to the gold star mothers and wives of Middletown was erected at Bayshore Village Senior Housing on Shoal Harbor Court, Port Monmouth. Present July 13, 1975, for the dedication were, from left to right, Mayor Peter J. Carton, Agnes Bleuitt, president of Bayshore Gold Star Mothers, Lorraine Conk, president of Monmouth County Gold Star Wives, and Colonel Harry I. Luftman, president of the Middletown Senior Housing Corp.

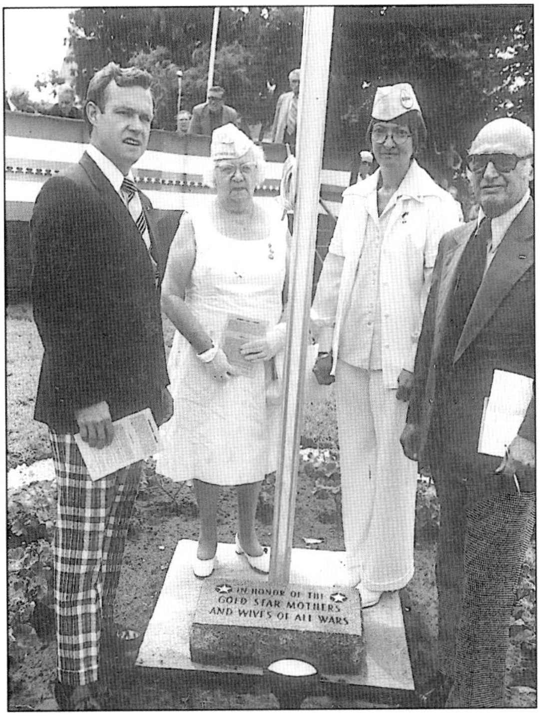

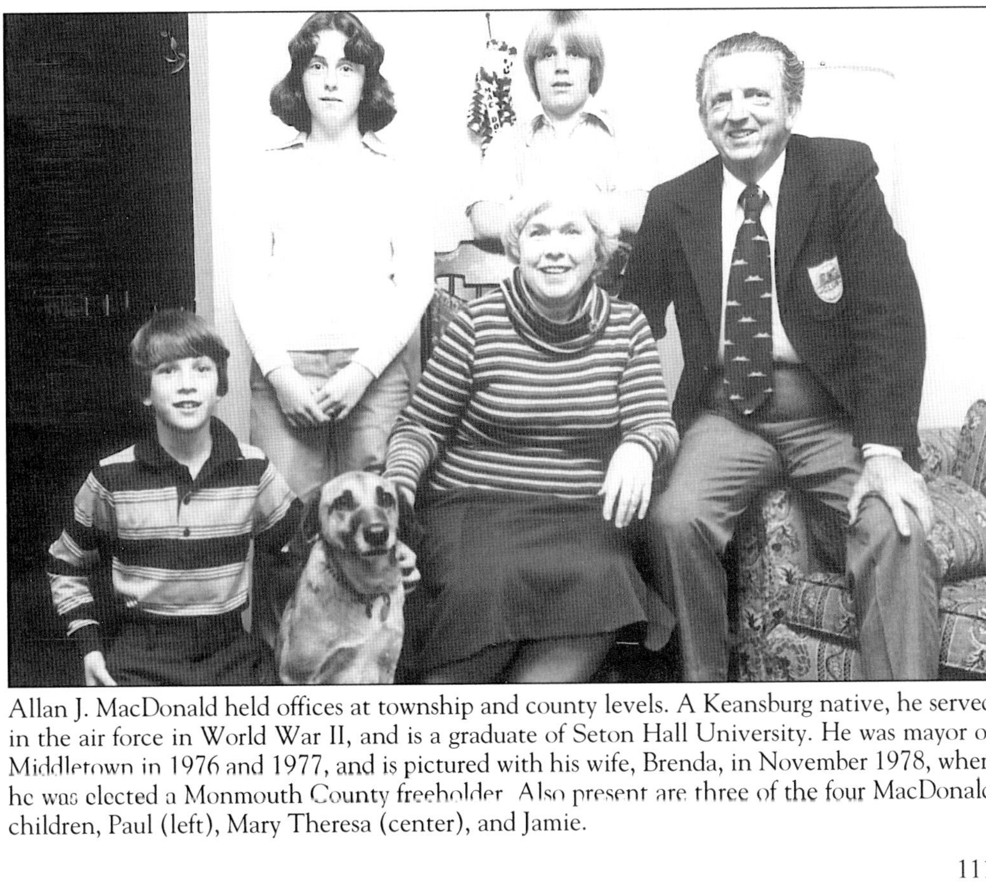

Allan J. MacDonald held offices at township and county levels. A Keansburg native, he served in the air force in World War II, and is a graduate of Seton Hall University. He was mayor of Middletown in 1976 and 1977, and is pictured with his wife, Brenda, in November 1978, when he was elected a Monmouth County freeholder. Also present are three of the four MacDonald children, Paul (left), Mary Theresa (center), and Jamie.

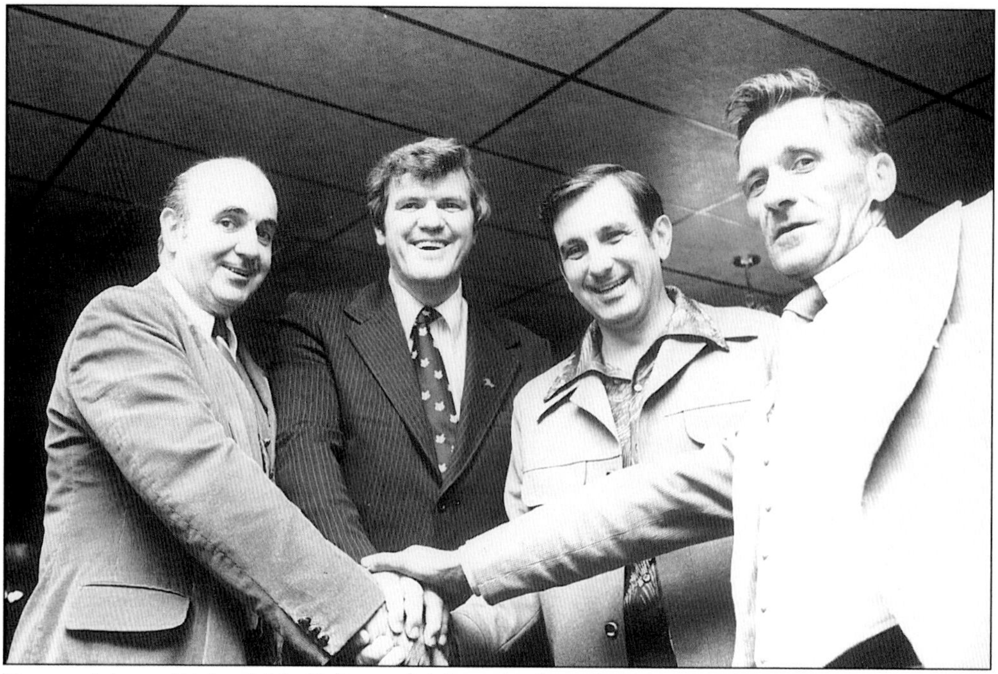

Deputy Mayor Richard V. Kelly and Mayor Robert J. Eckert, left and second from left respectively, won re-election to the township committee on November 7, 1978. Congratulating them are Joseph P. Caliendo, Middletown Democratic leader, to Eckert's left, and Patrick Gaynor, campaign manager.

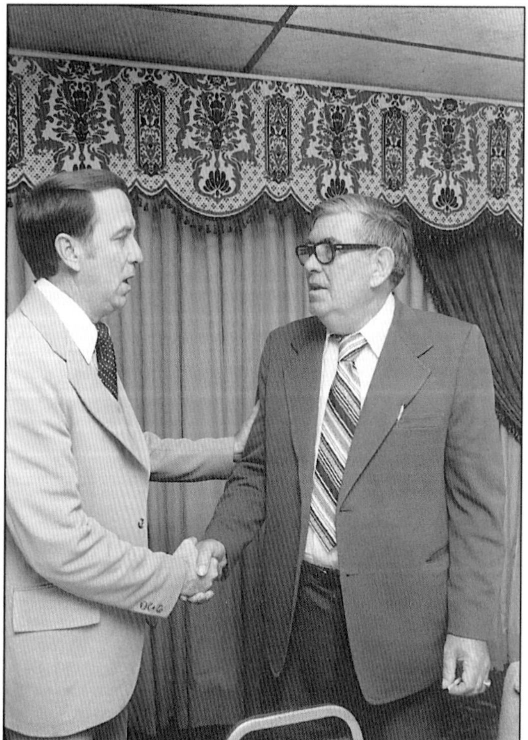

Frank A. Self, left, is congratulated by the former mayor Thomas J. Lynch, whom he defeated in the November 2, 1976 election for a seat on the township committee. The 84% voter turnout reflected that year's high interest in the race. Self attributed his victory to organization and hard work. At one time the only Republican on the committee, Self served as mayor when a Republican majority was restored, which has been unbroken since.

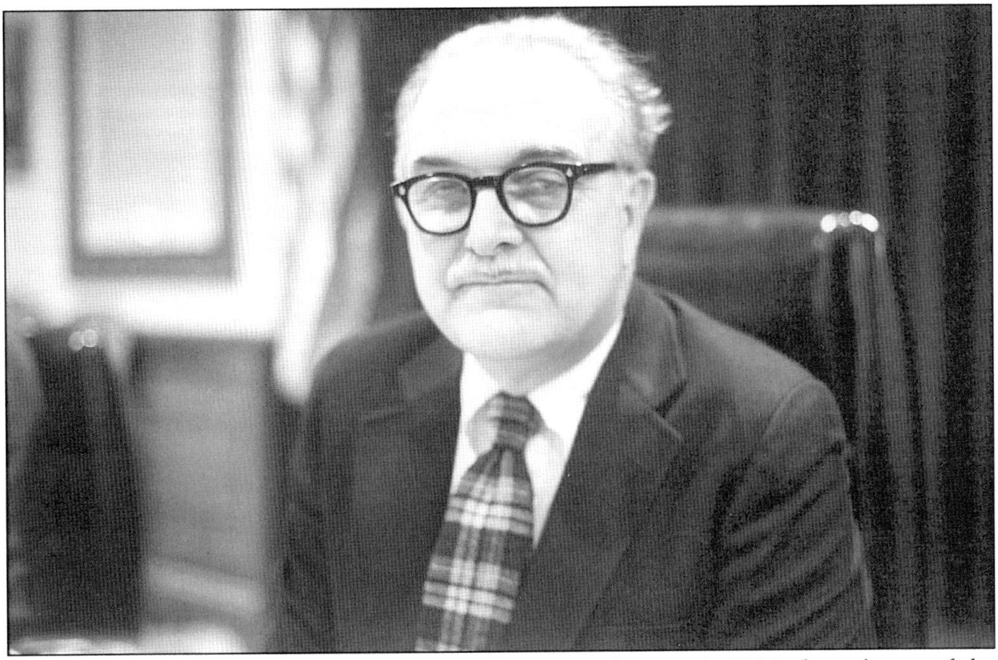

Robert B. Waller was selected mayor of Middletown on January 1, 1984, through one of the most bizarre acts of Middletown politics. He was expected to vote with his two Republican colleagues to select one of them, James F. Maher Jr., as mayor; a second of their majority would have been selected deputy mayor. Instead, he joined with the two Democrats to elect himself mayor and one of them, Richard V. Kelly, deputy mayor. Waller claimed the gesture was made to foster unity and cooperation—aims that were not achieved. He completed the third year of his committeeman term, and did not seek re-election; Maher was the 1985 mayor.

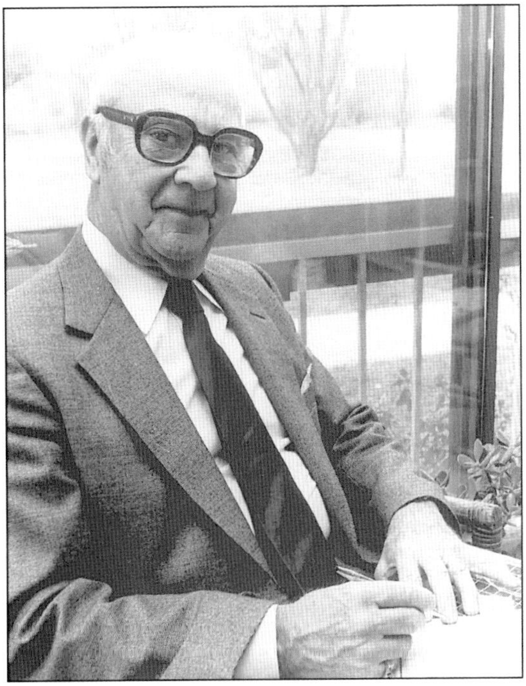

James F. Maher Jr. had two political careers. The first, in Weehawken, followed his return from the Army in 1948 to a town lacking housing for veterans. His first two races for council were unsuccessful, but he was appointed treasurer in 1951 and elected to the township council in 1952, serving eight years. Jim first ran for the Middletown Township Committee in 1981, served two three-year terms, and concluded his service in 1987 with a second term as mayor. He and his wife, Hattie, are retired in Shadow Lake Village.

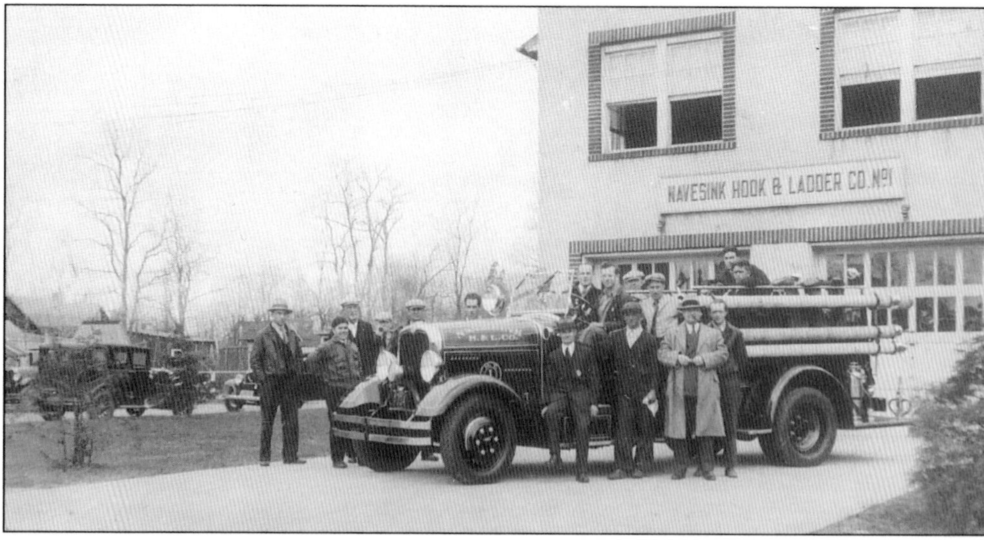

The Navesink Hook and Ladder Company Number One, Middletown's oldest fire company, was founded in 1886. It has had three homes on Monmouth Avenue, including a no-longer standing small garage across the street from their present location. Their current building was constructed behind this one, which is their second home. Many of its members are pictured there *c.* 1940s, with their 1936 Seagrave engine. (Collection of John Rhody.)

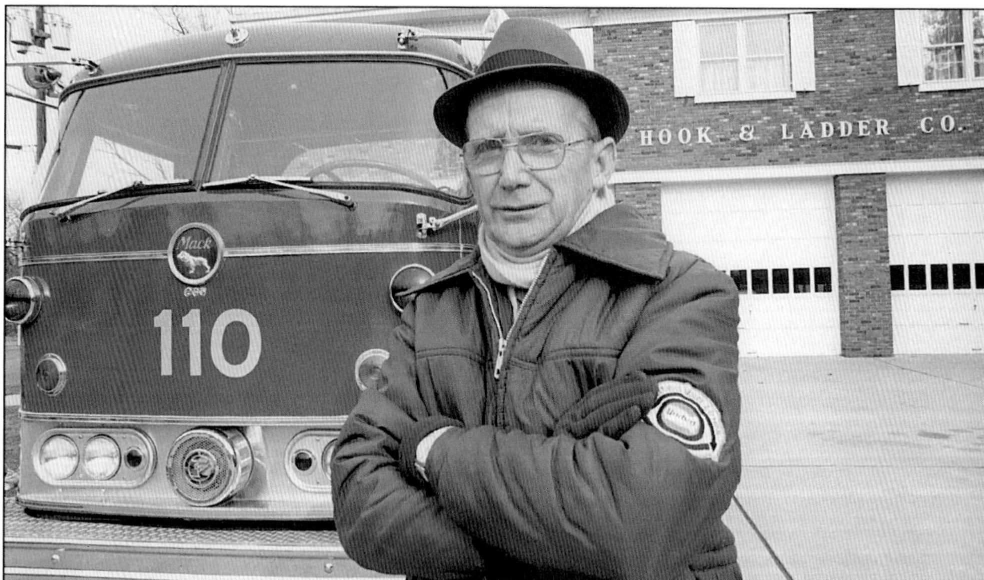

Edwin F. Banfield, born 1917 in Atlantic Highlands, moved in 1921 to the Locust area where he still resides, and followed his father and uncle into the Middletown Volunteer Fire Department. He is pictured in1976 in front of his Navesink Hook and Ladder Company, which he joined in 1943. He served 28 years as secretary, also having held the offices of captain, engineer, and trustee. Ed has held numerous positions in the township department and firemen associations at county and state levels, and has been called a legend in his town. The Banfield Moving and Storage Company, a fixture on Church Street since 1961, made its last move in April 1999. If Ed, "retires" from business, his status as one of the township's longest-serving firemen will still continue.

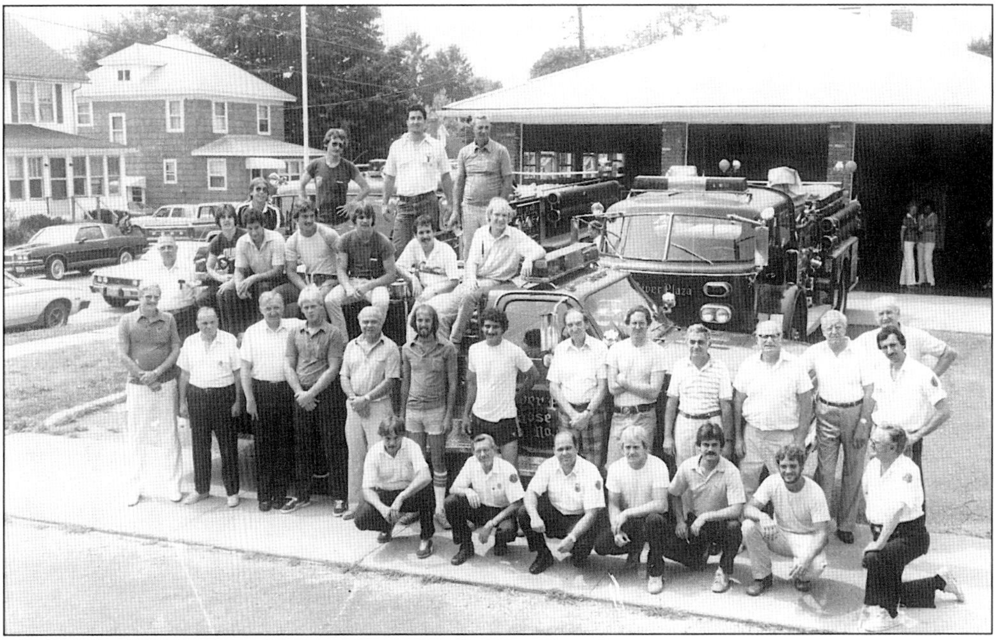

River Plaza Hose Company Number One, organized in 1926, was accepted as Company Number Nine of the Middletown Township Fire Department. The members are seen in 1982 in front of their *c.* 1960 Carpenter Street home, the second on the site.

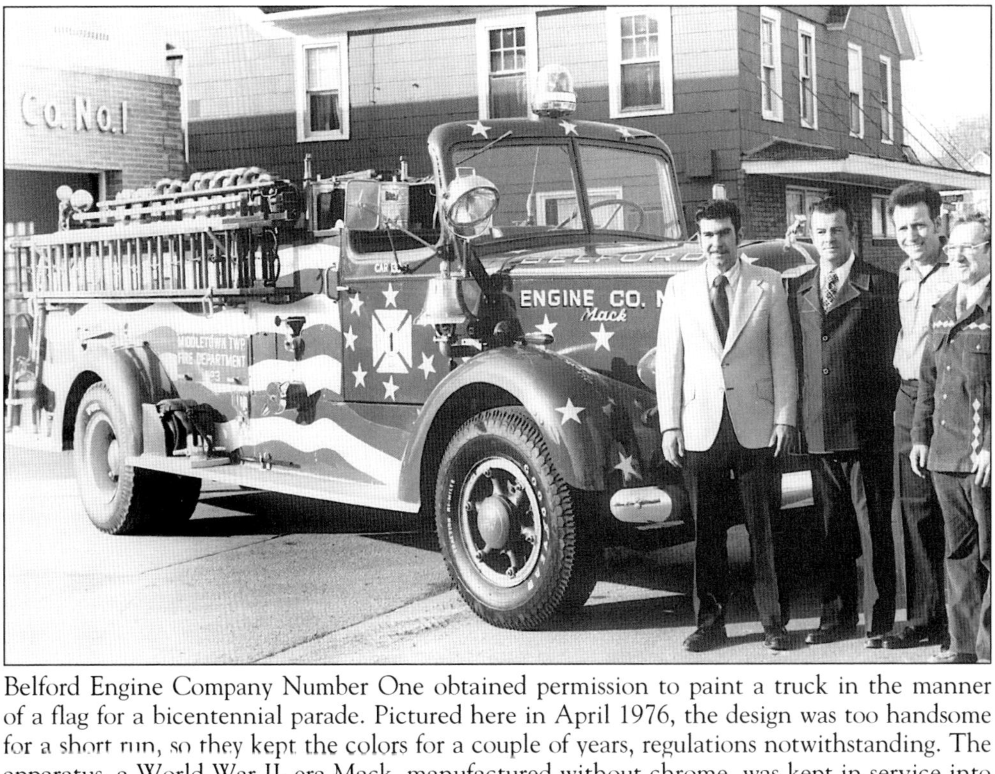

Belford Engine Company Number One obtained permission to paint a truck in the manner of a flag for a bicentennial parade. Pictured here in April 1976, the design was too handsome for a short run, so they kept the colors for a couple of years, regulations notwithstanding. The apparatus, a World War II–era Mack, manufactured without chrome, was kept in service into the 1990s.

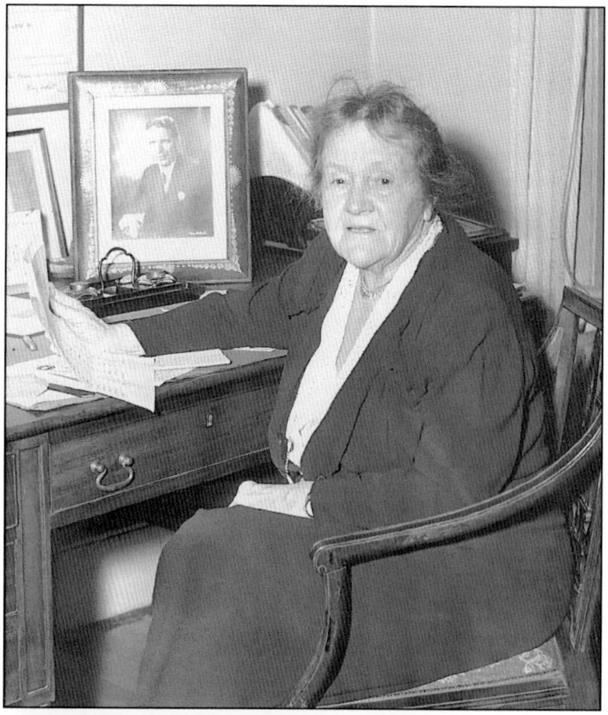

Geraldine Livingston Morgan married Lewis Thompson in 1896, taking residence at Brookdale Farm shortly thereafter. Their first child arrived in 1897, as she assumed her lengthy lifelong role as mistress of Brookdale. Thompson became active in Republican politics, and was well known for her philanthropies, taking a particular interest in children, education, and health. She died in 1967; this picture was taken around the late 1950s.

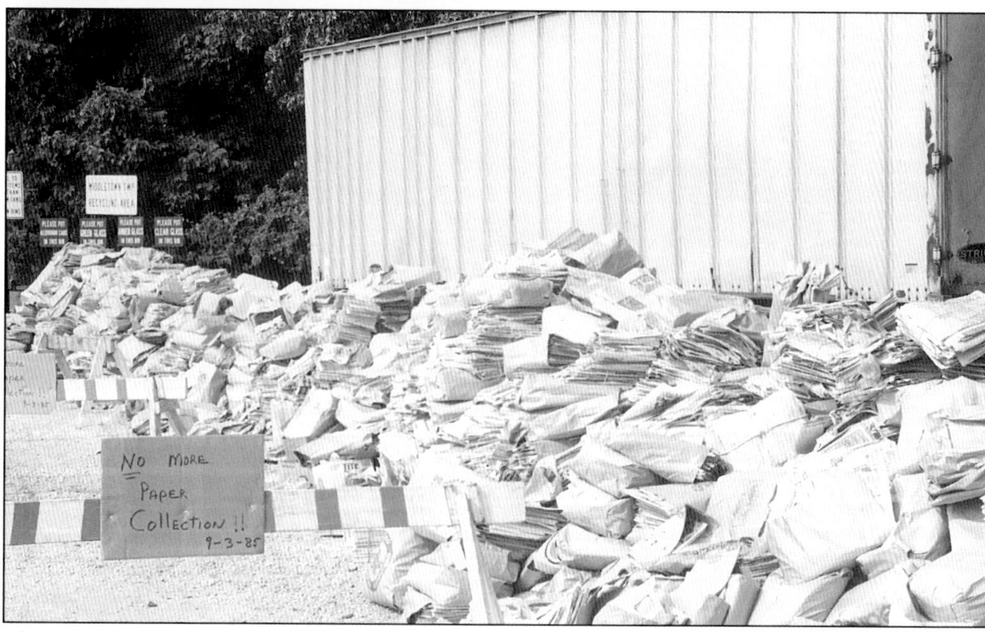

This August 4, 1985 picture, shows a site on the north side of Highway 35, opposite Bradlee's store, and is a reminder of how far recycling has come in recent years. It had been voluntary at several drop-off points, such as this one, which collected newspapers, glass, and aluminum cans (in barrels obscured by paper in the left background). Recycling these materials is now mandatory. Curbside collection is made, while a major drop-off point exists at the Kanes Lane Public Works yard for both materials required to be recycled and several other recyclable materials acceptable on a voluntary basis.

Postal service has been continuous at the Navesink office since 1866 (although it was known as Navesink for its first 22 years). The office does not provide delivery service, but was a community center when located on the corner of Navesink and Monmouth Avenues in the "red store." Postmaster Thelma Reiss, who made it a festive place at Christmas, is seen there in 1972. The office relocated to the first of its Highway 36 strip shopping center locations in the 1980s.

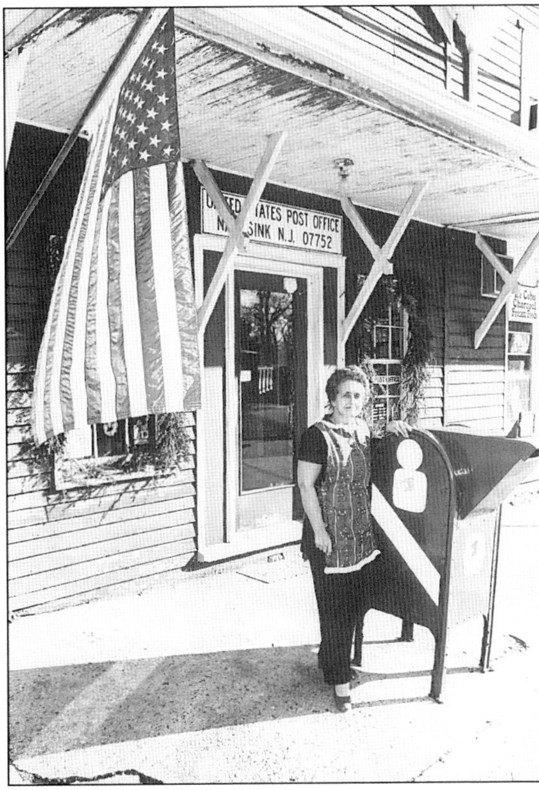

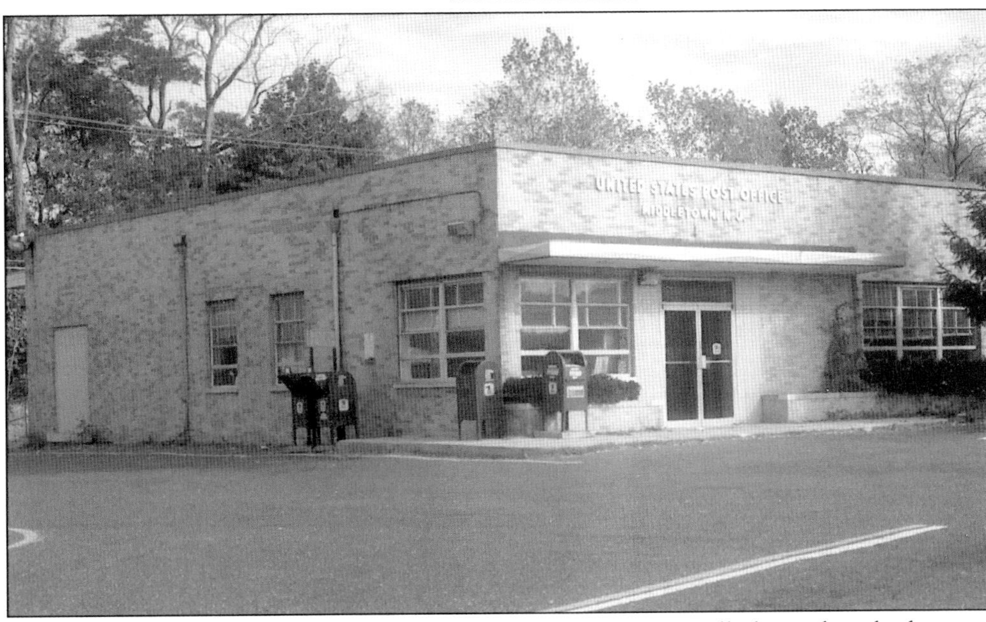

The early Middletown Post Office, established in 1812, was typically located in the home of the postmaster. It had a Kings Highway locale prior to the December 1955 move to Kings Highway East, north of Highway 35, where it is pictured in 1985. The office remained there until relocating to 1601 Highway 35, the present location, in the late 1980s. The former post office, unchanged on the exterior, is now home to *The Courier* newspaper.

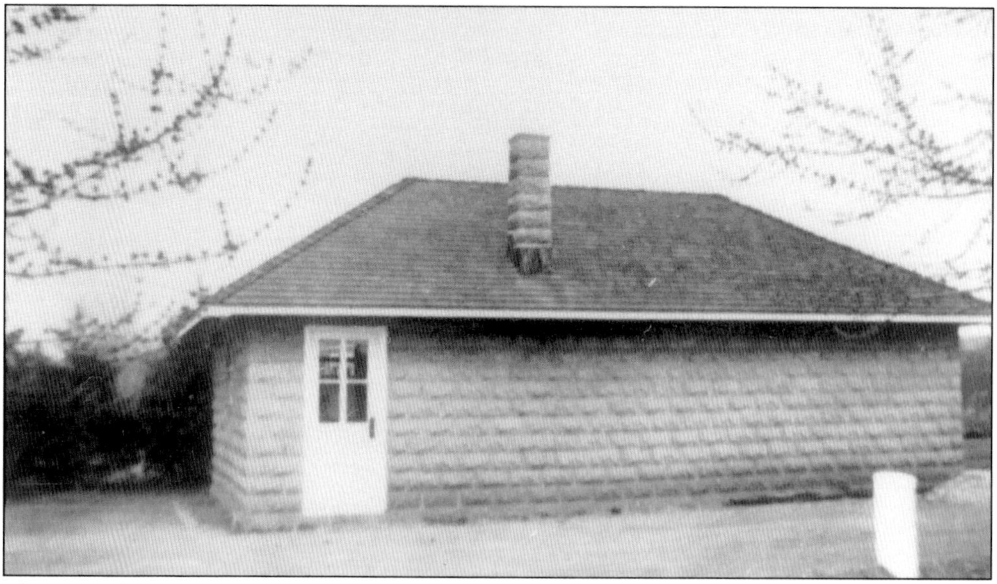

The township's first "jail" (actually it was more of a local lock-up) was built in 1929 at Campbells Junction, for which the township committee authorized a $2,000 expenditure that March. The building, later used by Wasserman's store for storage, is visible seen in the aerial in Volume II, p. 99, as the tiny white building facing Main Street. This undated view is perhaps c. 1930s.

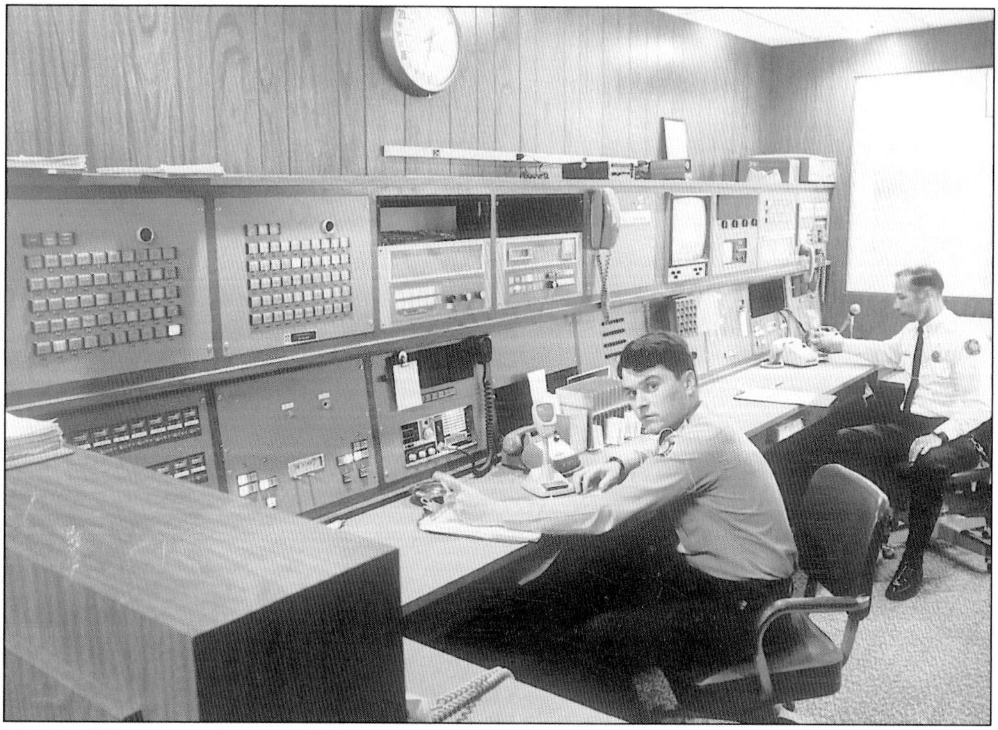

The Middletown Police installed a new dispatching console in 1974. Policemen took turns on the dispatch assignment at the time, a function now handled by non-officers. The township's communications capabilities today include a mobile unit transportable to emergency sites.

Seven

Around Town

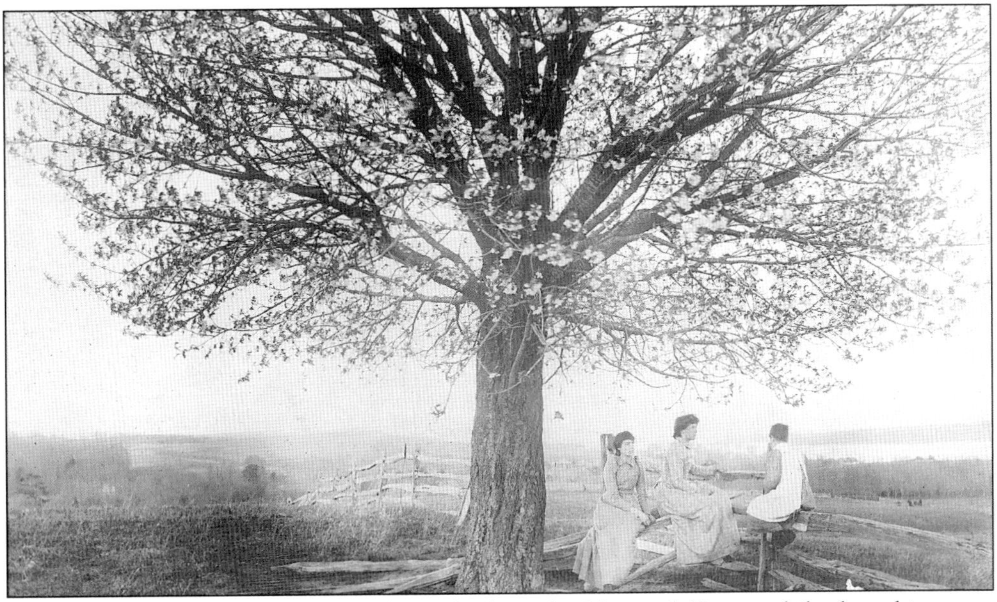

This scene is probably Cooper Road, overlooking the Navesink River, while the subjects are unidentified. The setting represents the township at the beginning of the 20th century, a rural, agrarian, perhaps pristine, pastoral landscape. Should it have remained that way? Do not respond "yes" if you live in a 20th-century house.

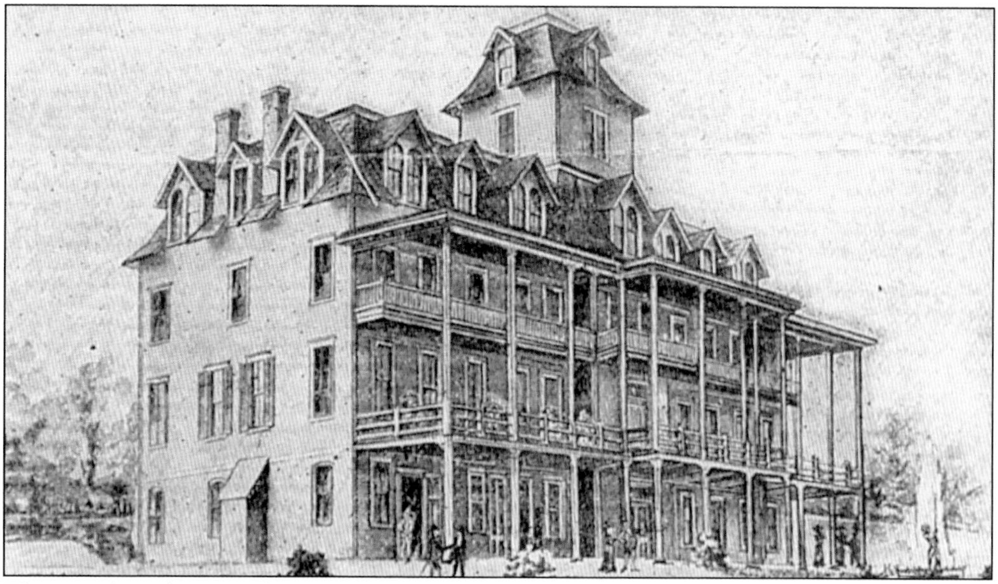

The Hotel Andrew on the south side of Hillside Avenue, east of Serpentine Drive, was the second on the site, replacing one that burned in 1885. The large structure, elaborate in its day, was probably expanded over time, and is often identified with neighboring Atlantic Highlands. The place served as the township's high school for the 1912–13 academic year, while the Leonardo building was under construction. The long-vacant hotel, seen in a sketch on its 1910 brochure, was destroyed by fire in 1929. (Special Collections and Archives, Rutgers University Libraries.)

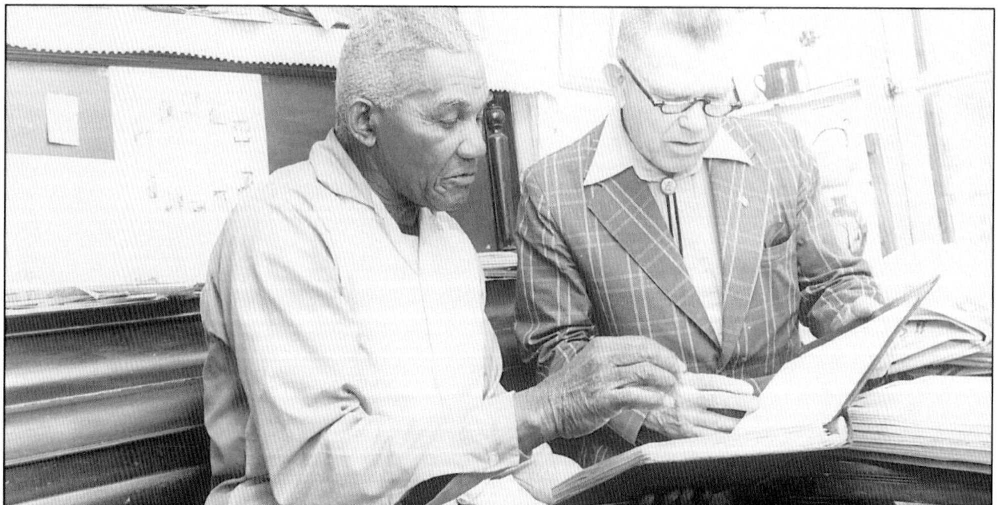

John Sutton, born 1888 in Lebanon, PA, came to the area in 1910 after working as a trapeze flyer in a circus. He became a gardener, was a longtime resident in the Hillside section, and also worked for the Jersey Central Power & Light Company in nearby Atlantic Highlands. Sutton was a long-distance walker (he took an annual birthday jaunt to Red Bank), enthusiastic philatelist, and a person whose congeniality made him a popular man about town. He is shown here at left showing Bob Bramley of the *Red Bank Register* mementos of his career, which included helping reveal in the 1920s the existence of a Ku Klux Klan unit near his Prospect Avenue home.

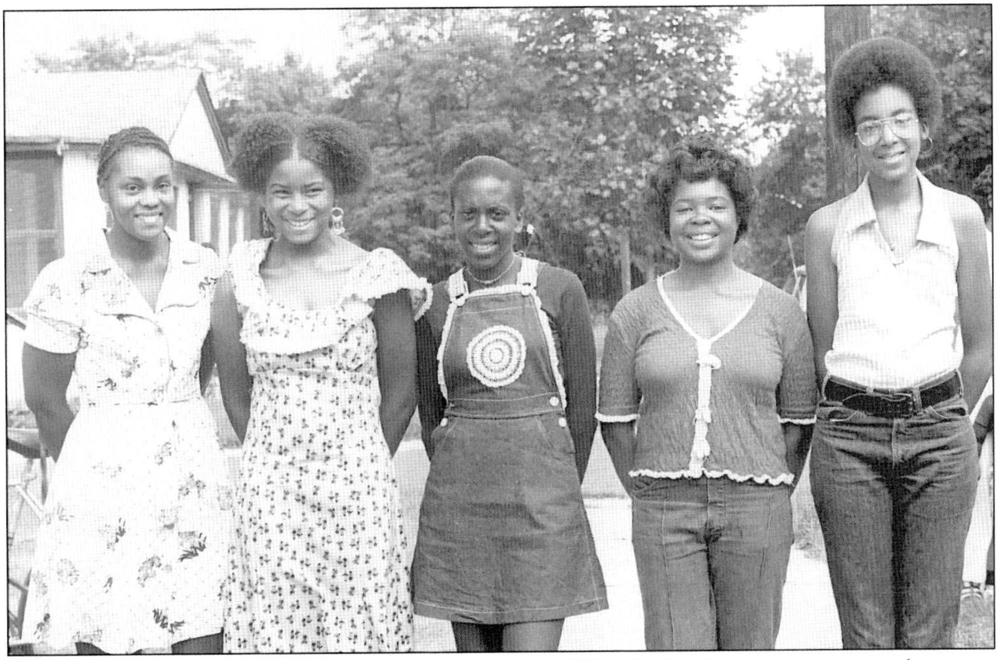

Quinn Chapel, AME Church, 109 Prospect Avenue, Hillside, held a competition to designate "Miss Quinn" as part of a July 1974 fund-raising campaign. The contestants were, from left to right, Dolores Bishop, Regina Brown, Susan Thompson, Sandi Keyes and Karen Byrd. The criterion for selection was a novel one, the title was to go to the contestant who raised the most money.

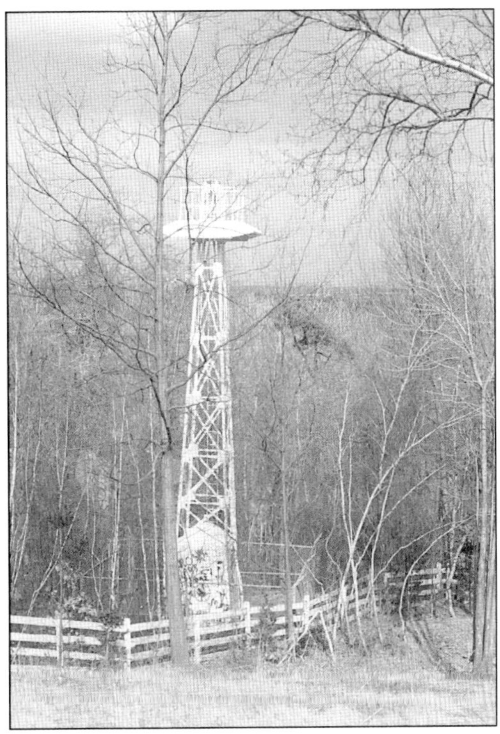

The Chapel Hill Light, originally atop the keeper's house, marked the Sandy Hook Channel when aligned with the Conover Beach Beacon (Volume I, pp. 81 and 28, respectively). The former was replaced, at an unknown date, by a steel tower containing a green light that gave an eerie glow to Stillwell Road travelers until extinguished c 1990. The unlit tower remains in place.

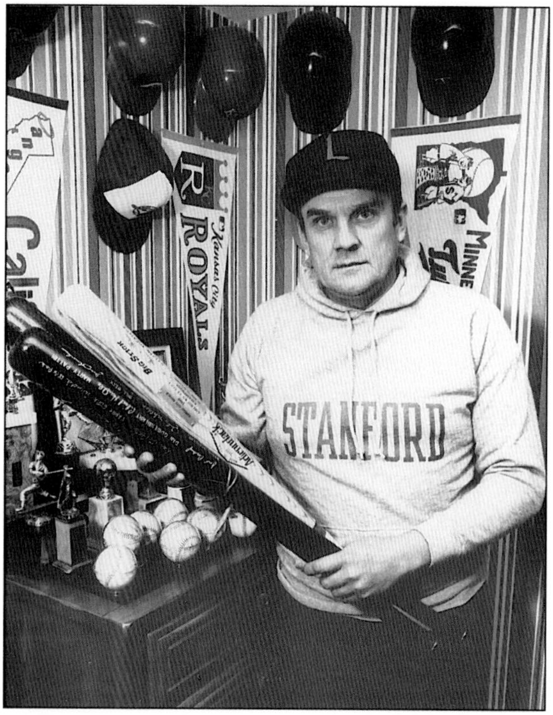

William Gustave Kunkel, born 1936 in Hoboken NJ, reached the major leagues with Kansas City Athletics in 1961, concluding a three-year career with the Yankees in 1963 with a lifetime pitching record of 6-6. He later resided in Leonardo, enjoying a longer American League career as an umpire. Bill and the former Maxine Nordby had three children. Their son Jeff, a baseball standout at Middletown South and Rider College, reached the major leagues with the Texas Rangers. Bill died in 1985; his memory is commemorated by the Bill Kunkel Memorial Park on Brevent Avenue.

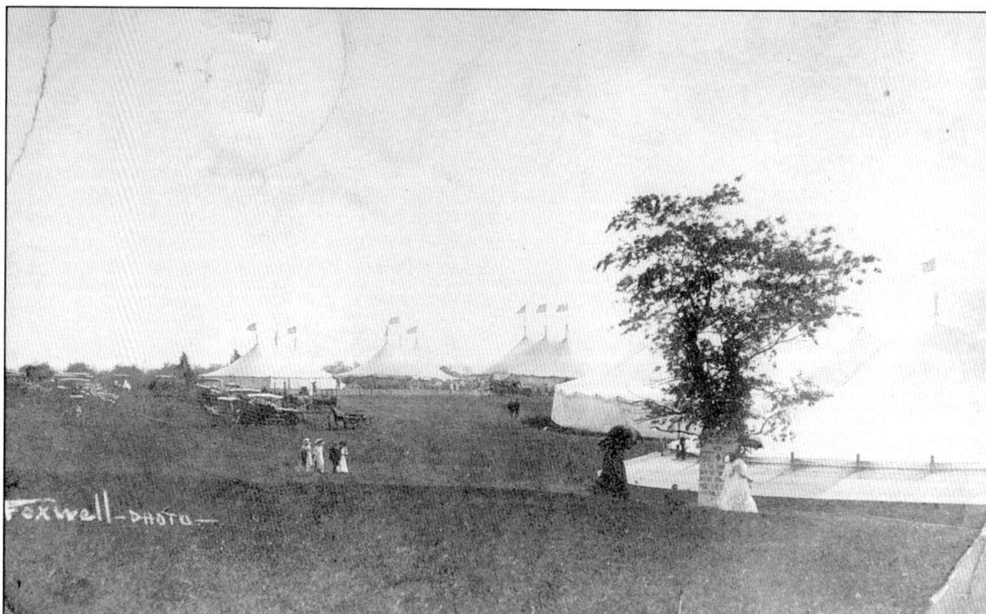

The Monmouth County Fair Grounds were often described during the event's run in the years surrounding 1910 as being located in Red Bank. Few may know, therefore, that they were in Middletown, on an extensive tract on the south side of Highway 35, east of Oak Hill Road. Some exhibitors and fair officials were gentlemen farmers, including J. Amory Haskell and Melvin A. Rice, as well as local-producing agriculturists. The grounds are seen here on a 1909 Foxwell photographic postcard. No reminders of the grounds remain; the property is developed with housing and commercial structures. (Collection of John Rhody.)

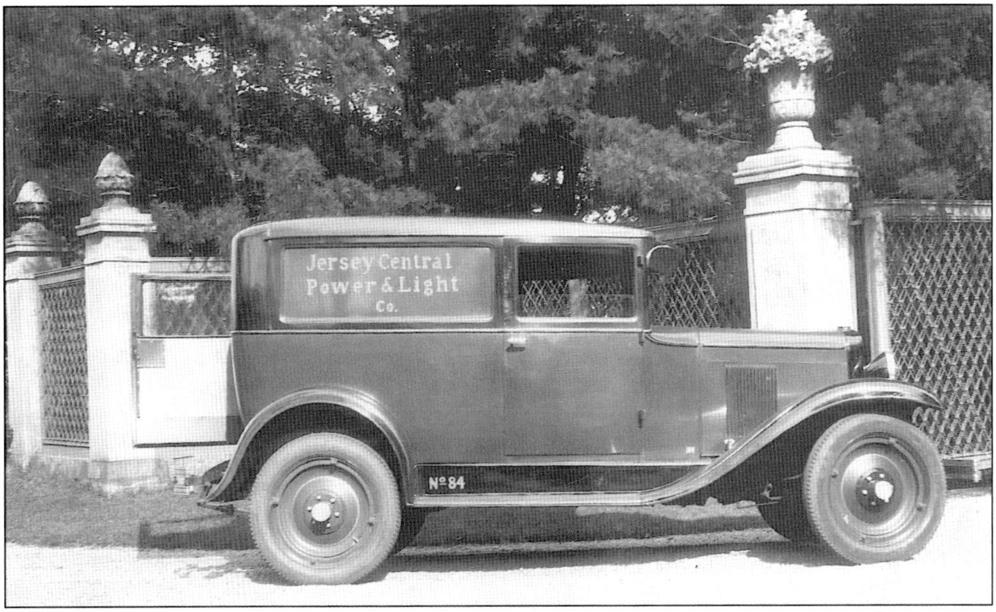

A new Chevrolet belonging to the meter-reading department of Jersey Central Power & Light Company was photographed outside the Timolat house at 776 Navesink River Road in June 1929.

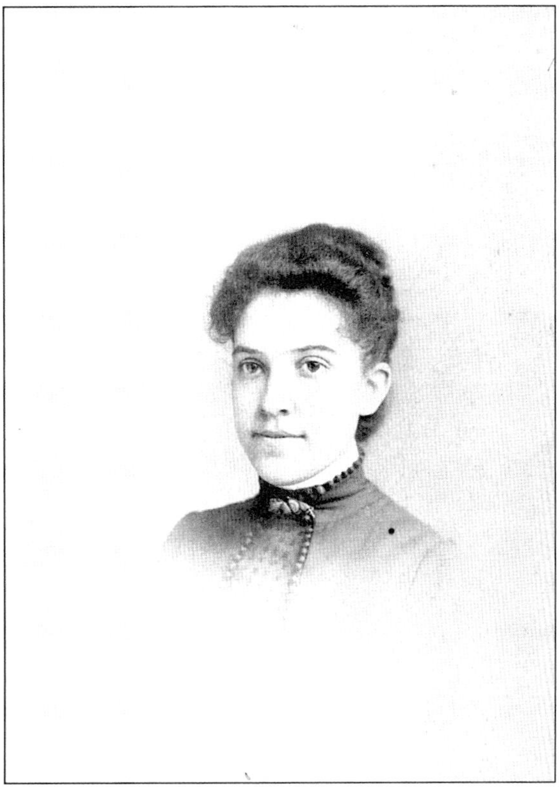

Louise Hartshorne was born in 1866, a direct descendant of Richard Hartshorne, a major 17th-century landowner and Middletown public office holder. She was an 1884 graduate of St. Mary's Hall, Burlington. She served Christ Church, Middletown, in various capacities, including 60 years as treasurer, as their organist, and for many years, as their Sunday school teacher. Miss Hartshorne was active in numerous organizations, including the Middletown Library, the Rumson Garden Club, the Diocesan Women's Auxiliary, and the Monmouth County Historical Association. She also had an informal, but influential role as the social arbiter of Middletown village, one whose approbation was necessary for a newcomer's "acceptance." Hartshorne died in February 1956. (Collection of the Monmouth County Historical Association.)

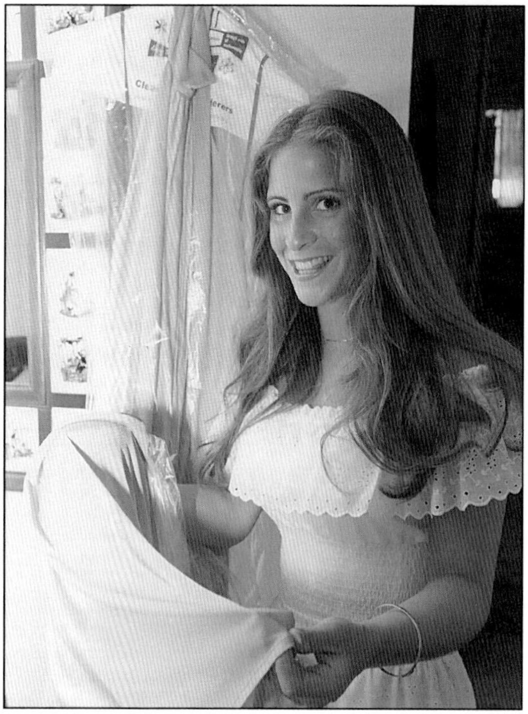

Diane Addonizio, then 18, won the Miss Monmouth County beauty pageant on May 12, 1978. The Middletown High School South graduate is pictured that June preparing for July's Miss New Jersey talent-oriented competition. Diane took a scholarly interest in political science and a performing interest in dramatics to the contest.

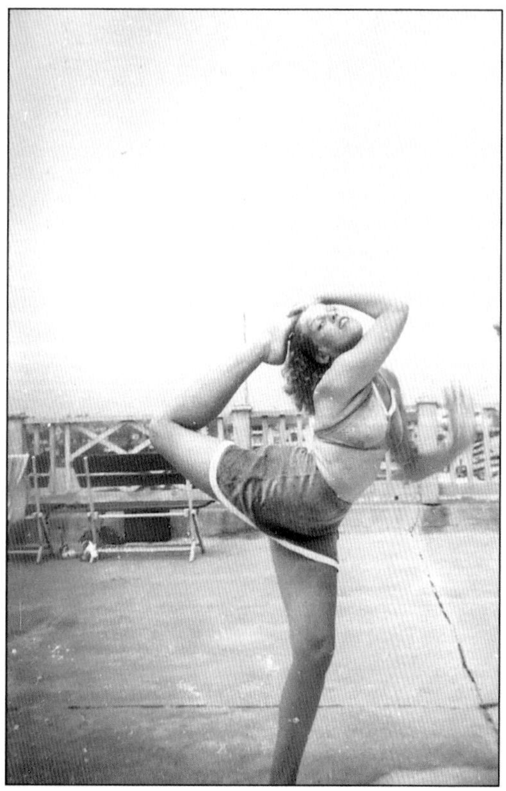

Personal flexibility is a useful quality in many respects. Katherine B. Meyer Richards exhibits an unusual form of it at Port Monmouth in 1945. Pulling that feat (or should it be feet?) deserves historical commemoration! The photograph was lent by her daughter, Sandi von Pier.

Patricia Flynn, a resident of Valley Drive, Navesink, won designation as Miss Middletown in 1974. She entered the contest as a lark, but was delighted with her success. The then 22 year old was more focused on her teaching career at Our Lady of Perpetual Help School in Highlands. The local beauty, an able gymnast and pianist, also had an interest in drama and acting.

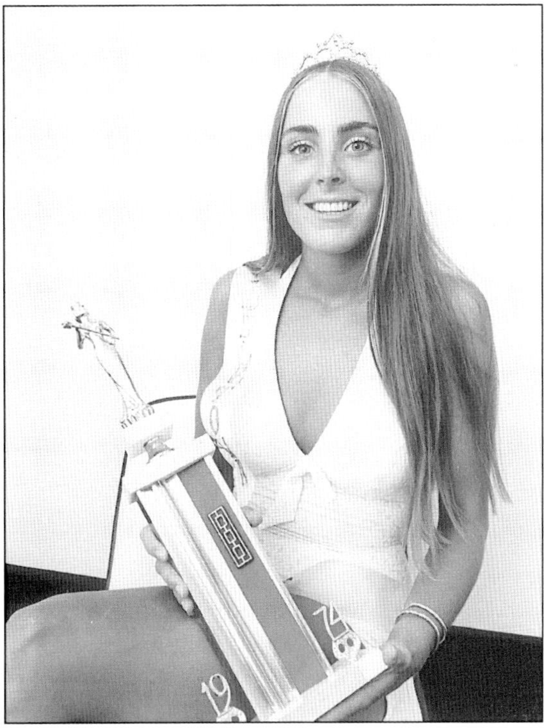

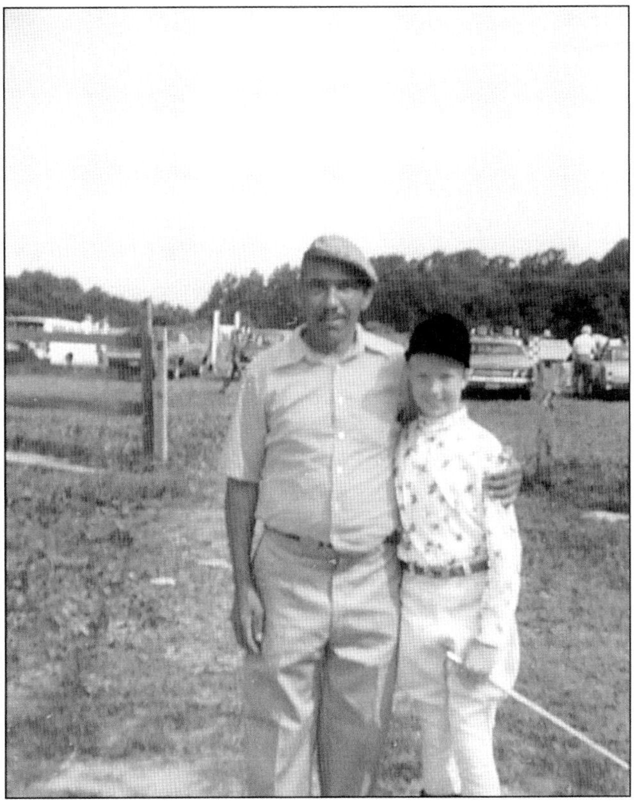

Congo Jones began his equine career as an eight year old, exercising race horses, and becoming a groom, trainer, and an aid to foaling mares. He worked at noted local horse farms, including those of the Whitneys and Paysons. Jones also raced steeplechase horses in England and cared for polo ponies. He opened the Congo Jones School of Horsemanship in 1952 on Newman Springs Road, taking a special interest in his younger students, instilling the courtesies of horsemanship, as well as the skills of riding. His kind nature is remembered fondly by many, including by the pictured student from the 1970s, Sandi Richards von Pier.

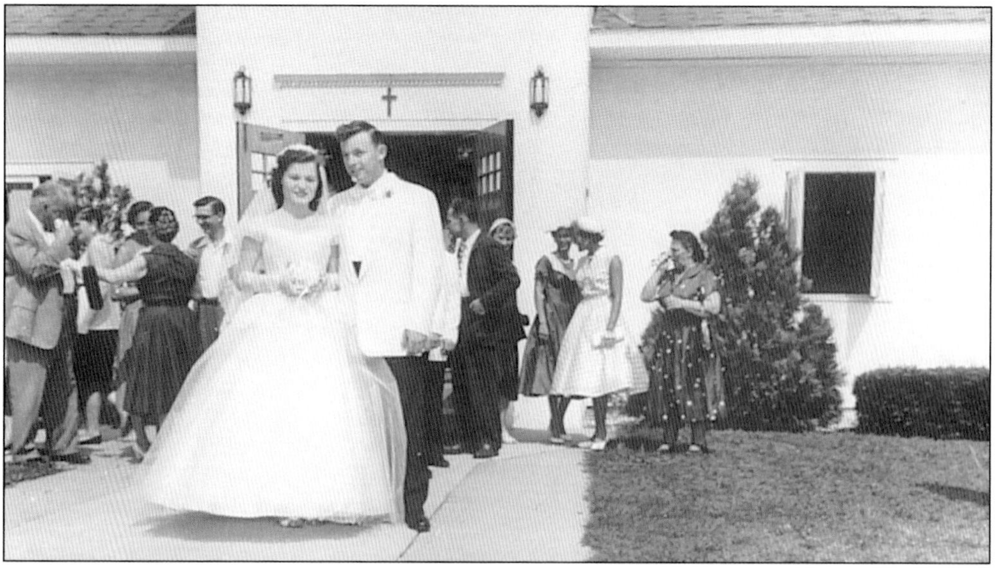

Harold Solomon and the former Margaret Papa are pictured outside St. Catherine's Church following their July 2, 1955 wedding. They proceeded to Sea Bright for the reception, where guests were startled by an unexpected visitor, a 550-pound sand shark dressed in a wet suit, brought on a stretcher by the groom's fellow first-aiders. Their finely finned friend, finding his humor value one joke, and his culinary value nil, was unceremoniously dumped in the Shrewsbury River.

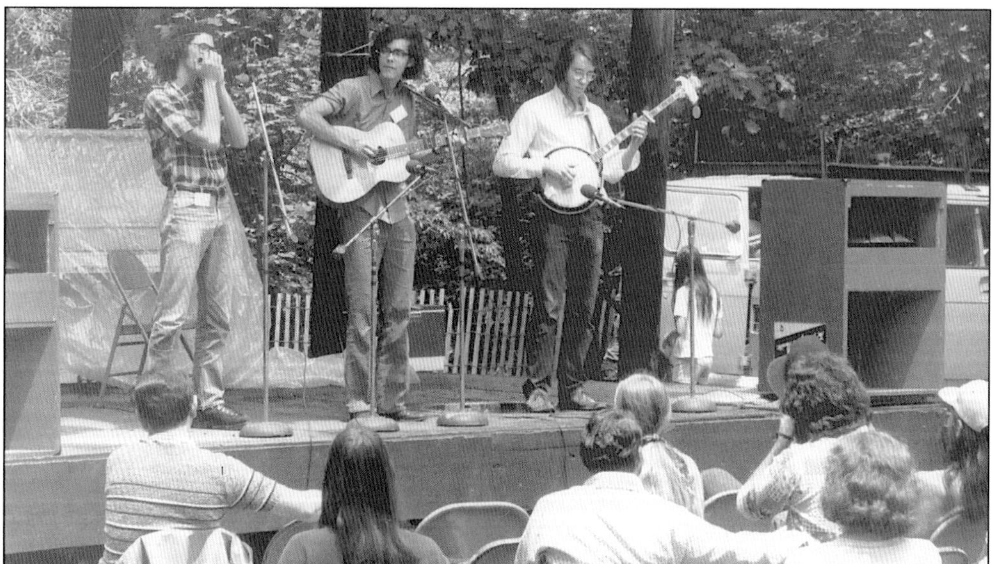

A shared interest in folk music attracted Dr. Richard Levine and his wife, Marlene, to each other at the University of Pennsylvania in the early 1950s. Having attended various folk festivals, they established the Middletown Folk Festival in Bodman Park in 1968, an event held annually through 1984 (it is pictured here in 1974). It grew in popularity, became a two-day event in 1969, and during its peak years of 1975–80, drew attendance in the 2,500-3,000 range. The Levines drew diverse groups of musicians, while their efforts attracted a variety of grants and commendations.

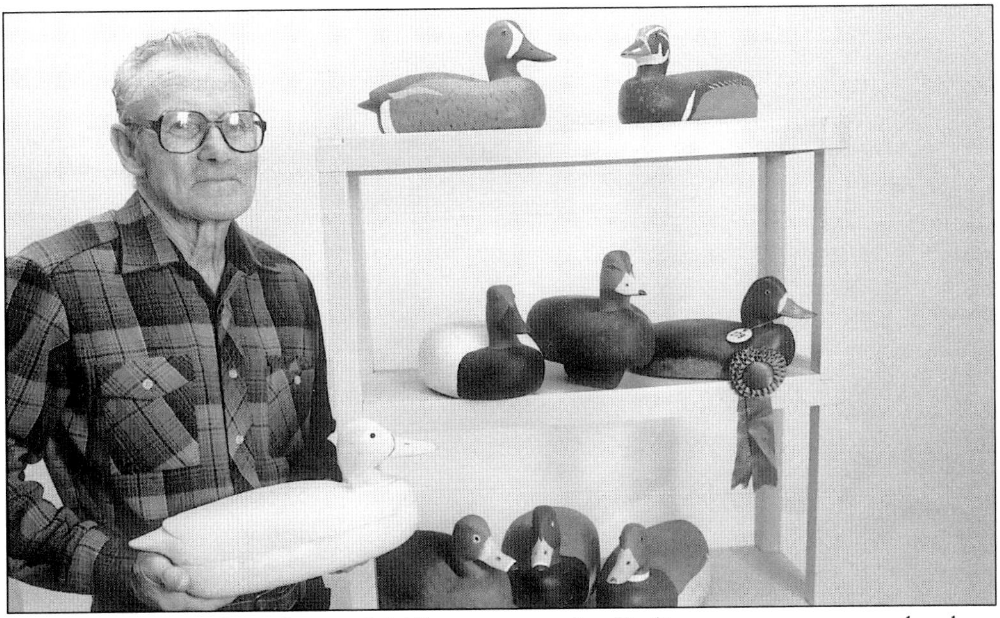

William "Sonny" Schoor, born in Middletown, moved to Burlington county as a youth, where he learned duck-carving from a noted local artisan. His early work was utilitarian for decoys, but after a long career, including work in fishing and defense, Bill, who had returned to Port Monmouth, began carving as an art form. He is pictured in 1984, with his highly realistic, award-winning birds.

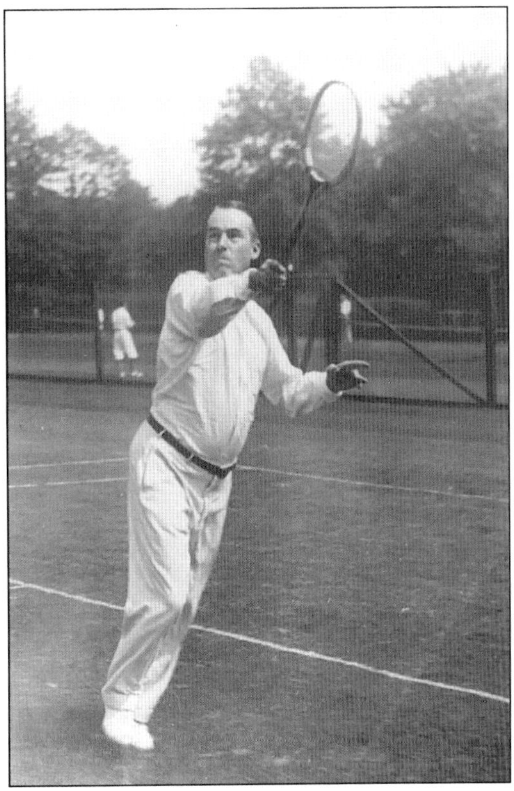

Holcombe Ward, who moved to Monmouth County c. 1915, attained early tennis prominence as a Harvard undergraduate, winning the intercollegiate and Eastern doubles championships with Dwight Davis in 1899. He graduated in 1900 and played against England on the first Davis Cup team that year, and again in 1902, 1905, and 1906. He was associated with the New York textile firm of French and Ward, retiring in 1937, and was later active as a board member of the Monmouth County Red Cross, heading fund drives during World War II. Ward lived on Navesink River Road and also headed the United States Lawn Tennis Association and the Seabright Lawn Tennis and Cricket Club. (Collection Seabright Lawn Tennis and Cricket Club.)

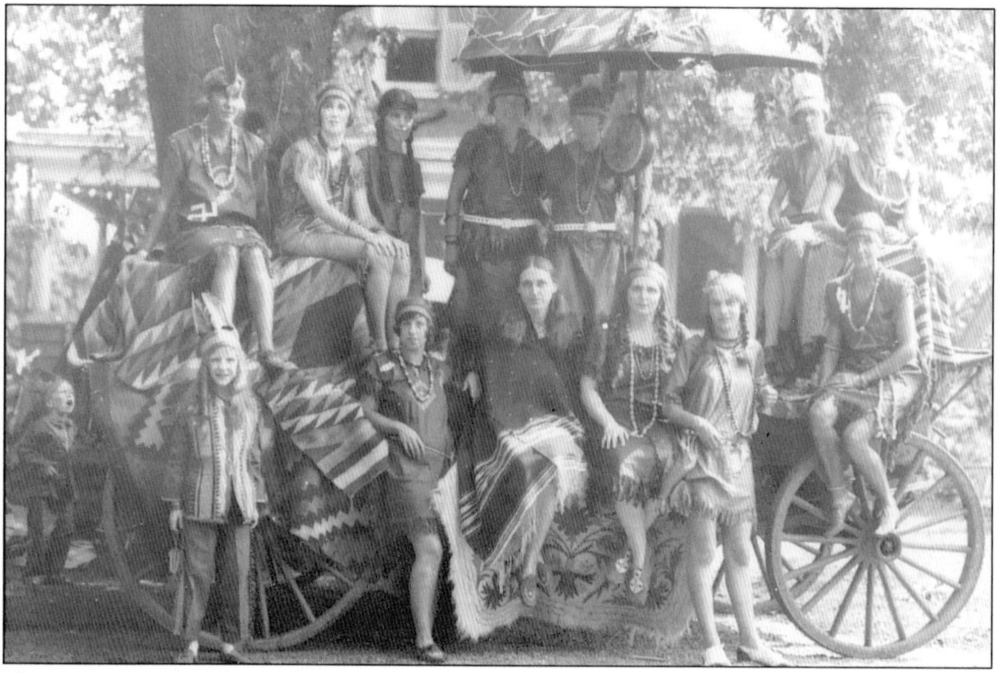

This event was the Christ Church Pirate Fair, although one could wonder when looking at the participants' attire why it was not the Indian Fair. Jane Hendrickson Bartlett, the lender of this 1920s picture, is the third from the left in front. To her left are Jean Thoms, Mrs. Hance, and Susanna Bennett Maguire. In the back row, Ruth Mandeville and Helen Linde are third and fourth from the left, while Mrs. Garrett Conover is at the far right.

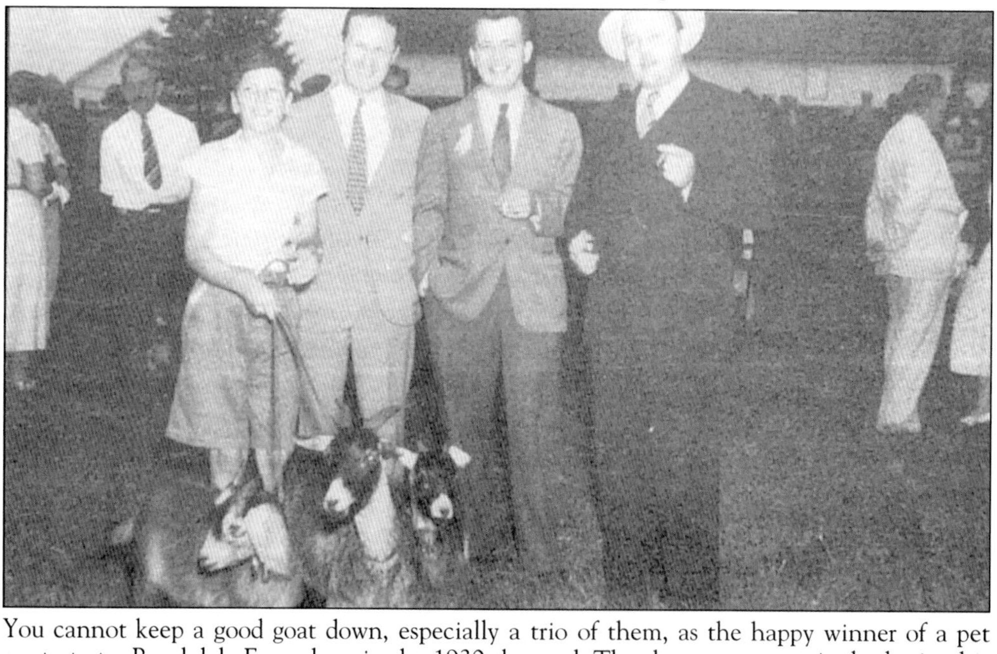

You cannot keep a good goat down, especially a trio of them, as the happy winner of a pet contest at a Brookdale Farm show in the 1930s learned. The three men, seemingly sharing his pride, are, Harold Kelly (left), Dr. Thatcher Parker (center), and Patrick Shannon. The latter was an editor of the *Jersey Shore Pictorial*, which first published the photograph in 1937.